Edward Guide to Everyday Life, 1900-1914

By Evangeline Holland

plum bun
publishing

Introduction

In the wake of *Downton Abbey* and *Mr. Selfridge*, the 21st century has experienced a bit of an Edwardian revival. The first wave of nostalgia for the early twentieth century occurred in the years after the First World War, and it swept through again—much stronger—in the 1970s, a time of much social upheaval and hardship. Historians and pop culture commentators in Britain and America alike have struggled to understand or explain why *Downton Abbey* in particular has struck a chord with millions of people worldwide. In 2011, A.N. Wilson, esteemed broadcaster and historian blasted *Downton Abbey* as "sanitised version of the past" and that it glorified "an ordering of society that was hateful in real life." [i] Nicoletta Gullace, associate professor of history at the University of New Hampshire, offers another viewpoint:

> "Women in the early 20th century were...demanding education, professional opportunities, and the vote. What we've given up, though, is a certain gentility and graciousness of living." [Downton Abbey] is "full of familiar things like running water, telephones, indoor plumbing, central heat, and steam travel, yet the very rich still displayed courtly manners and lived in unimaginable luxury and opulence. We are also connected to that time period more intimately, since it was not, in fact, so very long ago[.]"[ii]

Today this debate seems a lot of fuss about nothing, but you would be surprised to discover that the Edwardians themselves would have looked upon our interest with a benign smile. The turn of the century was, after all, an era of sublime confidence and vigor—with the Edwardians at its center. In the Western World, the Edwardian era was a time of great social change and of a solidification of the power of the ruling elite. The French, with their eloquent and perceptive turns of phrasing, characterized the years between 1880 and 1914 as La Belle Epoque (the beautiful epoch) and *Fin de siècle* (a period of degeneration and of hope for a new beginning). Certainly no other time in history has witnessed such decadence and pessimism aligned with such optimism and hope.

Nevertheless, the Edwardians marched into the twentieth century with more optimism and hope than pessimism. Wealth was abundant and nearly tax free, Society was no longer the small, exclusive circle confined to the aristocracy, travel was cheap and easy (no passports or visas required, save at the Russian and Ottoman borders, and the Gold Sovereign was taken everywhere), and advances in flight, science, and industry made everyone confident that improved technology would bring peace. More importantly, Great Britain was the most powerful nation in the world. The maxim coined for the Spanish Empire of the sixteenth and seventeenth centuries now rang true for the British Empire. From London to Cape Town to Bombay to Vancouver and back again, the sun never set on the fluttering Union Jack. Granted, British might was tested by the small colonial skirmishes throughout the nineteenth century, but Jolly Old England was still "Home" to millions of subjects of various creeds, colors, religions, and class.

The purpose of the this book is to give a general portrait of this long-ago age, and to hopefully spark your imagination and interest in looking up more information!

E.H.
January 2014

---

[i] Hooton, Christopher. "Downton Abbey 'is B*******, Basically', Says Historian A.N. Wilson." *Downton Abbey Is B******* Basically Says Historian A.N. Wilson Comments*. Metro, 17 Sept. 2011. Web. 28 Dec. 2013.

[ii] Wright, Lori. "UNH British Historian Explains Appeal of Downton Abbey | UNH Today."*UNH British Historian Explains Appeal of Downton Abbey*. UNH Today, 24 Jan. 2013. Web. 28 Dec. 2013.

Contents

PART III: SOCIETY

Part I: Everyday Life

The Edwardian Home

The Edwardian home differed little from the Victorian home, save that of decoration and purpose. Where the Victorians filled their homes to the brim with knickknacks, chair and sofa coverings, heavy furniture, plants, and carpets, the Edwardians gradually began to adopt the streamlined and open-air aesthetics preached by those in the Arts & Crafts movement.

Changes

Most aristocrats continued to live alongside the clutter and antiques accumulated after centuries, but members of The Souls, a clique made up of the aristocratic intelligentsia, were keen to move against the tide of their peers, and Percy and Madeleine Wyndham—the heart of the clique—commissioned Philip Webb to Clouds House in Wiltshire to fulfill these principles. Overall, aristocrats and the Americans who entered their world, preferred the lavish and the opulent, and had homes built or redecorated for this purpose.

The middle classes, newly "genteel", were prime targets for the manufacturers churning out imitation Jacobean or imitation Empire style furniture. Yet their homes served a much different function when compared to the wealthy and upper class, for they did not entertain on a huge scale, nor could they afford huge homes to house 10+ servants. As a result their homes were more utilitarian and less focused on public rooms, and they were also much more likely to live in houses with up-to-date appliances such as electric stoves or central heating, to make up for the lack of domestic staff.

Lower down the scale, the housing of the working class and poor varied greatly, with some existing in cramped and poorly ventilated slums, some in cottages on country estates, and others in the newly-created housing estates built for the improvement of the poor.

The housing of the underclass was a leading topic for Edwardian reformers, and during the 1890s and 1900s, the Councils of England's major cities took steps towards providing homes for the working class. Birmingham, Leeds, Bradford, and Manchester took the lead in providing municipal flats, but any plans for widespread council housing was checked by political antipathy and developers' greed. Liverpool, which was one of the fastest cities in 1900, pursued an aggressive policy of expanding its boundaries.

Between 1895 and 1914, eight suburbs were swallowed to create Greater Liverpool, and a major program of building council flats quickly followed. Between 1905 and 1906, a thousand three-story tenements had been built at a rate matched only in Glasgow (Scotland). However, it was the London County Council that surpassed all other efforts, via their Architect's Department.

According to Charles Booth's survey of the London poor, a million out of 4.5 million lived in grossly inadequate housing. The inhabitants of slums faced poor sanitation, lighting, and space on top of neglected buildings inspectors considered hazardous. This doesn't even take into account the numbers of homeless families dependent whose meager earnings couldn't even pay for the type of cheap and shoddy lodging already mentioned. The first housing project of the LCC was to house sixty people just off Holborn. The following project was much larger—housing 418 people in Southwark—and by 1908 flats in housing blocks had been built on twelve estates and housed 17,000 people.

An example of the transformation of a slum into a housing estate, was that of the notorious London slum, the Old Nichol, which was cleared and redeveloped in the late 1890s.

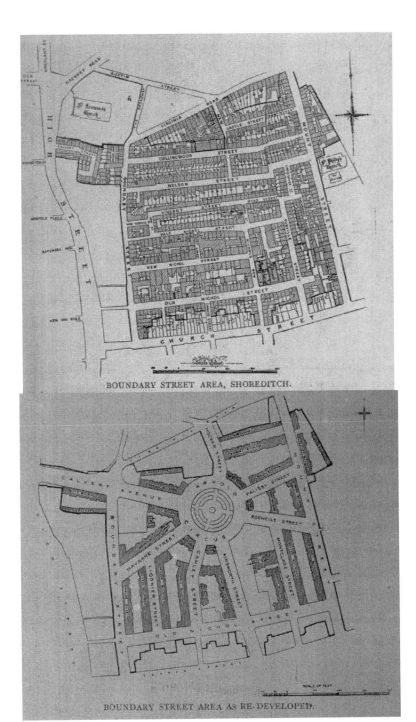

BOUNDARY STREET AREA, SHOREDITCH.

BOUNDARY STREET AREA AS RE-DEVELOPED.

In their zeal for housing reform, the LCC cleared slums but also displaced tens of thousands of Londoners who had nowhere to go when evicted.

The cold-blooded manner in which these Londoners were displaced, many of whom clung to their homes until the bitter end, is described by George Sims:

"When a slum has been levelled to the ground a huge block of working class dwellings generally rises on its site. These buildings are wanted. Many of them are excellent. But up to the present they have hardly succeeded in solving the great problem, because the evicted or displaced tenants, practically left without any superior accommodation, are driven into worse.

After notice had been served upon them some began at once to look about for other accommodation. But the larger number, because it is the nature of the slum dwellers to live only for to-day and to trust to luck for to-morrow, did nothing.

At last came the pinch. The authorities served the last notice, "Get out, or your walls will crumble about you." The tenant who after that still remained obstinate soon realised that the end had come. The roof, the doors, and the windows were removed while she (it is generally a woman) still remained crouching in a corner of the miserable room which contained the chair, the table, the bed, the frying pan, and the tub that were her 'furniture.'

Eventually the position became dangerous. When bricks and plaster began to fall in showers about her, and the point of the pickaxe came through the wall against which she was leaning, then at last she scrambled for her belongings and went out into the street, where a little crowd of onlookers and fellow sufferers welcomed her sympathetically.

Sometimes a whole family, the head having failed or neglected during the period of grace to find accommodation elsewhere, is turned into the street. I have seen families sitting homeless on their goods, which were piled high in the court. Guarding their household gods sat women with infants in their arms. They sat on, hopeless and despairing, and saw their homes demolished before their eyes.

Now and again the heap of bedding and furniture was diminished. A man would return and tell his wife he had found a place. They would gather up their goods and go. But all were not so fortunate. I have seen a woman with a child in her arms and two children crouching by her side sitting out long after nightfall by her flung-out furniture, because the husband could find no accommodation at the rent he could afford."

Despite these unfortunate circumstances, the new council flats were clean, bright, airy, and were fitted up with up-to-date appliances. In fact, not only new houses and council estates possessed the latest in fittings, but middle-class villas, elegant apartment flats, and even the town houses and country estates owned by the well-to-do. Electricity was wired in the upstairs (some more conscientious masters had it wired belowstairs as well), new plumbing, telephones installed, and water closets added to the layout. The most opulent transformation occurred in the bathroom, where the wealthiest had their baths amongst heated town rails, metal holders fixed to the wall for tooth brushes, mirrors over the pedestal wash basins, tiled floors (white or blue were the vogue), frosted glass windows, and marble walls. Some even featured the newfangled needle shower.

The *Daily Mail* tapped into the zeitgeist for new and improved housing for the lower and middle classes and founded the Ideal Home Exhibition in 1908. The exhibition featured whole rooms in the latest styles, and dedicated entire sections to home life (kitchens, sitting rooms, etc). They even featured a competition to build the "ideal home", and the Arts and Crafts Movement featured heavily amongst all displays. This concerted effort to uplift the poor had its roots in the Victorian era, but by the turn of the century Socialists and reformers alike demanded more than mere charity bazaars and drumming up donations; they preferred action.

The Salvation Army, founded by William and Catherine Booth in 1865, combined militant charity with Christianity, and out of this was born the settlement movement. The most famous of these was Toynbee Hall, founded in 1884. The aims of this movement were for the poor and rich to live together more closely. Situated in the poorer districts of London, middle and upper class volunteers lived in the settlement and ran programs providing food, shelter, and education for the poor amongst them. The first settlement homes were aligned with universities and a particular Anglican theology (High Church, Low Church), though later ones were founded by philanthropists (such as author Mrs. Humphry Ward, who founded the Passemore Edwards Settlement in 1898). The settlement movement was also a place for women to shine, and many houses dedicated to poor women and children were instituted by women's colleges and groups. In the Edwardian era, the poor had begun to take a role in their own reform, and many settlement halls were the site of debates and lectures run by working class men.

Also attracting interest for their dedication to social reform: the Fabian Society. Founded also in 1884, it became preeminent society for English socialism in the Edwardian era. Sidney and Beatrice Webb wrote many pamphlets and studies of the poor and of industrial Britain, and lobbied for the types of reforms popularized by Lloyd George—minimum wage, universal health care, and old age pensions. Famous Fabians included Virginia Woolf, H.G. Wells, Annie Besant, and George Bernard Shaw, the last of whom imbued many of his plays with his political beliefs. Lectures and public speaking engagements at Essex Hall were always packed, and gave a voice to the Labour Party.

This transformation from Victorian sentimentalism was extraordinary, and though many supported traditional class structure, an increasing number of people considered actions better than words when it came to social change. The people at the top may not have realized it, but society had begun to move beyond them long before WWI.

Heating
The basic home was heated by fireplace or, for the lower and working classes, the cooking range. Wealthier and more up-to-date homes were fitted with gas, and heated the home through a gas radiator--or, if fitted with electricity, electric radiators or even central heat.

Lighting

Gas lighting was first introduced in London in the early 1800s, and it became widely used in the mid-Victorian era. A large majority of society were slow to adopt electricity, both because of mistrust and its expense. The upper classes and aristocracy also tended to be wary of electricity (and even modern plumbing)—because it would lighten their servants' burdens.

The Bathroom

For a room so intimate and created for the expulsion of bodily excrement, the Edwardians were inordinately obsessed with bathrooms and plumbing. It was quite commonplace to discuss one's digestive system and "regularness," and during a house party in the country, the best hostesses paid close attention to the number of guests invited per bathroom.

The bathroom was also a frequent bone of contention between American heiresses and their new English family, and many butted against the centuries-old traditions of hip baths, chamber pots, and privy closets. The most progressive of English eventually discovered the delight and convenience of bathrooms via luxury hotels, new or updated country houses, and ocean liners (and were alerted to the health benefits of modern *sanitary* plumbing). An up-to-date bathroom became *de rigueur* for anyone with pretensions to fashion, or at the very least, desirous of guests who looked forward to a Saturday-to-Monday at an otherwise ancient country seat. According to *Houses and Gardens* by Mackay Hugh Baillie Scott:

In the development of the modern bathroom there is therefore no precedent in the tradition of the house, and in the average modern dwelling it will be well that the suggestion of spotless cleanliness and practical efficiency should be its salient characteristics. The floor and lower part of the walls of tiles, the bath and basin of white enamel with no pipes enclosed, with no dark corners to harbour dust and dirt, and the art of the bathroom as expressed in useless and dirt-concealing patterns rigorously excluded—such a scheme will, perhaps, represent the best that is possible for the average household.

...The bathroom should be so placed that the plumbing is reduced to a minimum, and the whole system is as simple and compact as possible, free from possible damage by frost, and capable of repair in all its parts without interference with the structure of the house. The quality of mystery has its artistic value in the house, but in the matter of plumbing it will probably only be appreciated by the plumber.

The modern bathroom was neatly and uniformly tiled, with porcelain fixtures, and marble wainscoting. Of the fixtures, the simplest bathrooms featured a toilet, a lavatory with bowl (the sink), bathtub, and mirror, whereas the most luxurious added a needle show, a fixed bath, heated towel rails, and other exquisite details to this room. The earliest bathrooms added to country houses or town mansions were usually converted linen closets, but by the mid-1900s, architects, and those who commissioned their services, considered the bathroom a room just as worthy of individuality and space as a bedroom or sitting room.

The Kitchen

The kitchen was not a place where design details were considered important to a home owner, but to the housewife, the cook, and the chef de cuisine of a large hotel, its layout and equipment were of the utmost importance. In the 1907 edition of *Mrs. Beeton's Household Management*, noted that the requisites of a good kitchen were:

1. Convenience of distribution in its parts, with largeness of dimension
2. Excellence of light, height, and ventilation
3. Easy of access, without passing through the house
4. Walls and location so arranged that the odours of cookery cannot spread about the house (the Victorians and Edwardians had a phobia of kitchen smells!)
5. Plenty of fuel and water, which, with the scullery, pantry and storeroom, should be so near the kitchen as to offer the smallest possible trouble in reaching them.

The issue of sanitation was also one of importance, and it was advised that walls be made of white glazed tiles and floor coverings of oil-cloth and linoleum. However, this varied depending on the architecture of area—for example, flags of smooth stone were cemented together to form a smooth floor in the north of England, the kitchen floor usually consisted of unglazed red tiles in the Midlands, and on the east coast, floors were frequently laid with red or yellow bricks.

Kitchen fixtures were simple and utilitarian, and a well-constructed sink of either wood lined with zinc, stoneware, or lined with cemented tiles were recommended. A large work table was the most important article of furniture, and the drawers at each end contained the cook's tools, such as knives and spoons, and small utensils and implements in constant use. The last, but by far the most important of the kitchen requisites was the kitchen range, or kitchener, which was used for cooking, heating water, and so on.

The kitchen range was a range, either open or close, that was fixed in its place with brickwork, the kitchener was a range entirely independent of its surroundings and stood on four legs, and the gas range or stove was similar to the kitchener, but was, of course, run with gas. Oil stoves and cooking by electricity were also popular options, though the latter was incredibly expensive to run.

A kitchen in tip-top form always contained a full array of utensils. There were the stewpans and saucepans of tin, copper, brass, enameled iron, and wrought steel; the boiler for boiling large joints, hams, and puddings; the digester, a small stock pot; the stock pot itself; the braising pan; the double or milk saucepan (a small bain-marie); steamers; fish-kettles; fish fryers; the frying pan; the bain-marie; the dripping pan; the gridion; and the dutch oven.

Other must-have utensils were weights and scales, a mincing machine, steak tongs, knives, a colander, a pestle and mortar, a chopping board and bowl, preserving pans, sieves, coffee and pepper mills, baking dishes, tartlet pans, vegetable cutters, an egg poacher, freezing machines, water filters, refrigerators, etc.

The Dining Room

Brothers and influential architects Sir Banister Fletcher and Herbert Phillips Fletcher provided Edwardian home buyers with guidance on purchasing, fitting, and decorating in their book, *The English Home*. Of the dining room, they firmly advised:

"This should have a warm yet subdued treatment in order to give it a quiet and cosy appearance. The walls should be divided only into two, as it is seldom possible in small houses to have a dado as well as a frieze. The lower part may have a dado of wainscot oak, or of stamped leather, and a moulded dado-rail may be formed to act as a chair-back and prevent the chairs rubbing against the wall surface.

Pompeian red is a good colour for the dining-room, but a subdued grey-green is preferred by many as a better background for pictures. There should always be a moulded picture-rail from which the pictures can be hung by means of hooks, for nothing looks more unfurnished and untidy than nails knocked into walls at different heights to support them. Pictures, moreover, can be easily taken down and cleaned and rehung if there is a picture-rail on the same level with, or not much higher than, the top of the door architraves. The picture-rail may be combined with the cornice where there is no frieze or in cases where a dado is provided, and the panel moulding may be utilized for this purpose where panelled walls are used.

The woodwork may be painted and varnished with a floor border in a darker colour, and a Turkey carpet covering the centre of the room has a pleasant effect. The table and chairs should be simple and harmonize with the style of the room. In furnishing the dining-room care should be taken not to have the table too large, and thus leave only a narrow passage round the room and a cramped space by the fireplace, which will make waiting at table a difficult operation.

The ceiling can either be plain or treated in ribs of a geometrical pattern, or with the beams showing.

The Drawing Room

This room, which also usually serves as a music-room, should usually be treated in a lighter key than the dining-room, and the walls may be divided into two by a deep frieze, possibly treated with figure-work of a lighter colour; but in larger rooms the walls may have a triple division. A chair-rail and dado may be dispensed with because the chairs in this room are usually arranged about the room in twos and threes for conversational purposes, and cabinets, small tables and bookcases may be placed against the walls.

Water-colour drawings are especially suitable, for they go well with the lighter treatment of this room. The woodwork should harmonize with the walls and ceilings, and may either be painted a cream-white with a finishing coat of eggshell enamel or, if it can be afforded, polished mahogany doors surrounded by architraves painted white are effective. Ceilings are as a rule best finished in white with moulded cornice and decorative bands.

Drawing-room furniture often consists of a collection of chairs and bric-a-brac of all styles brought together in a happy-go-lucky fashion, without any attempt at a homogeneous idea; but this suggestion of a furniture dealer's shop should be avoided.

Easy-chairs should not be much more than a foot in height, and may be upholstered in a simple texture in harmony with the general scheme of decoration. The primary object for which a chair is made should not be forgotten, and gimcrack constructions which, under the name of "Art," are foisted on the unwary customer only to give way under a person of more than usual weight should be avoided.

The Bedroom

The bedrooms should have the fitments designed by the architect, and they should form part of the room, as this will economize space and give it a finished appearance. Although it means additional preliminary expense, this will, however, be saved in subsequent expenditure on wardrobes and other furniture.

A bedroom floor may be stained a warm colour, and light hand rugs may be placed at the bedside before the looking-glass and wash-hand stand. Fitted carpets are a great mistake, for besides harbouring a great deal of dirt, extra domestic labour is required in sweeping them.

The walls may be finished in distemper of suitable tint, which, of course, should vary with the aspect of the room, as it goes without saying that a room facing south may be treated with a cooler tint than one facing north. The ceiling may be left plain white, or one may get a severe shock on waking from some intricate geometric stencil-work, such as one often sees in Italian hotels.

The Library or Study

The library should be treated in a manner somewhat similar to the dining-room and should have a subdued and cosy appearance.

The tops of the bookcases, which should have glass fronts to prevent dust settling on the books, should not be more than five or six feet from the ground, so that books may be easily reached, the top being used for casts or statuettes, etc. The library window sills may start from the top of these bookcases so as to exclude the outer world, and give the room the secluded character which conduces to study. One window, however, should be low enough to enable one to see out when seated, as this gives the room a cheerful appearance.

The Breakfast or Morning-room

Should, of course, be sunny and cheerful in character, and a light-coloured paper or distemper is suitable for the walls. The floor boards may be stained round the borders and a bright central carpet used. A moulded picture-rail and deep frieze are appropriate, and the latter treated in figure subjects on a light ground looks well.

Furnishing the Home

- *The Hire-Purchasing System*, wherein the buyer paid for their furnishings on an installment plan.
- *The Stock Furnishing System*, wherein the buyer took a list of what they wanted for each room, and purchased it all at once at a discounted rate.
- *The Craftsman's System*, wherein the buyer commissioned artist-craftsmen like C.R. Ashbee, C.F.A. Voysey, and others who owned their own workshops (typically aligned with the Arts and Crafts or Art Nouveau movements).
- *The Reproduction Method*, wherein the buyer purchased inexpensive furnishings in popular styles and modes (Sheraton, Chippendale, etc).

Bibliography

Aslet, Clive. *The Edwardian Country House: A Social and Architectural History*. London: Frances Lincoln Limited, 2012.

Bell, Yvonne. *The Edwardian Home*. Princes Risborough: Shire, 2005.

Dutton, Ralph. *The English Interior 1500 to 1900*. London: B.T. Batsford, 1948.

Flanders, Judith. *Inside the Victorian Home: A Portrait of Domestic Life in Victorian England*. New York: W. W. Norton, 2003.

Freeman, Mark. *The Edwardian Rural Poor*. London: Pickering & Chatto, 2005.

Service, Alastair. *Edwardian Interiors: Inside the Homes of the Poor, the Average, and the Wealthy*. London: Barrie & Jenkins, 1982.

Sparrow, Walter Shaw. *Hints on House Furnishing*. New York: John Lane, 1909.

Yelling, J. A. *Slums and Slum Clearance in Victorian London*. London: Allen & Unwin, 1986.

Cooking & Eating

According to British restaurant critic, Giles Coren, "a hundred years ago, British food was in its golden age, with the arrival of the great restaurant, the celebrity chef, exotic new dishes, and gargantuan twelve course meals."

Leading the way was, of course, King Edward VII. When Prince of Wales, he had swept aside both the lengthy meal times, encouraged service à la russe, and introduced, via his great appetite, the trend for copious, rich, luxurious eating habits. By the time he came to the throne, "his aristocratic and upper middle-class subjects were set on an annual collision course with raging dyspepsia."

Edwardian Gastronomy

The restaurant dinner, popular in Paris since the time of the French Revolution, had reached British shores by the 1880s. At first the act of dining in public was viewed warily—gentlemen were already accustomed to dining away from home at their clubs, men of the middle-class in steak shops and those of the working-class at oyster shops or food stands along the streets.

For ladies, the thought of eating in a place where strangers could gawk and stare was abhorrent. The breaking down of social barriers contributed to the custom of "dining out" by the 1890s. No longer were private, in-home suppers indicative of who was "in" and who was "out", and both ladies and gentlemen eagerly partook of the opportunity to leave their homes to see and be seen in the glamorous setting of a restaurant of the highest class.

To cater to this influx of diners, luxury hotels such as Claridge's, the Cecil, the Ritz and the Savoy, began to remodel their dining rooms into chic restaurants, fitted with terraced dining, winter gardens and separate supper rooms for private parties. An American influence came with the introduction of the "bar" and the "grillroom", which was a room set aside for informal dining.

The advent of this new transatlantic society left one restaurant clinging to the English tradition of formal evening attire. To dine in the Savoy's restaurant, or even to be served coffee in the adjoining foyer, it was absolutely essential that a lady wore a dinner gown sans chapeau and her escort a dress suit. Anyone who did not follow this command was liable to be refused entry, as an earl and his countess were to discover one night in 1907.

With these restaurants came the celebrity chef. Not since Antoine Carême ruled the stomachs of the Regency era's celebrities had the British shores experienced the artistry of a chef de haute cuisine. His successor? Auguste Escoffier, a Nice-born chef who simplified and modernized Carême's methods and contributed to the development of modern French cuisine. Escoffier formed a partnership with Cesar Ritz in 1890, and the two men moved to the Savoy Hotel in London and from there, established numerous hotels, including the Hotel Ritz across the world. In 1898, they opened the Hotel Ritz in Paris, and The Carlton in London the following year, where Escoffier also introduced the practice of the à la carte menu.

Escoffier had a rival in the form of a woman: the former scullery maid and proud Cockney, Rosa Lewis. The proprietress of the Cavendish Hotel, she had begun her culinary career in the London house of the Comte de Paris, the Orleanist pretender to the French throne. From there she went from the kitchens of the Duc d'Aumale, to the Duc d'Orleans, and at one time, simultaneously controlled the kitchens of White's Club and W.W. Astor's home, Hever Castle. It was when Lady Randolph Churchill acquired Rosa's services that she began her ascent to fame. Anecdotes tell of the Prince of Wales, upon being introduced to Rosa by Lady Randolph as an excellent cook, never doubted it, exclaiming "Damme, she takes more pains with a cabbage than with a chicken. . . . She gives me nothing sloppy, nothing colored up to dribble on a man's shirt-front."

Rosa became the first freelance cook, and was available for hire by any person who could afford her services. With Bertie's endorsement and her food witness to her talent, she became much in demand, with hostesses vying to obtain her services for country house parties throughout England. As she grew in importance, Rosa began to travel about with a chorus of assistant cooks attired exactly as she was, in spotless white with tall chef's hats and high laced "cooking boots" of soft black kid, to support the ankles during the long hours spent preparing dishes.

During the Coronation year of 1902, Rosa produced 29 suppers for just as many large balls, and often came home in the wee hours of the morning without a wink of sleep. With the money saved from that year, she bought the Cavendish Hotel in Jermyn Street, where she earned a fortune catering to the vital needs of the aristocracy: privacy and excellent food. A private dining room was available for use, where swells could bring their lady friends, and there were permanent suites for those inclined to live outside of their homes.

Exotic dishes were created to meet the demand from aristocratic gourmands. The ultimate Edwardian recipe? A rich, extravagant dish comprised of pate de fois gras stuffed inside of a truffle, which was stuffed inside of an ortolan, itself stuffed inside of a quail. Escoffier invented the Pêche Melba and Melba Toast in the 1890s, both dishes named for the strident soprano Nellie Melba, and Rosa Lewis invented a delicious quail pudding for King Edward.

Because meal times were pushed back by the close of the 19th century, other, smaller meals were inserted into the day to fill rumbling bellies. Lunch was inserted between breakfast and dinner, ladies added the afternoon tea. Another sort of tea—with hot muffins, crumpets, toast, cold salmon, pies, ham, roast beef, fruit, cream and tea and coffee—found its way into the more active and informal program of the country house.

The Edwardians never stopped eating. From the time they rose, to even the times they awoke in the middle of the night, food was ready and available. A typical English breakfast consisted of haddock, kidneys, kedgeree, porridge, game pie, tongue, poached eggs, bacon, chicken and woodcock. Luncheon included hot and cold dishes: cold fowls, lamb, pigeon, cold pie and ptarmigan, puddings, cheeses, biscuits, jellies, and fruit.

Supper now served *à la russe*, this allowed a greater sample of dishes available, and the number of courses grew. During the height of the Edwardian period, to sit down for a ten to fifteen course meal was quite the norm. Of course one wasn't required to partake of each course, nor was it expected, but the parade of dishes: hors d'oeuvres, soups, salads, vegetables, meats—poultry, game, beef, mutton, and pork—, seafood, puddings, breads, savories, and fruits, if not the number of wines offered to compliment each course, is enough to make our 21st century stomachs queasy.

And it didn't end there. Hostesses expecting the King were well advised to provide snacks consisting of lobster salad and cold chicken to serve at eleven, and even after dinner, a plate of sandwiches, and sometimes a quail or cutlet, was sent to his rooms. At night, dainties were left outside of guests' rooms during country house parties, in case someone felt a bit peckish. Despite the expense put into creating these elaborate meals, those of smaller means weren't left out of the general smörgåsbord.

This was also the apogee of name brands and modern processed foods such as Marmite (1902), Ty.phoo tea (1904), Colman's Mustard (1903), bouillon cubes made simulate beef extract by Maggi (1908) and Oxo (1910), instant coffee (1901), Bird's Custard Powder (est. 1837), Jacob's water biscuits (1881), HP Sauce (1903) and Cadbury's Milk Chocolate (est. 1824). The appearance of refrigeration made dining much easier too.

This trend for gargantuan meals obviously had its downsides. At the end of the season, these Edwardian gastronomes found their digestion so wound in knots, a month-long jaunt to the Continent was deemed necessary. And the annual trek to Austrian or German watering spots like Bad-Ischl or Carlsbad, were added to the general round of the season. Here ladies and gentlemen were put on strict diets and forced to exercise daily.

At the end of the treatment, or "cure", they would return to their homes a bit trimmer and with better digestion, only to begin the round of eating once more. Fortunately for the ladies, the standards of beauty praised the ample, womanly curves created by nature and enhanced with corsets, which gave them the signature "S" shape most assiduously admired by the men of the period.

English Food and Drink

English cooking had a bad rap during the 19th and early 20th centuries. Caricatures of the typical Englishman ("John Bull") poked fun at his florid face, his avoirdupois, and his bad manners when eating a meal consisting of a joint and boiled vegetables. In contrast, the typical Frenchman was even-complected, with a graceful figure, and impeccable and elegant table manners as he sat to dine at six course meal of the most aromatic and delicately prepared dishes.

The mania for French cooking began with Antonin Carême, chef de cuisine to the Prince Regent, who simplified meals and organized dishes into distinct groups, and solidified under Alexis Soyer, whose feasts dominated the imaginations of the early Victorians. French haute cuisine reached its pinnacle beneath the magical fingers of Auguste Escoffier, who became one of the leaders in the development of modern French cuisine. Yet, beneath the canapés and ragoûts, traditional English cooking retained its position on the tables of not only the poor and working classes, but on the menus of aristocratic and royal houses.

Traditional English cuisine was influenced by England's Puritan roots, which shunned strong flavors and the complex sauces associated with European (Catholic) nations. Most dishes, such as bread and cheese, roasted and stewed meats, meat and game pies, boiled vegetables and broths, and freshwater and saltwater fish, had ancient origins, and recipes for the aforementioned existed in the Forme of Cury, a 14th century cook book dating from the royal court of Richard II. Not surprisingly, English cuisine had its regional dishes, the most famous being Cornwall's Stargazy Pie, Derbyshire's Bakewell tart, Lancashire's hot pot, Leicestershire's Stilton cheese, and Devonshire's clotted cream.

An Englishman was most proud of his meat and game, and even after dining à la russe surpassed service à la française in popularity, the host of a supper party considered carving a roast or a joint or a fish an art, and practically a divine right to show off at the table. In historical fiction, the meat most often mentioned is mutton. Though meat in its various incarnations are typically described in an unappetizing manner, in truth, mutton is to lamb what beef to is veal–that is, meat from a sheep older than two years–and far from being cold and congealed and otherwise disgusting, mutton was very versatile: one could boil it, broil it, bake it, roast it, fillet it, stew it, braise it, and fry it.

Due to game laws, other extremely popular meats such as venison, hare, partridge, pigeon, and pheasant, and so on, were restricted to the wealthy, since the land on which game (and the lakes and rivers where fish was found) were owned by English aristocrats or the Royal Family, and shooting and hunting permits were expensive. However, the Sunday roast, a traditional meal served on that day and consisting of "roasted meat, roast potato together with accompaniments, such as Yorkshire pudding, stuffing, vegetables and gravy," was a meal common in all English households, with variations depending upon taste and budget.

Another most English dish is pudding. This is not the familiar milk-based chocolate or tapioca Jell-O brand seen in American supermarkets, but a rich, starchy, and typically savoury dish. Some puddings, such as rice pudding or Christmas pudding, were for dessert, but the best-known (Yorkshire pudding, suet pudding, blood pudding, etc) derived from English cooks devising ways in which to utilize fat drippings or leftover meats or blood.

During the British Raj, English cooks began to borrow from Indian dishes, creating a fusion cuisine known as "Anglo-Indian." By the end of the 19th century, Kedgeree, Mulligatawny soup, curried meats, and chutney became such a staple on the English menu, the dishes were absorbed into the national English cuisine.

But let us not forget that most English of cuisine: Tea! Though tea was drunk in vast quantities by the English since the 17th century, it was when afternoon tea was devised by the Duchess of Bedford in the 1840s, that tea consumption increased. In 1911 alone, the people of the United Kingdom as a whole, consumed 296,000,000 pounds, or six and three-quarters pounds per person, of tea!!! Only Russia, which consumed 147,132,000 pounds of tea came close to that figure. Strangely enough, the French considered tea a medicinal drink, preferring coffee, though ardent Anglophiles gamely indulged in their "fif o'clock."

Consumed with the tea were scones (Scottish in origin); dropped scones (which look like small pancakes) dipped in honey, crumpets (which look like English muffins); pikelets ("a British regional dialect word variously denoting a flatter variant on crumpet or muffin. In the West Midlands [and to some extent, the Yorkshire area] it is a term for crumpet. A crumpet in this area is similar in appearance [but not taste] to a North American pancake; light sandwiches (watercress, cucumber, ham, etc); and small cakes and pastries, all of which were displayed on tiered stands. Another form of tea was the "high tea," which does not denote a fancy tea party, but a somewhat substantial meal of cold meats, tea, cakes, and sandwiches. Farming or working-class families mostly ate this, though, as the supper hour was pushed back to the late evening in the Edwardian era, English people of all classes tended to indulge.

And so, English cooking, despite its preponderance of heavy meats, savory delights, and brow-raising names (Toad-in-a-hole, anyone?), is far from deserving of its bad reputation. After all, many of our most famous English (and American) heroes and heroines dined daily upon these dishes and I feel secure knowing that Jane Austen, Anne Bronte, and Charles Dickens wrote their masterpieces nourished by their Mother Country's cooking.

Luncheon, according to Lady Colin Campbell, has been defined as an insult to one's breakfast and an outrage to one's dinner. For most of the 19th century, three meals—breakfast, dinner, and supper—were considered sufficient, but the shift in dinner time to later in the day called something more substantial than a glass of madeira and a slice of madeira cake. This small meal was first called "nooning", and was consumed during the regular visiting hours of Regency era ladies (between 11 and 4). By the 1850s, "lunch" or "luncheon" became a part of the standard meal times of the day, and by the 1880s, society witnessed a plethora of lunches: hunting lunches, race luncheons, shooting luncheons, etc. Etiquette, of course, sprang around this new mealtime. According to Mrs. Humphry:

"The toilettes of the ladies are also more like dinner dresses than those usually worn in the afternoon. Here, with us, ordinary afternoon dress is the rule for ladies. In town, in the season, a man is expected to Luncheons wear either a frockcoat or a cutaway black coat. If he has been regularly invited to lunch he leaves his hat and stick in the hall. In the country, a man wears a country suit, or riding dress if he has ridden from his own home to his hostess' house.

All the guests are shown into the drawing room, where the hostess receives them. They retain their hats and, in winter, leave furs or heavy wraps in the hall or dining room. Gloves are usually removed and Guest when sitting down to table. The hostess may or may not have hat or bonnet on. If she has just come in from shopping or driving, she very probably will be in outdoor dress.

At a very formal luncheon, however, she will be in indoor dress; since outdoor costume might be interpreted as having reference to some intention of going out immediately after, and would be considered as a hint to her guests to leave early.

The routine of the meal is very simple. When the table is laid, all cold dishes are placed upon it, so as to have the service simplified as much as possible. One of the charms of lunch is that the servants are not in the room after the sweets have been brought in and handed round. In some houses, when the meal is a very elaborate one, the servants remain to hand fruit or ices, but the general custom is for them to leave the room and shut the door, having left everything ready in the shape of plates, knives, forks, spoons, &c. The meal is never expected to be a very elaborate one. Soup or fish may precede a joint or an entree, or a dish of game.

The joint is getting quite unfashionable among the smart. Rather small chicken pies or dishes of a French character are more acceptable than anything heavy or solid. Where the minage is of an important kind, the carving is done by the butler at a side-table, just as it is at dinner. Wine is not so much drunk at lunch as it used to be. Claret is, however, generally at hand. At many tables aerated waters are the usual beverage at this meal, even in houses where wine is always served at dinner. When gentlemen are present, they often like a glass of beer at luncheon. But even when no wine is habitually used, wineglasses are laid at each cover, which is prepared exactly as for dinner.

There is now such a rage for champagne that many people would regard a lunch as very incomplete without that wine. The hostess has to consider all these various views and decide what course she shall take in the matter.

The meal over...the rest of the party adjourn to the dining-room where coffee is usually served, and it is generally half-past three or nearly four before the guests leave. When guests are leaving, the hostess rings the bell, and sometimes walks with them as far as the drawing-room door. The servants have presumably been trained to hand each lady her coat and sunshade or umbrella; each gentleman his hat, overcoat, stick or umbrella; also to call a cab or summon the carriage, as the case may be."

The working classes kept to the three meal tradition of breakfast, supper, and dinner, mostly because they hadn't the leisure time to spare and since they worked early and went to bed early. Supper was also called High Tea, or Meat Tea in northern England and Scotland (though in common vernacular, it was just Tea), which typically consisted of "tea with sugar, bread heaped with butter, jam, preserves, cold meat, cheese or an egg." Among the poorer classes, the meal might be nothing more than a pot of tea with a bloater or herring, but on excursions or on holidays, "it might become the occasion for eating fish and chips, a dish which, it has been claimed, originated in Oldham in the 1860s."

As stated before, the English had drunk tea since the 17th century, but the Duchess of Bedford popularized afternoon tea in the 1840s. This ritual spread down and up the social ladder (with the exception of the poor and working classes) until it became an expression of one's leisure time and social status. Afternoon tea served multiple purposes, all of which had little to do with a repast before dinner.

Lady Colin Campbell's etiquette book lists two classes of tea—great tea and little tea, the latter which comprised of "handed tea" or "afternoon tea", and "high" or "meat" teas in the former (this was shared by the rich and poor, but was considered more a country entertainment than an actual necessary meal by the rich).

The High or Meat tea described by Lady Colin was considerably more substantial than the one eaten by the poor: "bowls of old china filled with ripe red strawberries, and jugs of rich cream by their side. Glass dishes containing preserved fruits of different colours, such as apricots, strawberries, marmalade, &c., take their stands at short intervals. Cakes of various kinds— plum, rice, and sponge; and then within easy reach of the "tea-drinkers" are hot muffins, crumpets, toast, tea-cakes, and what not.

At one end of the table the tea-tray stands, with its adjuncts; at the other the coffee is placed, also on a tray. The sideboard is the receptacle of the weightier matters, such as cold salmon, pigeon and veal and ham pies, boiled and roast fowls, tongues, ham, veal cake; and should it be a very 'hungry tea,' roast beef and lamb may be there for the gentlemen of the party."

There were also servants in attendance, who carved the meat and prepared the tea, and frequently this meal was capped by a small dance or a game of charades.

The Handed, or Afternoon tea, was part of a lady's "At Home", which was the designated hour and day when she would receive callers. If so inclined, one would drop by for tea and find the hostess in the drawing room where she served tea to her callers and provided food of a daintier fare:

"In winter, muffins and hot buttered cakes, sometimes buttered toast, are provided, with mixed biscuits and tempting looking little cakes from the confectioner's. Plain bread and butter, brown and white, are always provided, and the slices are usually rolled so that they can be lifted without the glove or finger coming in contact with the butter. Foie gras sandwiches are always appreciated, and in summer sandwiches made of cucumber or cress are liked."

Alcoholic beverages were just as commonplace as tea, with beer and ale the staple of the working glasses, and fine wines the province of the wealthy. During the Edwardian period, cocktails— the American influence—invaded English restaurants and homes, and according to a 1910 issue of *The Sketch*, the smartest homes served them before lunch or dinner. Punches, mixed drinks containing fruit or fruit juice, with the option of alcohol, were de rigueur for balls where large amounts of drink were needed to quench hundreds of thirsty dancers.

Other drinks popular with the Edwardians were coffee (though not as popular as it was in America and in France), champagne, and aerated (mineral) water. The last of these rose in stature with the growth of health consciousness and the fad for hiking and mountaineering. The most popular brand was Perrier, a company owned by Sir Saint-John Harmsworth, the younger brother of Lord Northcliffe of the *Daily Mail*. He launched a huge campaign in his brother's papers touting the chicness and Frenchness of the aerated water to the *Daily Mail*'s readership. Soon bottled mineral water flooded the market, and the 1907 Army & Navy Catalog lists two pages worth of brands.

Cooking Schools and Domestic Training
Many would argue that the Edwardian era was the age of modern
cookery. Not only were chefs lifting the preparation and
consumption of food to the highest art, but due to falling food
prices and rising incomes, the opportunity of dining on the best
cuisine expanded to the middle classes.

Though women were mostly boxed into the field of domestic
science, they too influenced the rise of culinary arts and a health
consciousness. Rosa Lewis, the "Queen of Cooks," was the most
visible Edwardian woman, and Marthe Distel, a French journalist
who founded the culinary magazine *La Cuisinière Cordon Bleu* to
teach the principles of French cuisine to upper-class women, had a
lasting impact when this magazine led to the formation of *Le
Cordon Bleu* cooking school. However, the most influential woman
in the food industry was Mrs. Agnes Marshall.

The 1880s and 1890s witnessed the beginnings of the domestic
science movement, and the charismatic and determined Mrs.
Marshall fit into this female-oriented movement, boosting the
National Training School of Cookery's pupils from forty within
two years of purchasing the school to thousands for day-, month-,
semester-, or year-long courses. Her pupils included cooks
wanting to increase their skills (or, cooks dispatched hastily by
their employers to learn how to prepare edible meals), middle class
women desiring to run a tip-top household, and even aristocratic
women picking up a unique hobby. The curriculum "offered
specialty instruction in cooking, including lessons in curry from an
English colonel who had served in India and classes in French
haute cuisine taught by a Cordon Bleu graduate."

Over the following ten years, Mrs. Marshall expanded her
empire adding an employment agency and registrar for cooks, a
kitchen shop where food prepared by students was sold to the
public, cookbooks, a weekly newspaper called *The Table*. She also
sold "specialty foods, utensils, cutlery, cast-iron equipment, and
cooking supplies including baking powder, flavorings, vegetable
food colorants, leaf gelatin, and in 1888, an edible cornet à la crème
(ice cream cone) made with ground almonds." This last item, and
her ice cream molds which ran up to a thousand shapes and
varieties, earned Mrs. Marshall the moniker "Queen of Ices" in

response to her passionate devotion to ices, ice creams, and frozen desserts.

With so many things to juggle, it was amazing that Mrs. Marshall had the time to lecture, but she did, scheduling six talks per week in Birmingham, Glasgow, Leeds, Manchester, and Newcastle, and a second tour went to twelve additional cities. Her live demonstrations, held on consecutive Saturdays in London, drew rave reviews and even more fame, though oddly enough, she found little success in the United States (her nearest rival there was Maria Parloa).

She began to wind her career down a notch by the mid-1890s, turning from lecturing, cooking, and writing, to charity, initiating Yule dinners for the poor and maintaining winter soup kitchens. After writing one more cookbook, *Fancy Ices*, Mrs. Marshall retired to Pinner, her estate on the River Pinn, where she lived until her death from a riding accident in 1905, just a month short of her fiftieth birthday.

Mrs. Marshall and her empire faded from view and memory as the twentieth century wore on, "but her influence and opinions endured even longer. She denounced canned food and the substandard meals served in railway cars and depots. She campaigned for the availability of fresh produce and trained kitchen staff. Her prognostications foresaw the acceptance of dishwashers, the expansion of automobile travel, the advent of supermarkets, fad diets, chemical purification of water, refrigerated trucks, and the popularization of the ice cream freezer."

The Epicure, sub-titled "A Journal of Taste," chronicled the domestic science and cookery movement in England. Each issue featured recipes, articles on food chemistry and preparation, spotlights on the latest cookbooks, new trends in table setting, feeding the poor, the food manufacturing trade, and descriptions of the various cooking schools and domestic science programs mushrooming across the country. During the 1890s and 1900s there were numerous exhibitions, lectures, and programs focused on nutrition, cooking demonstrations, food purchasing, and other domestic matters. 1906 was the year of the 17th Universal Cookery & Food Exhibition, which was held at the Royal Horticultural Hall and boasted Queen Alexandra as its patroness.

"The main features of the Exhibition have been retained as on former occasions; there will, however, be several new additions which are likely to add considerably to the educational value of the forthcoming Exhibition. The High-class Cookery Section, which was hitherto styled the "Artistic," has been divided into two groups, one for exhibits of ornamental character, and one for classic and modern cookery exhibits, where ornamentation, especially the nonedible, will be rigidly excluded. The whole of this section has been entirely remodelled and re-classified. Soups and sauces have also found a place this year, so that this part of the Exhibition ought to prove exceptionally interesting.

Larger space having been secured for still exhibits in the Cookery and Confectionery Sections, and for competitive demonstrations, the scope for exhibitors will be greater on the present occasion than has hitherto been possible, and it is anticipated that the increased number of competitors who have promised to take part will reap some benefit by having better accommodation and opportunities for the display of their exhibits.

In consequence of this the space for exhibits of a purely commercial character has to be considerably reduced. Several of the more important trade spaces have already been booked by former exhibitors, and there is only a comparatively small number of spaces now available for trade exhibits.

The Demonstrative Competitions should be specially interesting as well as instructive, there being several novel competitions and contests announced.

The innovation introduced last year of giving cash prizes with some of the medals will, as far as possible, be continued, and the gold medals will be solid gold—no silver-gilt or gold-plated medals will be awarded, the Committee having renounced this practice, which at its best cannot be considered as satisfactory. The prize list shows a most liberal supply of valuable scholarships, cups, gold, silver and bronze medals, which are offered for competition in the various classes.

The prizes so far offered represent a value of nearly £400—which the Committee have every reason to hope will be substantially increased by the end of the present month.

Arrangements have been made for a series of up-to-date lectures and demonstrations to be given daily in the Lecture Hall.

These include: A demonstration lecture, by Miss Stubbs, of the Midland Dairy Institute, entitled, "Milk, Butter, and their Products"; a demonstration lecture by Mr. E. P. Veerasawmy, M.C.A., entitled, "Indian Dishes: Fish, Flesh, Poultry and Vegetables"; three demonstrations on artistic confectionery by Mr. F. Dingle, M.C.A., and Mr. Emile Merz, M.C.A.; a lecture by Mr. Tom Sedgwick, entitled, "German Methods of Fruit Preserving"; a demonstration on "The Art of Sauce Making," by Mr. Iwan Kriens, M.C.A., and two special demonstrations by Mr. C. Hermann Senn, G.C.A., assisted by Mr. Ph. Heuline, M.C.A., on " Luncheon and Supper Dishes, Hors d'CEuvre, and Savouries."

As usual, both cooks from H.M. Army and Navy will be fully represented at the Exhibition. The War Office has given permission for soldier-cooks from the battalions of the Guards in the London districts and from Aldershot, also from regiments of the Household Cavalry, to take part in the competitions in Army cookery.

The Lords Commissioners of the Admiralty have been pleased to give permission for three cooks' ratings, with their instructors, from each of the three ports, to attend the Exhibition for the purpose of taking part in the competition for Navy cookery. The party will be in charge of a lieutenant, who will be responsible for the arrangements, the attendance of the men, and their accommodation in town.

At the recommendation of the Sub-Committee of the group for Cookery in Elementary Schools, it has been decided that each school competing must send six pupils, and that these must be of one class, and not picked out from several classes. Following is the syllabus of dishes selected for this competition :—1. Lentil Soup and Rock Cakes; 2. Rhubarb Tart, Boiled Potatoes; 3. Fried Plaice, Porridge; 4. Roast Beef, Pancakes; 5. Irish Stew, Fried Sausages and Bread; 6. Cornish Pasties, Lemonade."

Bibliography

Bailey, Adrian. *Mrs. Bridges' Upstairs Downstairs Cookery Book*. New York: Simon and Schuster, 1975.

Blakeston, Oswell. *Edwardian Glamour Cookery without Tears*. London: Hugh Evelyn, 1960.

Broomfield, Andrea. *Food and Cooking in Victorian England: A History*. Westport, CT: Praeger, 2007.

Colquhoun, Kate. *Taste: The Story of Britain through Its Cooking*. New York: Bloomsbury, 2007.

The Countess of Warwick. *Life's Ebb and Flow*. New York: W. Morrow, 1929.

Cowles, Virginia. *Gay Monarch: The Life and Pleasures of Edward VII*. New York: Harper, 1956.

Marshall, A. B., and Robin Weir. *Mrs. Marshall: The Greatest Victorian Ice Cream Maker: With a Facsimile of The Book of Ices 1885: With Additional Chapters*. W. Yorkshire: Published for Syon House by Smith Settle, 1998.

Pearsall, Ronald. *Edwardian Life and Leisure*. Newton Abbot: David & Charles, 1973.

Shapiro, Laura. *Perfection Salad: Women and Cooking at the Turn of the Century*. New York: Farrar, Straus, and Giroux, 1986.

Tannahill, Reay. *Food in History*. New York, NY: Stein & Day, 1973.

Wilson, C. Anne. *Eating with the Victorians*. [Stroud, Gloucestershire]: Sutton Publications, 2004.

Household Budgets

In 1901, the Cornhill Magazine published a series on family budgets ranging from the lowest workman to the comfortable income of £10,000 a year. The following are excerpts from each tier of budgets.

Workman

The budget must be considered in terms of weekly expenditure. The yearly or half-yearly balance-sheet, formal or informal, is for the man who reckons his income by the year, not for him who lives from Saturday to Saturday on weekly wages. The class we are considering is one of men earning from twenty or twenty-five to forty shillings a week, and for our instance we put the sum at thirty shillings, not as the average of a full week's wages, which would be a little higher, but as a general average, allowing for missed time, slack periods, and the like.

Our particular example is of a man—a married man, of course—living in a humble though decent neighbourhood in London, at no very great distance from his work. We will suppose the children to be three, and of school age, though this need not hinder us from glancing as we pass at the effect on the exchequer of an increase both in numbers and in age.

Rent varies of course with a dozen circumstances, but it is no very uncommon thing to find our thirty-shilling-a-week workman paying it to the amount of ten shillings a week—precisely a third of his income—or even more. At seven shillings we will fix our man's rent. For that he will get three rooms—not very big rooms, as a general thing— being the half of one of the six-roomed houses that make the bulk of the streets in East London. The relatively higher rent of small houses arises from an excessive demand, and from the fact that a workman *must* live within a reasonable distance of his work.

The 'missis' begins the other side of the account by going shopping on Saturday evening, taking her husband with her—he is a docile husband, this—to wait outside shops and carry the heavier parcels. The whole Saturday marketing expenditure [is] eight shillings and fourpence-halfpenny. Thus:—

	Shillings (s.)	Pence (d.)
Grocer's	1	8
Cheesemonger's	1	11
Butcher's	2	7
Fishmonger's	0	10
Greengrocer's	0	6
Baker's	0	10½
Total	8	4½

So that when the landlord takes his seven shillings on Monday morning, more than half the week's money will be knocked down.

The remaining household expenses: As to food, there will be bread to get for the rest of the week, and this will cost one-and-threepence. This, with the three loaves already bought, allows one loaf a day. The joint of meat will probably hold out, in one shape or another, over Thursday's dinner, and then something else—fish, sausages, or what not— will be bought for Friday and Saturday. This, with what is called a 'relish ' for tea or breakfast—it may be fish, or an egg, or a rasher of bacon—on an occasion or two in the latter part of the week—the whole of the additional meat and fish, in short—will cost two shillings. Extra vegetables will be needed, some of them for Thursday's stew, and the cost of these may be put at ninepence.

In the matter of fuel, expense will vary, of course, with the season. The workman is afflicted with a sad lack of storage-room, and this fact alone would be sufficient to condemn him to buy coal by the hundredweight. This means, of course, that he cannot avail himself of low summer prices to lay in a stock, and he must pay the current rate, however high. Moreover, the current rate with the small dealers of whom he buys is apt to be above that of the merchants who quote by the ton, while the quality of the coal is anything but correspondingly high.

Except on washing days only one fire will be used in the winter, for the cooking is done in the living room. In the summer a fire is only used when heavy cooking is to be done, a small oil stove sufficing for the occasional boiling of a kettle or the frying of a rasher of bacon. Taking one thing with another the year round, fuel—coal and wood—will cost our workman two shillings a week.

Paraffin oil, for lamp and stove, will cost sixpence for the week, and perhaps one packet of Swedish boxes of matches will be used—especially if the workman smoke, as he usually does— and these matches will cost three-halfpence. Soap, starch, blue, and soda will cost sixpence a week, and blacking and blacklead three-halfpence. The washing and ironing will be done at home, of course, but clothes will be put out to mangle at a cost of threepence. Pepper, salt, mustard, and so forth—' cruet allowance,' in fact—will average at three-halfpence a week.

With this we come to the end of strictly household expenses, and we find, as I calculate, that since the transactions of Saturday, seven-and-seven-pence-halfpenny more will have been spent, making, with the rent and the money spent on Saturday, a total of one pound three shillings. So that now there is left from the week's wages a sum of seven shillings available for clothes, clubs, insurances, beer, tobacco, fares, newspapers, books, holidays, renewals of furniture and utensils, postage, petty cash, amusements, charities, dissipations, savings, investments, and as many more things as we may imagine it will buy.

The income and expenditure account of the week, then, will stand thus:—

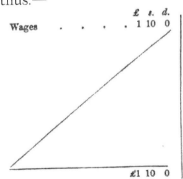

	£	s.	d.
Wages	1	10	0
	£1	**10**	**0**

	£	s.	d.
Rent		7	0
Meat and fish		5	5
Bread and flour		2	1½
Grocery		1	8
Cheese, butter, bacon, and eggs	1	11	
Greengrocery		1	3
Firing		2	0
Oil and sundries		1	7½
Allowance for clothes		2	0
Club and insurance		1	0
Beer and tobacco		2	9
Balance in hand for contingencies, petty cash, &c.		1	3
	£1	**10**	**0**

Lower Middle Class

Amongst the earners of a yearly wage of from 150l. to 200l. we find certain skilled mechanics; bank clerks; managing clerks to solicitors; teachers in the London Board Schools (in 1895 there were about 800 male teachers receiving from 150l. to 165l. per annum) ; the younger reporters on the best metropolitan papers; the senior reporters on the best local papers; second division clerks in the Colonial, Home, and India Offices. Also, the second-class examining officers in the Customs; senior telegraphists; first-class overseers in the General Post Office; Government office-keepers; sanitary inspectors; relieving officers; many vestry officials; clerks under the County Councils; police inspectors; chief warders of prisons; barristers' clerks; photographers employed in the manufacture of process blocks; assistant painters in the leading theatres; organists, and curates in priest's orders.

For the expenditure of a yearly income of from 150l. to 200l. per annum, the example chosen is that of a cashier in a solicitor's office—a man of high character, good education, and high ideals, who, from his fourteenth to his fortieth year, has earned his living in his chosen profession. For ten years he has been married to the daughter of a once well-to-do farmer, who for some time before her marriage had found it necessary, in consequence of agricultural depression, to go out into the world and earn her own living in a house of business. In her father's house she had learned the domestic arts.

Our typical couple are fortunate in having but two children—fortunate not merely because there will be fewer mouths to feed but because the wage-earner's mobility will not be unduly checked. The size of his family is of peculiar importance when a man is young and coming to find out his powers and capabilities. It is only with a small one that he will be able to make a favourable disposition of his labour. With an increasing family he will find it harder and harder to move about in search of his best market.

It is in the proportion of his income that must be expended on the item 'Rent' that a man of small means is more particularly handicapped. To the worker in the City of London, where, as a matter of fact, our solicitor's clerk worked for twenty years, or in Westminster, where he worked for four, one of three courses is practically open. Either he must live within easy distance in lodgings in some such locality as Trinity Square, S.E., or Vincent Square, S.W., or in one of those huge blocks of flats to be found in the neighbourhood of London's heart in such districts as Finsbury, Lambeth, or Southwark; or he must go further afield and find an inexpensive house in one of the cheaper suburbs, Clapham, Forest Gate, Wandsworth, Walthamstow, Kilburn, Peckham, or Finsbury Park. That he will be well advised in adopting the latter course there can, I think, be no possible doubt, and this although he will have to add to his rent the cost of travelling to and fro.

In the first place he will be able to house himself at a lower rental; in the second place his surroundings will be far more healthy; in the third place his neighbours will be of his own class, a matter of chiefest importance to his wife and children, the greater part of whose lives must be spent in these surroundings. There are thousands of snug little suburban sixroomed houses which can be had for a weekly rental of from 10s. to 12s. 6d. a week, and it is in these that the vast majority of London Benedicts who earn from 150l. to 200l. a year are to be run to earth. Those who live in lodgings or flats near by their work pay a higher rent for two or three small rooms. And when we get into what we may call essentially the clerks' suburbs— Leytonstone, Forest Gate, Walthamstow, and such like—it is astonishing what a difference an extra shilling or two a week will make in the general character of our surroundings.

Our specimen couple were fortunate in being enabled to live in a twelve-and-sixpenny house, in a very different road from the road of ten-shilling houses, by the fact that a relative rented one of their rooms. A parallel arrangement is of course open to any couple who care to take in a lodger.

Having then decided upon a home in the suburbs, the next expenditure which has to be faced is the wage-earner's railway fare to and from his work. In all probability the distance will be from four to six miles. This would mean at least sixpence a day spent in travelling, were it not that all the railway companies issue season tickets at reduced rates. Some of them, however, do not offer these facilities to third-class passengers. We must, therefore, in a typical case put down at least 7l. a year for a second-class 'season.' A ticket of this sort has of course the further advantage of covering the expense of extra journeys to town for churches, picture galleries, or Albert Hall concerts on Sundays, or for evening lectures or amusements on weekdays.

Our wage-earner has now to face the very considerable expenditure which, in the budget at the end of this article, comes under the three headings dealing with Dress. And in approaching this matter we must remember that not only has dress 'a moral effect upon the conduct of mankind,' but, so far as the individual is concerned, has very often a determining effect upon his success as a wage-earner. Here he is clearly at a disadvantage compared with the man who works with his hands and who only has to keep a black coat for high days and holidays. Thus, through the action of certain economic laws, the average 'lower-middle' bread-winner is forced into an extravagance in the matter of clothes out of all proportion to his income.

Plain living will be a matter of course on an income of 150l. a year, but this does not necessarily connote cheap food. The thoughtful housekeeper will instruct her husband to call in before leaving town at some such market as Leadenhall, or to do her marketing for her at one of the great central stores where he will pay cash. Because of the rapid sale get goods of the best quality and of the freshest at prices well worth comparing with those of the small local dealer, who will be only too anxious to book orders and deliver goods. The same will apply in the matter of fish. In some districts, she will find large local stores only second to those to be found in the City.

	Shillings (s.)	Pence (d.)
Meat and Fish	7	0
Greengrocer	1	3
Milk	2	6
Bread	1	6

Grocery	6	0
Total	18	3

Total Budget—:

	£	s.	d.
Rent (26*l.*), rates and taxes (5*l.* 3*s.* 5*d.*)	31	3	5
Railway travelling	7	0	0
Life insurance and benefit club	4	8	3
Newspapers, books, &c.	4	10	0
Gas, coal, coke, oil, wood, matches	9	17	0
Summer Holiday	5	0	0
Tobacco	2	5	0
Birthday and Christmas presents	1	10	0
Stamps and stationery		12	0
Food	47	9	0
House expenses	5	4	0
Boots	6	0	0
Tailor	6	0	0
Dress for wife and children	13	0	0
Balance to cover doctor, chemist, charities, &c. . .	6	1	4
	£150	0	0

It may be interesting to compare with Mr. Layard's model budget the following statement of the manner in which an annual income of about 250*l.* is expended by a family consisting of two adults and two children (aged six and three respectively), with servant. The family reside in a south-west suburb of London noted for its shopping facilities, and the household is run on temperance principles. For the facts and figures the Editor is indebted to one of the greatest living authorities on domestic social economy.

	£	s.	d.
Rent, including rates and taxes (half-share of 52*l.* house)	33	0	0
Housekeeping expenses	90	0	0
Breadwinner's lunches and frequently teas in town .	30	0	0
Clothing (this is low as sewing-machine is much in evidence in this household)	17	10	0
Servant's wages|	12	0	0
Coal and gas (gas cooking stove)	7	10	0
Life and fire insurance premiums	10	5	0
Church-sittings and small subscriptions . . .	3	5	0
Season ticket (third class)	4	10	0
Holidays	12	0	0
Doctors, about	3	0	0
Repairs and additions to furniture , . . .	4	0	0
Sundries; amusements, bus fares, garden, newspapers, magazines, books, postages, presents, volunteering, &c., &c., say	10	0	0
	£237	0	0

Eight Hundred a Year

To those who usually start marriage on such an income, the professional man, or the younger son with a narrow berth in the

Civil Service and vague prospects in the direction of a too healthily constituted uncle, it is a sum upon which the two ends which must annually be drawn together can be made to meet with comfortable success or inconvenient uncertainty, according to the requirements and habits of the couple who have the spending of it. Such a couple have usually to consider, to a certain extent, what is vaguely called "keeping up appearances".

First of all comes the house-rent, a figure which depends partly upon the size of the house, partly upon the locality in which it is situated. In the choice of a house there are two things to be considered, the house itself and its locality. The advantages of the two are interdependent; that is to say that it may be necessary to sacrifice something in the first in order to gain something in the second and *vice versa*. It is not wise, I am sure, to live at too great a distance from the haunts and habitations of the world to which one belongs; to do so draws down the curses of friends and increases expenditure in cab fares. Go right away, into a suburb or the country, beyond the range of London calls altogether, or choose a neighbourhood which, if visiting is to take place at all, does not involve too great a tax upon the strength and time of the wife and the purses and patience of her friends.

Fashionable neighbourhoods, naturally, do not come within the limits of possibility, or desirability either, for reasons other than the question of rent, one being that tradespeople charge much higher prices in such neighbourhoods; my radius is determined, therefore, by the solid reality of cab fares and the sum total of the weekly books, not by considerations of the social standing of one's front door. Thus Bayswater is within, but Shepherd's Bush without the circle; Kensington is included, but Hammersmith unadvisable; Bloomsbury, especially for theatres, is convenient, but Kilburn is too far away.

Having taken your house and put down 130*l.* out of your 800*l.* for rent, the next question is the question of servants. Two is the right number, a cook at 20*l.* a year, and a house-parlourmaid at 18*l.* With two such servants, if they are well-meaning and fairly intelligent, a woman can have her house properly kept and her household conducted with order and daintiness, *if she chooses.* which means that she must be willing to supervise and interest herself in the details of the establishment.

We come now to the sum necessary for housekeeping expenses. In this, I include food; household necessaries, such as lamp-oil, candles, soap, and the like; washing and window-cleaning. These expenses ought to be, and with careful management can be, covered by 4l. a week, and I would divide the items as follows:

	Pound (£ or l.)	Shilling (d.)	Pence (s.)
Washing	0	12	0
Window-cleaning	0	1	4
Meat	1	0	0
Groceries	1	0	0
Bread	0	4	0
Vegetables	0	3	6
Milk	0	3	6
Eggs	0	2	6
Butter	0	4	6
Fish	0	4	0
Bacon	0	3	0
Total	3	18	4

The rates and taxes, housekeeping, and servants being accounted for, we will pass on to the husband's side of the household, which means wine and tobacco. If he drinks claret, his wine bill cannot well come to less than 30l. in the year; altogether, whisky, claret, port, sherry, and brandy come to £20 2s. If he is but a moderate smoker, smokes tobacco at 6s. 6d. a pound, and allows himself 100 cigars and 200 or 300 cigarettes in the year, he will cover his expenses in this direction with 10l.

The husband needs more pocket-money than the wife, and the wife needs more clothes than the husband. He must certainly have his 12s. a week, and that means 30l. a year, or a little more—to be quite accurate, 3l. 4s. Then he will spend 40l. on clothes, so that his personal allowance cannot be less than 70l. The wife will require less pocket money; she must content herself with 20l. a year, and out of that she must pay her club subscription, if she belongs to a club, her expenses of locomotion, and the cab fares to and from the dinner parties. Her dress, on the other hand, will cost more than her husband's, and we must allow her, I think, 50l., so that the sum employed by each in personal expenses is the same, that is to say, 70l. a year.

Then there is the doctor, and as under this heading we will include the dentist and the chemist's bill, we cannot set apart less than 30l. Coal will come to 12l. in the year, and gas, or its equivalent, to 9l.

The full budget works out to:

	£
Rent, rates, and taxes	130
Housekeeping	208
Servants' wages	38
Husband's allowance	70
Wife's allowance	70
Repairs	50
Holidays	50
Doctor	30
Wine	20
Tobacco	10
Coal	12
Gas	9
Stationery	5
Postage &c.	13
Entertaining &c.	35
	£750

Eighteen Hundred a Year

The expenditure of an income of £1800 a year will vary a great deal in detail according to whether it is spent in London or the country.

In London: The house rent, which, on an income of 1,800*l*., in most cases had better not exceed 200*l*., including rates and taxes, may very easily mount up to 350*l*. Say that the young couple decide on the more fashionable locality, and weight their income with a disproportionately high rent. Under these circumstances I think the disposition of their income and general expenditure would work out into something like the following table :—

	£	*s.*	*d.*
I. Rent, rates, and taxes	360	0	0
II. Housekeeping, including living, washing, lighting	550	0	0
III. Repairs, insurance, cleaning, painting, &c.	100	0	0
IV. Coal	60	0	0
V. Dress (man and woman)	200	0	0
VI. Wages, including beer, for four servants	130	0	0
VII. Wine	60	0	0
VIII. Stamps, newspapers, stationery, &c.	30	0	0
IX. Doctors, dentists, accidents, journeys	100	0	0
X. New house linen	20	0	0
XI. Charities	40	0	0
	£1,650	0	0

Speaking in a general way, every maid represents an additional sixty or seventy pounds a year, and every man another seventy or eighty. These sums cover all expenses connected with a servant, including wages. It is generally worthwhile to increase wages to keep a good servant, and few things are more extravagant than changing servants; but no one gets what he wants by offering wages above the average.

A large class of people who keep three servants, even if they increase them to four. add a kitchenmaid, or an up-and-down girl, rather than a lady's-maid. I am inclined to think that in early years of married life a lady's-maid, besides being a great comfort, partly pays herself by the saving of dressmakers' bills, and turning old things into new. It is fancy things made at home that really pay, not petticoats and under-linen. The lady's-maid, too, must undertake the mending of house linen.

In the Country: For the young, the energetic and the ambitious, towns are best at first, and they can gravitate towards the country as they grow older. This surely is one of the greatest inducements for saving, and in no sense is it a mean or lowering object. We will begin now with our changed table of expenditure for life in the country. The most important reduction will be in the house-rent.

TABLE—COUNTRY.

					£	s.	d.
I.	Rent, rates and taxes	.	.	.	180	0	0
II.	Housekeeping (living, washing, lighting)	.	.	.	450	0	0
III.	Repairs, insurance, cleaning, painting		.	.	100	0	0
IV.	Coal	.	.	.	80	0	0
V.	Dress (man and woman)	.	.	.	180	0	0
VI.	Wages, including beer (four servants)		.	.	130	0	0
VII.	Wine	.	.	.	50	0	0
VIII.	Stamps, newspapers, stationery	.	.	.	30	0	0
IX.	Doctor, dentist, accidents, journeys	.	.	.	100	0	0
X.	New house linen	.	.	.	20	0	0
XI.	Charities	.	.	.	40	0	0
					£1,360	0	0

Furnishing in the country can be done even more simply and sensibly than in London. If washing house linen is more, cleaning of curtains and chintzes, &c., is infinitely less; three months of London making things much dirtier than a year in the country. If the garden is carefully and knowingly stocked to supply the wants of every month in the year the saving in the weekly books is considerable, as nothing ought to be bought except potatoes, and the plentiful supply of vegetables for many months in the year considerably reduces the butcher's book. Everyone who has space in the country should keep pigs; nothing so prevents waste or actually pays better. A garden makes a very great saving in the weekly books, and enables a family to live well with much less meat.

Ten Thousand a Year

The most ordinary way of possessing an income of 10,000£. a year is to derive it mainly from land to be taxed and rated on it, and to have about 4,000l. or 5,000l. to spend. This is the case of the man who inherits a large property, but, as this man is in no way the master of his own income, and as his receipts and expenses generally diverge in opposite directions—his income gradually diminishing as the demands on it increase. As the subject of this article is to be £10,000. a year to spend, and, as it would be impossible to enter into individual vagaries, I have chosen for an exemplary budget the expenditure of an ordinary well-favoured couple, who have been left 10,000l. a year, with a solid capital behind and no inherited burdens.

For housing, you will likely choose the medium-sized 'mansion,' either in London or the country—or in both, according to taste. One of moderate size in an accessible part of London would represent from 450l. to 500l. a year, its rates and taxes about 150l., and its up-keep, painting, and repairs, an average of 200l. a year.

As far as the country part of your life is concerned, it is impossible to do more than generalise. One man will want to hunt, another to shoot; fishing will be the elixir of life to a third, politics the dry bread which nourishes a fourth. But, whatever his country pursuits or his intellectual interests, the man must content himself with about one-fifth of the income with which to satisfy them— that is, between 2,000J. and 2,500l. a year; this sum should provide him with a very fair amount of interest and variety in whatever lies his particular fancy.

As the size of your house was more or less decided by the size of your income, so the scale of your housekeeping will be practically decided by the size of your house. Suppose there are fifteen or sixteen people in the house, three in the kitchen, three men and a boy, two housemaids, a lady's maid, and either two nurses and babies, or a governess and child—four or five in the dining-room—two in family and two or three guests—a fair average for the books, if flowers and vegetables are provided by the country house, would be from 20l. to 22l. a week, to include servants' beer and washing, and all household washing, also the board of two servants, in whichever of your houses was empty.

Regular entertaining and amusements would count as extra, and, as this would mean shooting-parties in your country house and big dinners in London (the cost of a dinner of sixteen people is about 15l., including wine), 350l. a year would be none too much to allow. The wages of about twelve or fourteen servants would average between 350l. and 400l., and the upkeep of a London and country house in linen, muslins and chintzes, quilts, cushions, &c.,

and repair of wear and tear, would be close upon *200l.* in the case of the man with a London and country house; in the case of the man who rents a shooting it would be rather less.

600l. yearly would provide the upkeep of a good working stable for London or country—two pairs of horses, and two ponies or hacks.

Both the man and the woman would require *4:50l.* for clothes, private expenses, and subscriptions; and then another bugbear rises, in the shape of education. For the sake of argument, suppose there to be three children, two boys and a girl. As babies, *200l.* would easily cover their expenses; but hanging over you would be the training of their youthful minds. Having *10,000l.* a year, you would not have the shadow of an excuse not to give them the best of everything. You would lay by *300l.* a year against the evil day when Eton claimed them for her own, and when they cost you nearly all their weight, and certainly all their worth, in gold. You would have accumulated in this manner, in the first ten years of their existence, £3600 towards carrying them through private and public school life. the girl can be kept through those twenty years for rather over *100l.* a year.

Public rates and taxes are the final twist of the torture screw, and they will grind out of you close upon *500l.* This would be taking the income tax at *8d.* or *9d.* in the pound; anything over that, like the present 1s. *2d.*, would be an 'adverse circumstance,' to be met by the margin—another proof of the desirability of having one.

BUDGET.

	£
Country property expenses	2,200
London house, inclusive of rates and taxes, decorative and other repairs	800
House books, inclusive of beer and washing and household washing	1,200
Wages	400
Coal	130
Lighting	70
Liveries (indoor)	70
Butler's book, for all postage of letters, parcels, hampers, cabs, &c.	130
Stationery and small bills	150
Wine	200
Entertaining and amusements	350
Upkeep of two houses in linen, chintzes, general wear and tear, &c.	200
Dress and private expenses (450l. each)	900
Education and children's clothes	500
Stables	600
Small journeys and visits	150
Illness	100
Taxes (income tax and others)	450
Charities	400
	9,000

Below Stairs

Edwardians of means and/or status could not function without servants. The basics of everyday life–heating, lighting, cooking, cleaning, and washing–were all incredibly labor intensive, and the presence of housemaids, parlourmaids, cooks, scullery maids, footmen, butlers, etc were also a status symbol, for they represented a particular level of income.

There was no shortage of prospective servants, with the 1901 census showing that a little over two million women out of the total British population of thirty-seven million were employed in domestic service, and the 1911 census showing an increase to 2.1 million servants out of a population of forty-one million.

Compared with factory workers and farmers, whose wages were less than forty shillings (from which 2/3rds were spent on food), domestic servants, who were provided with board and lodging, did better on the whole (the usual allowance of food for each servant per week was 1/2 lb. of butter, 1/4 lb. of tea, 1 lb. of loaf sugar, 1 lb. of cheese, and a daily pint of beer. There was no restriction as to bread, but many ruled that all bread must be a day old before it was eaten).

The **butler** was the senior servant in the household who kept charge of the wine cellar, the serving of meals, the silver, and the general arrangements for the reception of guests. He saw to the fires in the sitting rooms, attended to his employer's literary needs so far as newspapers are concerned, and acted as valet to his master if no valet was kept. A butler's average wages ranged from £50 to £100.

The **housekeeper** was the senior female servant, who supervised the women staff (though she knew better than to meddle with either the cook or the nanny), was responsible for the cleaning and the laundry, and presented the menus daily to the mistress of the house for her approval. A housekeeper was invariably called "Mrs." because of the relative power/prestige possessed by a married woman. Her wages averaged £40-70 per year.

The **cook** ruled the kitchen and the kitchen- and scullery-maids beneath her. A cook's wages varied from £18 a year to £500 or more, and their duties in the household were quite as varied as their pay. The dining-room was her special charge, and to this was usually added the care of the hall, the doorsteps, and the kitchen staircase, in addition to her own special realm. She was also a "Mrs." whether married or not, or known informally as "Cook." Some homes employed a *chef de cuisine* (male) instead of a cook (female), and his wages could be astronomical when compared to hers. Rosa Lewis's reputation was an anomaly only because she was placed on equal footing with a chef.

With an average wage of £35-50 per year, the **valet** attended exclusively to the personal accommodation of his master. He waited upon him during all times of dressing and undressing; brushes, folds up his clothes, or places them in readiness for him. He saw to all repairs and put away clothes in a wardrobe when not in use, making sure to cover them with brown holland or linen wrappers to secure them from dust. Boots and shoes were cleaned by the under-footman, but each morning the valet placed them in the dressing-room for his master. While the housemaid cleaned the grate, lit the fire, and swept and dusted the room, he prepared the washing-table, arranged the shaving apparatus, and laid his master's clothing out for the day.

The sole responsibility of a **lady's maid** was to her mistress. Her duties were solely to care for the wardrobe of her mistress, to assist her at her toilette, to draw her bath, to lay out her clothes and keep her room tidy. Excellent sewing skills were a must, for the lady's maid repaired her mistress's clothing and hats, and was expected to smarten her attire when trips to the local seamstress or a fashionable dressmaker was either too expensive or too far away. A lady's maid also received her mistress's cast-offs, which, if sold to rag-pickers, could be a lucrative bonus to her annual wages of £20-30.

The head **housemaid** had charge of the linen and tidied the bedrooms of the lady and the gentleman of the house and a few of the spare rooms. A housemaid's wages ranged from £15 to £30, but an under-housemaid seldom exceeded £20—though sometimes where three or four were kept the second housemaid was paid highly, the wages of the first being in proportion. The under-housemaid was secondary to the head housemaid. Her duties were rather similar to the latter, though she lacked the opportunity to possess any real responsibility.

The duties of the **first footman** were as follows: he set the table for each meal, or brought the breakfast trays to the members of the family, other than his master and mistress, and attended to the front door during the morning. He rubbed up the silver daily, cleaning it thoroughly once a week, and kept the dining room in order. He attended to the lamps and lighting of the family fires, and after dinner, carried coffee to the library or drawing-room. When waiting on table, he passed the large dishes and gravies.

The **second footman** alternated with the first footman in attendance on the door. He cleaned the halls, took care of the breakfast and coatroom, served the children's table—should there be one—and attended to the dusting of high places. He occasionally helped to clean the silver and dishes, and when waiting on the table, he passed the vegetables, salad, and dessert, and after dinner, the cigarettes and cigars to the guests. The wages of footmen depended far more upon height and appearance than efficiency. A second footman of 5'6 would command £20-22, while one of 5'10 or 6 feet would not take under £28 or £30. A short first footman could not expect more than £30, while a tall man could command £32-40.

The lot of a **scullery maid** was tough. She rose the earliest in the house (sometimes as early as 4 am) to clean the grates and lay the household fires. But mostly, she was expected to wait on the cook, to wash up all pots, pans, dishes, plates, knives, forks, etc, to lay the table for the servants' meals, to wash vegetables, peel potatoes, and carry coals to the kitchen, and scullery. Her duties also consisted of sweeping the kitchen and scullery, dusting everything before the cook came down in the morning, and also charge of the front-door steps, area steps and area. For all of this, her wages ranged from £10-14 per year.

The position of **chauffeur** was relatively new in 1912, which meant his duties—and pay—varied based on the house and employer. He also existed in the in-between world occupied by the governess, since he was not a member of the household, yet he was not a member of the outdoor servants (and those employed in the stables tended to resent the presence of an automobile and the changes it entailed). At best, the chauffeur's duties consisted of driving the family and of maintaining the upkeep of the motorcar, and with board and lodgings included, his wages ranged from a lowly £10 to a very high £250, if he were very experienced.

In her memoirs, *Before The Sunset Fades* (1953), Daphne Fielding, ex-Marchioness of Bath, detailed the forty-three member staff employed at Longleat during the Edwardian era:
One House Steward
One Butler
One Under Butler
One Groom of the Chambers
One Valet
Three Footmen
One Steward's Room Footman
Two Oddmen
Two Pantry Boys
One Lamp Boy
One Housekeeper
Two Lady's Maids
One Nurse
One Nursery Maid
Eight Housemaids
Two Sewing Maids
Two Still Room Maids
Six Laundry Maids
One Chef
Two Kitchen Maids
One Vegetable Maid
One Scullery Maid
One Daily Woman

Such a large staff was not typical amongst all great country houses, but the scope and scale of the house, not to mention the entertainments and house parties and fetes held on the estate, required a large staff of mostly invisible employees to keep everything humming along. Outside staff usually comprised of coachmen, grooms, stable boys, gardeners, gamekeepers, and later the chauffeur/mechanic. Some households even hired their own dairymaids, who churned the butter, milked the cows (though some localities employed cowkeepers for this task), watched the cheeses, and made the cream. Included in the wages of domestic servants were allowances for beer, sugar, and tea, and they given annual gifts of cloth with which to make up their uniforms.

A further anecdote in Daphne Fielding's reminisces included the average day for servants in a country estate like Longleat:

- Each week three sheep of different species were butchered for the household, one Southdown, one Westmorland, and one Brittany, the last being used exclusively for small cutlets.
- Every morning the chef wrote out the menus on a broad slate and took them upstairs for the approval of Lady Bath.
- When the family moved to Berkeley Square for the London Season, seventeen of the staff accompanied them, together with eleven horses and five stablemen.
- The housekeeper and the house steward presided over the steward's room table at which the head butler, the cook, the lady's maids, the valets and the groom of the chambers used to eat. The remainder, the liveried servants and the under maids, had their meals in the servants' hall where the second butler and head laundry maid ranked the highest. The housekeeper had her own sitting room where she received the steward's room for tea.
- Twice a week, on Tuesdays and Thursdays, dances were held in the servants' hall. A pianist was engaged from the neighboring town and a buffet supper was produced by the kitchen and still room staff.
- The normal day at Longleat began with prayers before breakfast, at which the whole family appeared. The staff entered the chapel in single file in order of precedence. The village clergyman officiated.
- The first footman was considered to be the Lady's footman. It was he who stood behind her chair, and any chore that the Lady's maid required to have done for her mistress was his responsibility. The third footman was the nursery footman, at the beck and call of the nannies.
- The duty of the groom of the chambers was to care for the reception rooms, see that the writing tables were properly equipped, collect letters for the post, deliver notes and

messages, look after the fires and attend to the comfort and needs of the visitors.

All of this was just a fraction of the lives and duties of the domestic servants. Some stately homes, like the magnificent Chatsworth or Blenheim Palace, possessed even more staff, all of whom kept the great estates running smoothly and unobtrusively.

Much further down on the social scale, etiquette books and authors who advised on household management, such as Mrs. Beeton, gave this advice on the recommended number or variety of domestic servants one could afford based on income:

- About £1,000 a year—A cook, upper housemaid, nursemaid, under housemaid, and a man servant.
- About £750 a year—A cook, housemaid, nursemaid, and footboy.
- About £500 a year—A cook, housemaid, and nursemaid.
- About £300 a year—A maid-of-all-work and nursemaid.
- About £200 or £150 a year—A maid-of-all-work (and girl occasionally).

By the mid-Edwardian era, legislation was introduced to protect the rights of domestic servants, and the 1911 National Insurance Act solidified their right to health care and respect from their employers. Though the First World War did not break the tradition or need for servants, pre-war housewives had long been admonished by women's journals and newspapers and books about self-sufficiency, and the invention of household appliances gradually chipped away at the dependence on servants. Nevertheless, the character of the country house, or even the London mansion, was largely created by its large staff, and being "In Service" was considered a coveted position for the lower classes for a surprisingly long period in history.

The Engagement of Servants

The Every Woman's Encyclopaedia was a late Edwardian periodical aimed at upper-middle and upper-class ladies. The articles ranged from household matters to society to legal matters that pertained especially to women. The following advice was given for obtaining servants and setting a time-table of duties.

"It is no easy matter to secure quickly the treasure for whom you are seeking. Do not be in a hurry and take anyone; it only entails expense, much vexation, constant changes, and a bad reputation in the neighbourhood, because it is soon said that " no one ever stops with Mrs. So-and-so."

Better by far put up with temporary help than with someone who is unsuitable. It is a moot question whether it is better to find servants (1) through the medium of a registry office or (2) advertisements, or (3) through friends or tradespeople.

No. 1 answers well if you deal with a thoroughly good office where the head has a good reputation to keep up, and who charges a small booking fee of a 1s. or thereabouts, and then an engagement fee when the applicant is suited. No. 3 is not always practicable, as it is a slow method, therefore No. 2 (an advertisement in a first-class paper) is generally the best. State your requirements briefly, but plainly, and it is wise to conclude with the words " No registries," if you do not desire to deal with any, otherwise you are apt to be inundated with letters.

Interviews

A personal interview is necessary. No mistress is bound to pay the applicant's fare, unless she has agreed to do so beforehand, though sometimes an attempt is made to demand it.
During the interview it is wise to ascertain:
1. Why she left the last situation.
2. What wages she desires.
3. If her health is good.
4. What experience she has had.
5. What hours off and holidays she expects.
If possible, show the girl the house, kitchen, and her own room. Explain clearly all details of the situation, such as number in family, hours for rising and coming in, dress, and so forth, so that she knows what is expected of her.

Obtaining Characters

If the first interview is mutually satisfactory, the next move is to write to the lady who is to give the character. Written recommendations are to be avoided if in any way possible, as many false characters are thus obtained; the address of an empty house in a good neighbourhood being given, the care-taker of which is a friend or relative of the applicant. This friend opens the letter and replies in glowing terms about So-and-so's honesty, cleanliness, etc.

Wages

Wages are usually paid monthly, dating from the day on which the servant enters the situation. Keep a wage-book, enter each payment, and always require the payee's signature. Unless a special arrangement is made, remember no deduction may be made from wages for breakages, or for illness.

Holidays

No mistress can nowadays hope to keep servants unless she allows them reasonable and healthy relaxation. Usually one evening a week is given, between the hours of about 6 and 10, alternate Sunday afternoons and evenings, and, perhaps, an extra afternoon and evening once a month. The yearly holiday ranges from a week to a fortnight. Fresh air and exercise are as essential for the maid as for the mistress, and it is bad management and false economy to permit domestics to become unhealthy and discontented for lack of them.

A New Servant

Be sure and give her a good start. Before her arrival see that all the cupboards, apparatus, cloths, etc., belonging to her province are in good order. Hand her an inventory of everything over which she has charge, and a plainly detailed scheme of her daily and weekly work, hours, etc. A considerate mistress will also make sure that the maid's room, bed, etc., are clean and comfortable, and will be prepared to show a little indulgence for the first week, or until the girl has been given time to settle down and learn the various fads of the family.

General Time-Table
Daily Work in a seven-roomed house
Family – Master, mistress, and one child

6 a.m. – Rise, light kitchen fire, fill kettles, clean boots, sweep hall and steps. Sweep, and light dining-room fire, call family, and take hot water. Help mistress to lay table, and prepare breakfast.

8 a.m. – Have kitchen breakfast while family breakfast. Clear kitchen breakfast; tidy kitchen. Attend to bedrooms.

9 a.m. – Help clear dining-room. Wash breakfast things.

9.20 a.m. – Help make beds; receive daily orders. Dust bedrooms.

10.15 a.m. – Do special work for the day. Help in the kitchen, etc.

12.30 a.m. – Lay cloth for luncheon.

1 p.m. – Dining-room luncheon and kitchen dinner.

1.45 p.m. – Remove and wash lunch things. Tidy kitchen. Make up fire.

2.30 p.m. – Change dress. Put large clean apron over afternoon black dress and muslin apron, and do some light work, such as cleaning silver, sewing, ironing. Be ready to answer front door.

4 p.m. – Prepare drawing-room and kitchen teas.

4.30 p.m. – Carry in drawing-room tea.

5.15 p.m. – Remove and wash tea. things.

6 p.m. – Arrange bedrooms for the night. Help prepare dinner.

7 p.m. – Lay table.

7.30 or 8 p.m. – Serve dinner and wait at table {the amount possible depends on the skill of the mistress in organising and arranging this meal).

8.30 or 9 p.m. – Clear, and wash up dinner things. Tidy kitchen. Have supper.

9.45 p.m. – Take hot water to bedrooms and go to bed.

The mistress should see that the general reading, or going on some errand during servant has an hour off for writing letters, the afternoon or early evening each day.

Special Weekly Work

Monday Morning – Wash kitchen cloths, dusters, and any small articles done at home.

Tuesday Morning – Clean large bedroom.

Wednesday Morning – Clean two small bedrooms.

Thursday Morning – Clean dining-room, bathroom, and lavatory.

Friday Morning – Clean staircase, hall, and sweep drawing-room.

Friday Afternoon – Clean kitchen brasses, etc.

Saturday Morning – Clean kitchen range thoroughly, and do extra work in larder, etc.

Wages of a general servant vary in different localities from £12 to £24 per annum. Usually 1s. to 1s. 6d. is allowed for laundry expenses, according to the time allowed for getting up her own small things.

Dress. – Print dresses, with neat white aprons and caps, should be worn for mornings, and large coarse aprons should be used when stoves have to be cleaned or scullery work done. A black dress, pretty muslin apron and cap, should be worn in the afternoon. If low wages are paid, the mistress will often give the maid material for one black dress, or provide her caps, aprons, cuffs, etc.; but this is a voluntary matter.

Bibliography

Balsan, Consuelo Vanderbilt. *The Glitter and the Gold*. New York: Harper, 1952.

Evans, Sîan. *Life Below Stairs*. London: National Trust, 2011.

Fielding, Daphne Vivian. *Before the Sunset Fades, Recalled by the Marchioness of Bath*. N.p.: Longleat Estate, 1951.

Harrison, Rosina. *Rose: My Life in Service*. New York: Viking, 1975.

Horn, Pamela. *Life below Stairs: The Real Life of Servants, the Edwardian Era to 1939*. Stroud: Amberley, 2012.

Horn, Pamela. *The Rise and Fall of the Victorian Servant*. Dublin: Gill and Macmillan, 1975.

Lethbridge, Lucy. *Servants: A Downstairs History of Britain from the Nineteenth Century to Modern Times*. New York, NY: W.W. Norton, 2013.

Powell, Margaret. *Below Stairs: The Classic Kitchen Maid's Memoir That Inspired Upstairs, Downstairs and Downton Abbey*. New York: St. Martin's, 2012.

Smith, Nina Slingsby. *George, Memoirs of a Gentleman's Gentleman*. London: J. Cape, 1984.Waterson, Merlin. *The Servants' Hall: A Domestic History of Erddig*. London: Routledge & K. Paul, 1980.

Fashion
Women's Dress

"....A large fraction of our time was spent in changing our clothes." said Cynthia Asquith, and during the Edwardian era, men and women were expected to change multiple times a day, depending on their activity, the season, and their residence. A society columnist lamented this burden in a 1901 article titled "The Impossibility of Dressing on £1000 a Year":

"'How the poor live' has been the subject of countless articles, but the struggle for existence of the smart society woman—one of our "splendid paupers"—seems fated to take a back seat in the literature of the day. Consider the hard case of one, young and pretty, condemned to dress on a thousand a year.

The requirements of her set demand the purse of a Croesus and the powers of a quick-change artiste. On the sum named she needs the juggling abilities of a Chancellor of the Exchequer to make both ends meet. The annual campaign of smart society is arranged as follows. May, June, and July comprise the London season proper—in itself a costly campaign. In an ordinary year several Court functions have to be reckoned with, and there are always private parties of all sorts and conditions, big dinners and smart small ones, balls, concerns, the opera, plays, and so forth.

The daylight hours are occupied with race-meetings, garden parties, restaurant luncheons, morning walks, afternoon drivers, teas and bazaars, not to mention frolics at Ranelagh and outings to riverside Clubs. With August comes yachting and Cowes, succeeded by a trip on the Continent to Aix, Homburg, Marienbad, or St. Moritz. September brings Scotland, with an interlude of Doncaster races, while October is claimed by the Newmarket weeks. Then comes a run over to Paris for winter frocks and hats, and November has its regular round of country house visits, big "shoots," and smart race meetings.

Then London again, with its merry winter season bridge parties, theatre parties, and restaurant dinners. After Christmas comes the travel in search of sunshine to Egypt, Sicily, or the South of France. Nowadays we are nothing if not athletic, and most women do Swedish exercises, swim, golf, bicycle, or drive their motors. And for each and all of these pursuits and amusements the smart woman must have her suitable attire.

Costs

Ball or dinner gown: £40

"Little gown" (black, intended for restaurant or bridge dinners): £30-35

Velvet gown for November: £50-60

Six evening gowns with a couple of "little" frocks to act as accessories.

Drawing-room gown and train: £100+

Fancy dress: £300+

Tea-gown: £30

Tea-coat: £25+

Crepe de chine gown for summer: £35-40

Two morning frocks for the winter and two for summer

Country and Scotland: plain serges for rough weather, homepsuns for the heather, bicycle suits, driving coats, a "get up" for golf and another for the automobile, costumes for fishing and shooting, yachting gowns (£20+). Two of each frock.

Hats from London or Paris: £8-10

Russian sables (cloaks and wraps): £500+

Evening cloaks: £35-40

Silk petticoats: £4-15

Pocket handkerchiefs: £5 a dozen

Shoes: £2 a pair + 30 shillings for ornamental buckles

Walking boots, rough boots for walking with the guns or mountaineering, and special shoes for golf and cycling are required, and each evening gown demands its shoes to match, with paste diamond buttons (£2-3).

Gloves are given as presents during Christmas and for birthdays, but if not, a year's supply cost £20-30

Parasols and umbrellas: £7-10 for those with plain handles

Mysteries of the toilet, such as manicure, face, massage and hair-colouring, not to say a general "make-up," mean the expenditure of quite £100 a year. And to this must be added the purchase of scents, soap, cosmetics, perfumes, and powders for home use. Hair-dressing, with all its attendant expenses of hair-waving, new combs, pins, washes, and the many new arrangements in hair to follow the fleeting fashions, along represents much money.

This sketch of a smart woman's dress expenses computed on a moderate basis will go far to prove that £1000 a year spells poverty instead of riches."

Lingerie

The new silhouette of the Edwardian era required a much slimmer parcel of undergarments than before, and it was in this period that underclothing took on the sensual connotations of the word "lingerie".

Ornate, overtly sexual and colorful underclothes began to shift away from the boudoirs of courtesans and into the bedchambers of respectable housewives and independent women. Whereas Victorian underclothing had been functional, the sole function of Edwardian underwear was to attract and tantalize men.

Along with the word lingerie used in place of undergarments, other terms changed to reflect the emphasis on seduction; the shift was first called a *camisole* and then simply known as a "slip" by this period, drawers turning into *knickers* and petticoats into "frillies". This was the age of frou-frou, that exciting sound of chiffon and taffeta undergarments that *whispered* as a woman walked (though by the middle of the era, the sound of a swishing petticoat was deemed vulgar).

For the wealthy lady, the proper layer of lingerie was important and the corsetier and couturier one purchased one's lingerie from was a status symbol, its purchase acknowledging that the lady had a special someone for whom she flaunted her undergarments.

The fashionable woman was poured into at least seven layers of underclothing before she even dressed for the hour! Since they changed clothing five to six times a day, with even more if one was on vacation or at a Saturday-to-Monday, it was imperative that underclothing was both attractive and sturdy. When the lady awoke, her first layer of undergarment were the combinations, a kind of pant and vest in one piece which gained popularity in the 1870s with the introduction of the "Princess style" dress and greatly reduced the bulk that would have accompanied a separate chemise and pantaloons. Generally made of wool or a mixture of wool and silk, they came in a number of styles: strapless for evening wear, or with a skirt in the back to hide the slit in the pants.

Over this was laced the corset. The late Victorian corset fitted over the bosom and hips with curved busks that compressed the stomach and supported the spine. The S-bend corset of the early Edwardian era, called thus due to the peculiar arch of the back this corset produced, caused women to thrust their bosom forward and their hips backwards to give them the hourglass shape then popular. When skirts and bodices narrowed after 1908, the emphasis was now placed on an overall slimness, and corsets were designed to compress the waist and hips and no longer covered the bosom. They were also quite long, ending at mid-thigh, causing a slight difficulty in sitting and standing.

Next layer, the camisole. A kind of under-blouse that buttoned down the front, it gathered at the waist and was trimmed with lace around the neck and puffed sleeves. This was very fitted, with darts and seaming, and decorated with lace and trimming during the 1880-1908 period, and after, it was made quite plain, often with a square neckline. Over this, a pair of frilly knickers, which sometimes buttoned at the waist or tied with tapes. The last undergarment essential to a lady was the waist-petticoat, made of lawn or rustling silk. It was laid upon the floor in a circle and the lady stepped into the center, the maid lifting the petticoat up and tying it around the waist. Tightly-laced, secured and buttoned up, the lady was then ready to be attired for whatever occasion of her day or night.

The Hobble Skirt

Of all the fads in fashion of the Edwardian era, none was so provocative–or dangerous–as the hobble skirt. French couturier Paul Poiret claimed to have created the hobble skirt, but the narrow, nearly skin-tight skirt had its roots in the early 1880s, when fashion placed emphasis on the posterior hidden beneath a neat, erotic bustle. However, it wasn't until skirts began to narrow once more circa 1908/09 when the true "hobble skirt" made its appearance.

Between 1910 and 1913, the hobble skirt reigned supreme in fashion, obtaining popularity from the Oriental- and Directoire-inspired crazes. These skirts were extremely slim to the point of forcing women who wore them to take tiny, mincing "geisha-like" steps, and nearly barring them from independent movement (it is rather curious that as the suffrage movement moved to militancy, fashions for women became restricting).

Though the hobble skirt was denounced as unsafe, and some employers even barred their female workers from wearing them, a few factions approved of the trend: "Grandmothers think that the means justify the end, and that the hobble skirt will bring back to women the old grace. They will be compelled to shorten their strides, learn to place their feet in a straight line, and not throw them in or out in the slovenly modern way, and that the entire appearance of women will be thus benefited."

By 1912, the hobble skirt had become a tad more practical, with many concealing slits, hidden pleats, draping, and sometimes even Turkish trousers, beneath the narrow outer-skirt, which allowed greater movement than the hobbled walk initially characterizing the fad. Thank goodness, for the newspapers of the day reported countless accidents involving hobble skirts, with many women tripping, falling, and even breaking their legs while maneuvering in the skirt. To save face against the backlash, many Parisian couturiers began to characterize the trend as "American"!

To the rescue did come an American firm who, with great ingenuity, designed "Hobble Skirt" cars for city tramways. The correct name for these trams was Low Level Center Entrance cars or Hedley-Doyle cars after their designers, Frank Hedley, who was Vice-President and General Manager of the New York Railways Company, and James S. Doyle, Superintendent of Car Equipment. In 1912 they produced three prototype cars for the company–the sills of the doors were only about 8 inches from street level and once inside the floor sloped up into each saloon to give space under the floor for the bogies–and by 1914, tramlines throughout the world were equipped with "Hobble Skirt" cars.

Men's Dress

According to Mrs. Humphry, "It is a duty one owes one's friends to dress well" and "it is absolutely true, though in a very limited sense, that the tailor makes the man." Furthermore, she instructs, "if he commits flagrant errors in costume he will not be invited out very much, of that he may be certain."

Edward VII was a stickler in matters of dress, and was not above scolding his friends, Prime Ministers, and foreign dignitaries if they appeared in anything less than correct. These expectations kept the Edwardian gentleman as much on his toes as it did the ladies, and the introduction of sports, new leisure activities, and the growing number of decorated men (knighthoods, medals, etc) increased the pressure.

Unlike women's fashions, traditional articles of gentleman's clothing changed very little; the only concession to the passing of time were tiny details: a new cut to trousers, a new shape to a jacket, etcetera. As it had since the turn of the nineteenth century, colors remained fairly dark, the only places allotted for color, the waistcoat, the sweater and the tie. However, with the rise of sports such as hunting, yachting, cricket, polo and others, there came the introduction of sportswear.

For day, **morning dress** was de rigueur. To be seen in London attired in nothing less was an affront to sartorial sensibilities. Morning dress consisted of a **morning coat**, which was almost always single-breasted, of serge, worsted, cheviot or vicuna, and black or iron-gray; a **waistcoat**, either single- or double-breasted, which matched the coat or was of a lighter color; striped spongebag **trousers** (trousers of wool serge, baggy at knee); a **cravat**; and **silk hat** (though a bowler/Homburg could be worn). The **frock coat**, a double-breasted, knee-length coat of black or dark gray wool, was worn on formal morning occasions, though by the Edwardian era, it was more often seen on elderly men. By the 1900s, the **lounge jacket** began to replace both the morning coat and frock coat. Generally high of neck, with short lapels and double-breasted, the front curved away at the bottom.

For evening, men's attire was strictly composed of a **black dress coat, white waistcoat and trousers matching the coat.** The dress coat was double-breasted with a cut-away front and two tails at the rear. In 1900, the tails were knee length and the front cut away square at the waist, with two or three buttons on each front. The sleeves would end plain or with a cuff, and slit with two or three buttons also. There was also the choice to wear the **dinner jacket** if dressing for dinner at home or at a men's club. This was worn with a white shirt and a dark tie. As the era progressed, the dinner jacket was increasingly cut on the lines of a lounge jacket, and from it emerged the "**tuxedo**" (though this was the American term; the Continental term was "Monte Carlo").

Due to the King's fondness for lounge suits, sport jackets, **Norfolk shooting jackets** with front and back pleats, and knickerbockers in loud tweeds, there came a greater emphasis on comfort, and a greater obsession with sports. This was the epoch of polo, cricket, shooting and hunting, and in the 1890s, such new sports such as tennis, football, golf, cycling and motoring.

And of course each sport required its own set of clothing. Knits, flannel and tweeds were popular, with the color white most used for yachting, golf, tennis, cricket and polo. For cycling, shooting and golf, knickerbockers and plus-fours, a type of loose knee-breeches fastened at the knee with a band were favored, and for rowing, knit sweaters in team or school colors (e.g. light blue for Cambridge, navy for Oxford).

Typical outwear consisted of the **Chesterfield**, a single-breasted coat of herringbone tweed with velvet collar; the **ulster**, a slightly less-fashionable coat with shoulder cape or hood generally worn for travel; the **Raglan overcoat**, a long and full coat of waterproof material, made with side seams to allow access to trouser pockets; the **Inverness cape**, a waterproof coat with a cape-like front composed of two "wings" taking the place of sleeves and covering the arms—made of fur or fur-lined for motoring; and **mackintoshes**, a raincoat of rubber, tweed, cotton, parramatta, etc. Made of gabardine, the **trench coat**, was invented by Thomas Burberry in 1901 as an alternative to the heavy serge greatcoats worn by British and French officers. Though not in widespread use until the Great War, it was an optional piece included in a typical officer's kit.

Hats were also dictated by fashion and time of day. Casual hats for the day included the **Homburg**, a stiff felt hat with a dented crown and turned-up silk-bound brim; the **Trilby**, of a similar shape but with a softer felt; and the **Derby** (Bowler in America), with either curved or flat sides. The **top or silk hat** was worn with the frock coat, morning coat and evening dress, but as the first two were replaced by the lounge suit, the top hat was less seen in the streets; the **boater**, a flat-brimmed, flat-crowned straw hat worn in the summer; and the **opera hat**, also known as a "Gibus" after its inventor. This hat was of corded silk or merino and the crown was supported by a spiral spring that enabled the hat to collapse and fold quite flat.

The "tooth-pick", a shoe of black or tan with a long pointed toe, was worn, though boots were correct for dress wear. From 1910 on, shoes became more popular than boots, and about this year, the **American Boston**, or bull-dog toe was introduced. This had a blunt round toe with an upward bulge. Accessories for men included gloves, spats, scarves, umbrellas, walking sticks and various items of jewelry.

Gloves were essential for town wear, of tan kid for day, and suede or fabric for evenings. **Scarves** were of knitted silk or wool; some plainly colored, some striped. **Spats** of drill or box-cloth were in black, drab or white, and covered the top of shoe and ankle, fastened with four buttons and a strap and buckle under the foot.

The **umbrella**, when tightly rolled, doubled for a walking stick, and during the 1890s, became a fashionable substitute for it. **Walking sticks** of malacca and rattan were favorites for Town use, with crook, crutch or straight handles, very often mounted with silver bands and tips. Some sticks cleverly held in their recesses pencils, cigarettes, flasks, pipes or even devices for measuring the height of horses.

Watches were of the pocket type, open faced, half-hunter and full-hunter cases (with the glass protected by a metal cover; the half-hunter had a circular cut-out in the middle of the cover, with the hour chapters engraved around it; the hands could be partially seen through this cut out). They were made of gold, silver, nickel and oxidized steel. Matching Albert chains passed across the waistcoat, through a chain-hole, and the watch was placed in one pocket, the other end of the chain in the other.

Pins were of gold for ties and scarves, and made in many shapes. In gold or silver also, were cigarette cases and visiting card cases. Leather wallets, note cases (for pound notes) and purses were also worn by men. To round off other accessories were cuff links, key-rings, silver match-boxes, petrol and tinder lighters, cigar and cigarette holders of meerschaum or amber, and pipes and tobacco pouches were carried from time to time.

Basic Guidelines for Dress
Unless a gentleman's valet or tailor were incredibly uninformed, the basic guidelines for daily dress were quite easy to remember:
Morning Wear: the morning-coat or jacket, or the tweed suit is correct. After lunch: retain the morning wear or change into frock coat and grey striped trousers in a material known as "mixed cheviots."
Park suit: grey or light-brown frock-coat, with waistcoat and trousers to match. Can also be worn at Ascot.
Summer Wedding: grey frock-coat suit, silk hat, grey suede gloves, boots, light waistcoat, and dark grey tie.
Winter Wedding: black frock-coat and waistcoat, grey striped trousers, boots, grey suede or buckskin gloves
Summer morning in the Park: straw hat, or low hat and tweed suit, or a black coat and silk hat. Straw hats or low hats were never worn with black coats of any kind.
Informal Dinner: dinner jacket and black waistcoat
Theater dress: dress coat, white waistcoat, white tie, black trousers, silk top hat.

Children's Dress
There was a shift towards dress made specifically for children by the turn of the century, though it retained an echo of their parents' clothing.

Babies of both sexes were swaddled in long white lawn gowns until they learned to walk, and boys were "breeched"—or placed in short pants—as early as aged three in the 1890s. By the 1910s, the one-piece romper, undoubtedly a subtle reaction to increased masculinity/militarism *and* the loss of men in the Great War, had supplanted the fashion of placing toddler boys in skirts.

Once boys were of school age, the Eton suit—black jacket, knee pants, and round collars—, sailor suits, and modified Highland dress were worn. The "Russian blouse suit," or suit consisting of bloomers and tunic with wide starched collar, became popular around 1904 for boys between the age of five and nine. In general, styles of dress for boys followed the customs of Eton College, where they did not wear long trousers until around sixteen or seventeen, which was when Seniors at Eton were permitted to wear trousers and long jackets with tails.

Girls clothing mirrored that of women more so than boys to those of men, and the silhouette of their clothing mimicked the changes in sleeve size, skirt shape, and so on in ladies' dress. The feminine version of the sailor suit was highly popular, and girls also wore a form of Highland dress. When it came to skirt length, the younger a girl was, the shorter her skirt, which signified "keep away" to gentlemen. However, the age at which a girl put up her skirts varied—if a girl had a number of older unmarried sisters, the time was often delayed.

As with all matters in the Edwardian era, class also played a role in children's dress. Girls entering domestic service, mines, or factory work put up their hair and lengthened their hems long before upper class and aristocratic girls, and their clothes were cut down from their mothers or older sisters, or perhaps from secondhand shops. Boys typically wore rough, homespun breeches and jackets, with a woolen cap, and they too lengthened their trousers at an earlier age than the sons of gentlemen.

Bibliography

Anonymous. "The Impossibility of Dressing on £1000 a Year." *The Harmsworth London Magazine* Oct. 1902: 145-49. *HathiTrust*. Web. 28 Aug. 2012.

Barton, Lucy. *Historic Costume for the Stage*. London: Black, 1961.

Condra, Jill. *The Greenwood Encyclopedia of Clothing through World History*. Westport, CT: Greenwood, 2008.

Druesedow, Jean L. *Men's Fashion Illustrations from the Turn of the Century*. New York: Dover, 1990.

Humphry, C. E. *Manners for Men*. Exeter, Eng.: Webb & Bower, 1979.

Koda, Harold, and Andrew Bolton. *Poiret*. New York: Metropolitan Museum of Art, 2007.

Mansfield, Alan, Phillis Cunnington, and Valerie Mansfield. *Handbook of English Costume in the Twentieth Century: 1900 - 1950*. London: Faber and Faber, 1973.

Pearsall, Ronald. *Edwardian Life and Leisure*. New York: St. Martin's, 1974.

Webb, Wilfred Mark. *The Heritage of Dress: Being Notes on the History and Evolution of Clothes*. London: Times Book Club, 1912.

Communication & Correspondence

The Edwardian era witnessed a blossoming of ways and means to keep in touch with friends, loved ones, business associates, and others with whom one needed to correspond. The most popular communication method of the day were postcards, lavishly designed with photographs or illustrations of cities, sights, royals, or the most popular actors and actresses of the day.

The telephone frequently only penetrated the most up-to-date homes, not simply because of the expense but because many considered them intrusive. As such, the simple letter—folded, stuffed inside of a crisp envelope, and stamped—retained its prominence in methods of correspondence. Nevertheless, by the close of the Edwardian age, new technologies like the Marconigram brought the world much closer together than ever before. And of course the growth of aviation inspired the possibility of air mail—the first scheduled airmail service between Hendon and Windsor was established on September 9, 1911 in celebration of George V's coronation.

The General Post Office

The Edwardians were long past the days when the Penny Post was a novel service, and were accustomed to the well-oiled machine that moved letters, parcels, packages, and even crates across Town, the whole of Britain, and to the far-flung colonies.

The General Post Office was located at St. Martin's-le-Grand near St. Paul's Cathedral, and it served as both the main post office for London and the headquarters of the G.P.O. Here, between 6:46 am and 10pm, letters, packages, newspapers, etc were sorted, weighed, dispatched, and delivered *poste restante*. London was divided into eight postal districts— the Eastern, Northern, North Western, Western, South Western, South Eastern, East Central, and West Central—which each had its own post office, from which letters were distributed to the surrounding district. Mail was delivered constantly throughout the day, its frequency dependent upon the distance from the G.P.O., and a letter posted within the bounds of London could reach its destination in a mere two to three hours.

Mail was not delivered on Sundays, but letters could be delivered by express messenger for about one pence per mile.

Many of the head district offices were open from 8am to 8 pm, where letters could be posted in advance of the Monday morning mails. Other places for mailing letters, postcards, and packages were the numerous red pillar boxes dotting London's pavement, at railway terminals, and sub-offices in shops were postage was sold.

The Parcel Post was slow in comparison, but there were also numerous independent parcel delivery companies with quicker delivery. Other options for quicker delivery were the Commissionaires, made up of retired soldiers who also acted as interpreters and guides; the Boy Messengers Company; and the International Lady Couriers, a company that provided "ladies qualified to act as guides to the sights of London, as interpreters, as travelling companions, as aids in shopping or packing, etc." These lady guides kept a register of respectable boarding and lodging houses, engaged rooms at respectable hotels, exchanged money, purchased railway tickets, and otherwise provided a whole host of services for strangers to London.

Telegrams

The Post Office had control of all telegraph lines, save those used for private railways, in Great Britain. London possessed over 500 telegraph offices by 1911, and for 1½ pence per word (6 pence minimum charge), a message would reach its recipient almost immediately. Telegrams sent outside of Great Britain varied from one to six pence, depending on destination, but those reached their recipients just as quickly.

Italian engineer Guglielmo Marconi invented the Marconigram, or wireless telegram, in 1896, and it was widely adopted by private yachts and ocean vessels—including the ill-fated R.M.S. *Titanic*. These were more expensive than regular telegrams, at 6½ pence per word, which made their use amongst the upper classes and the wealthy that much more fashionable. In fact, it was the backlog of personal Marconigrams from the *Titanic*'s passengers that caused the overworked operator Jack Phillips to dismiss warnings of ice. The Marconigram dealt another blow to the ruling elite in summer 1912 over allegations of insider trading, which involved some of the highest ministers of Parliament and shook public confidence in their leaders.

Telephone

Both the National Telephone Company and the Post Office maintained the telephone service in London (until 1911, when the license of the National Telephone Company expired, whereupon the whole operation was taken over by the G.P.O.), and at the rate of two pence per three minutes' of conversation, one could telephone across London.

Call-offices could be found all over London, in post offices, shops, public libraries, underground stations, etc, and trunk lines—operated by the G.P.O.—allowed telephone communication to all of the principal British cities at three pence and up, per three minutes' conversation. The telephone line between London and Paris was established in 1891, and the charge was eight shillings per three minutes, with the price rising to ten shillings per three minutes of the call was placed to Bordeaux, Lyons, Marseilles, and St. Etienne.

The Deckert transmitter, or "Post Office Telephone," was introduced in the mid 1890s to replace the older Gower-Bell telephone.

FIGURE 43.

T.E. Herbert, a telegraph engineer describes it thus: "The wooden diaphragm is covered by the top board of the instrument. In the centre of this board a hole is cut, and a brass tube carrying a china mouthpiece is fixed. This mouthpiece concentrates the sounds of the voice, bringing them more forcibly upon the transmitter than if the diaphragm were left open...the great objection to the china mouthpiece arrangement lies in the fact that moisture is condensed upon it, and when the telephone is much used most unpleasant odours are present."

Bibliography

Browne, Christopher. *Getting the Message: Story of the British Post Office.* Stroud.: A. Sutton Pub., 1993.

Donaldson, Frances Lonsdale. *The Marconi Scandal.* New York: Harcourt, Brace & World, 1962.

Johannessen, Neil. *Telephone Boxes.* Princes Risborough: Shire, 1999.

Povey, P. J., and R. A. J. Earl. *Vintage Telephones of the World.* London: P. Peregrinus in Association with the Science Museum, 1988.

Robinson, Howard. *The British Post Office.* Princeton, N.J.: Princeton Univ., 1948.

Stray, Julian. *Post Offices.* Oxford: Shire, 2010.

Part II: Government, War, and the Country

Keeping The Peace

Barristers, Solicitors, and the Courts of Law

For a large portion of the nineteenth century, the law was the province of the gentleman—perhaps a third or fourth son of an aristocrat. The rise of the middle classes and the standardization of training for professions banished the relatively snobbish, lackadaisical approach to "taking the silk" and practicing law.

In the Edwardian era, the gentleman and the self-made man could be members of the Bar, as could residents of Britain's colonies (the law attracted many from the West Indies, South and West Africa, and India). Solicitors were just as diverse in social and ethnic background as barristers, since becoming a solicitor was no longer considered a step down from a barrister.

The law was focused around the Inns of Court—the Inner Temple and Middle Temple on the south side of Fleet Street, Lincoln's Inn in Chancery Lane, and Grey's Inn in Holburn. The inns each served the function as a society for the study and practice of law and as lodgings (chambers) for barristers. Each inn, which fiercely protected their individuality, were governed by "benchers," or the older members of each inn, and possessed a dining hall, chapel, library, and common room.

Candidates for the Bar were mostly University men, who studied law for at least three years and twelve terms, and four of these terms each year had to have been "kept" at his chosen Inn of Court. This was marked by "dining in the hall six days during each term." Members of the Universities of Oxford and Cambridge only needed to "dine but three days in each term." Previously, a candidate for the Bar "had only to attend a single function—a dinner—during each term and, having 'eaten twelve dinners,' he, ipso facto, became entitled to be called to the Bar, no matter how inadequate might be his knowledge of the law." During this time of study, the aspiring barrister had to pass, "from time to time, regular and strict examinations, prescribed by the Council of Legal Education."

When the budding barrister passed the necessary examinations, he was called to the Bar, a ceremony that consisted of "his attending court on a certain day where, seated with other neophytes, he [was] addressed by the judge (who [had], of course, been posted in advance), as follows:

'Does Mr. move?'

To this the young barrister bashfully assents, though naturally he has no real motion to make. By this brief colloquy he has at once been translated from the student to the barrister."

The total cost of study for the Bar amounted to about £140.

Solicitors entered their field through an apprenticeship after a preliminary examination determined whether the aspiring solicitor possessed the sufficient education. If he passed, he was apprenticed for five years to a practitioner—perhaps property law, or family law—, to whom he paid around 100-400 guineas, as well as official fees amounting to about £130. The apprentice solicitor began his career with "copying papers and performing minor services in the public offices" simultaneously with pursuing his study of law, which, by the late Edwardian era, had grown increasingly arduous.

The apprentice solicitor was required to take two examinations: the first, held by the Solicitors' Incorporated Law Society, tested his progress, and the second and final exam determined his qualification to be admitted to practice. Having thus acquitted himself well on this final exam, the solicitor was admitted by the courts and was "thereafter subject to the discipline of the Society and to that of the courts themselves, usually prompted by the Society."

After examinations, the responsibilities and practices of the new barrister and solicitor diverged. Thomas Leaming, an American lawyer, explains the differences between the two professions:

"The solicitor, or attorney, is a man of law business—not an advocate. A person contemplating litigation must first go to a solicitor, who guides his conduct by advice in the preliminary stages, or occasionally retains a barrister to give a written opinion upon a concrete question of law. The solicitor conducts all the negotiations or threats which usually precede a lawsuit and if compromise is impossible he brings a suit and retains a junior barrister by handing him a brief, which consists of a written narrative of the controversy, with copies of all papers and correspondence—in short, the facts of the case—and which states on its back the amount of the barrister's fee. The brief is engrossed or type-written on large-sized paper with very broad margins for notes, and is folded only once and lengthwise so as to make a packet fifteen by four inches."

The young barrister "is confronted with formidable obstacles, for he cannot look to his friends to furnish him with briefs. He can never be consulted nor retained by the litigants themselves. The only clients he can ever have are solicitors, whose clients, in turn, are the public. He never goes beyond his dingy chambers in the Inns of Court, where, guarded by his clerk, he either wearily waits for solicitors with briefs and fees, or, more likely still, gives it up and goes fishing, shooting or hunting.

The early ambition of the young barrister is to become a 'devil' to some junior barrister, who always has recourse to such an understudy, and, if the junior is making over £1,000 a year, he continuously employs the same devil. This term is not applied in a jocular sense, but is the regular and serious appellation of a young barrister who, in wig and gown, thus serves without compensation and without fame—for his name never appears— often for from five to seven years. The devil studies the case, sees the witnesses, looks up the law and generally masters all the details, in order to supply the junior with ammunition.

Before the trial the junior has one or more conferences with the solicitor, all paid for at so many guineas; occasionally he even sees the party he is to represent, and, more rarely, an important witness or two. The devil is sometimes present, although his existence is, as a rule, decorously concealed from the solicitor.

If the leader is absent, which frequently happens notwithstanding his fee has been paid, inasmuch as no case is deferred by reason of counsel's absence, the junior takes his place, while the solicitor grumbles and more devolves upon the *devil.*

Occasionally, indeed, both leader and junior may be elsewhere and then is the glorious opportunity of the poor devil, who hungers for such an accident, for he may open, examine, and cross-examine, and, if neither his junior nor his august leader appear, he may even close to the jury. The solicitor will be white with rage and chagrin, wondering how he shall explain to the litigant the absence of the counsel whose fees he has paid, but the devil may win and so please the solicitor that the next time he may himself be briefed as junior.

The devil is in no sense an employee or personal associate of the junior—which might look like partnership, a thing too abhorrent to be permitted. On the contrary, he often has his own chambers and may, at any time, be himself retained as a junior, in which event his business takes precedence of his duties as a *devil*, and he then describes himself as being "on his own."

Having gained some identity, and more or less business "on his own " from the solicitors, a devil gradually begins to shine as a junior, whereupon appears his own satellite in the person of a younger man as devil, while the junior becomes more and more absorbed in the engrossing but ever fascinating activities of regular practice at the Bar.

Reaching a certain degree of prominence, a junior at the common-law Bar may next "take silk;" that is, become a K. C, or King's Counsel, which has its counterpart at the Chancery Bar in becoming a *leader*. Whether a barrister shall apply for silk is optional with himself and the distinction is granted by the Lord Chancellor, at his discretion, to a limited, but not numerically defined, number of distinguished barristers. The phrase is derived from the fact that the K. C.'s gown is made of silk instead of "stuff," or cotton. It has also a broad collar, whereas the stuff gown is suspended from shoulder to shoulder.

Whether or not to "take silk," or to become a "leader," is a critical question in the career of any successful common law or chancery barrister. As a junior, he has acquired a paying practice, as his fee is always two-thirds that of the leader. He has also a comfortable chamber practice in giving opinions, drawing pleadings and the like, but all this must be abandoned—because the etiquette of the Bar does not permit a K. C. or leader to do 'a junior's work—and he must thereafter hazard the fitful fancy of the solicitors when selecting counsel in important causes. Some have taken silk to their sorrow, and many strong men remain juniors all their lives, trying cases with K. C.'s and leaders much younger than themselves."

The young barrister also had to choose whether he would take the Common Law Bar or the Chancery Bar, the former of which handled civil and criminal cases, and the latter of which handled such matters as trusts, wills, and guardianships. Common law barristers had their chambers chiefly in the Middle Temple and Inner Temple, and chancery barristers were largely in Lincoln's Inn. There were further specializations, "—although the divisions are not so marked—into probate, divorce or admiralty men." There was also what was known as "the Parliamentary Bar, practicing entirely before Parliamentary committees, boards and commissions." A curiosity of England was the lack of distinction between civil and criminal practice—common law barristers accepted both kinds of briefs indiscriminately.

Solicitors were exempt from the wearing of special robes and wigs, instead attiring "themselves in the conventional frock or morning coat and silk hat which is indispensable for all London business men. They all, however, carry long and shallow leather bags, the shape of folded briefs, which are usually made of polished patent leather." These wigs, introduced in the courts in 1670, made of human hair that needed to be curled and powdered, were replaced in 1822 by horse hair wigs that needed little curling and no powder.

The dress of barristers was the same for the Common Law Bar as for the Chancery Bar, but the details of both gown and wig signified "to the initiated much as to the professional position of the wearer." The junior's gown was made of "stuff," or cotton, and was suspended from shoulder to shoulder.

The K.C., or leader, wore silk gowns with broad collars (hence "taking the silk"), but when in mourning, he wore a "stuff" gown, but to preserve his distinction, he wore "'weepers'—a six inch deep, white lawn cuff, the name and utility of which originated before handkerchiefs were invented. Moreover, when in mourning his "bands"—the untied white lawn cravat, hanging straight down, which all barristers wear— have three lines of stitching instead of two. Under his gown, a K.C. wears a 'court coat,' cut not unlike an ordinary morning coat, though with hooks and eyes instead of buttons, while the junior wears the conventional frock coat."

Leaming turns his focus to the operation of the courts of law and the process of arrest and conviction:

Arrest and Hearing

Upon arrest, a preliminary hearing is first held at a police station where, as in most English proceedings, the testimony, with anything the prisoner may say (after he has been warned of the consequence of self-incrimination) is carefully reduced to longhand writing and plays an important part at the subsequent stages of the prosecution.

The next step is the hearing before a Police Magistrate at Bow or Marlborough Streets, or at any one of the like courts in London which, although of minor importance, are dignified tribunals. The court room is entered by two small doors, one for the witnesses and audience, the other for officials and solicitors, and there is another passage leading from the cells through which the prisoners are brought to a dock. This dock, as in all criminal courts, is at the far end of the room from the magistrate. The prisoner is thus isolated and can only communicate with his solicitor, if he has been able to retain one, by scrawling a note and passing it on to an officer.

The magistrate, appointed by the Crown or the Lord Chancellor acting in its behalf, is almost invariably a man of standing and repute, usually a barrister, whose ready dispatch of business shows great experience with crime, and whose kindness to the merely unfortunate testifies to his charitableness of heart. He wears no wig nor gown and is called in court, "Your Worship"; whereas judges of the High Court are called in court, "My Lord", and those of the County Courts, "Your Honor". All judges, however, are addressed in private life as "Mr." or, if they have one, by a title which is usually conferred upon judges of the High Court. Solicitors act for the more important prisoners but barristers are rarely seen and appear in ordinary street dress if at all.

If the accused be held for trial by the magistrate, the next step, as with us, is the presentation of the charge to the grand jury. The grand jury either throw out the indictment or find a true bill, in which event a jury trial follows at the Central Criminal Court.

Central Criminal Court, or the Old Bailey

At the corner of Newgate and Old Bailey streets, near Fleet street and not far from Ludgate Hill, stands a modern building, officially known as the Central Criminal Court, but popularly called "the Old Bailey." It occupies the site of the ancient Newgate Gaol and Fleet Prison, where, for nearly seven centuries the criminals of London expiated their crimes. There they were tried and, if convicted, hanged on the premises, or—a scarcely better fate—thrown into Newgate Prison, which, from time immemorial, was so overcrowded, so ill-ventilated and so poorly supplied with water that it was the hot-bed of diseases designated as "prison fever." At a single session of court the fever had been known to carry off fifty human beings; not only prisoners, but such august personages as judges, mayors, aldermen and sheriffs.

The present fine structure is exclusively a court house to which prisoners are brought for trial and confined in sanitary cells beneath the court rooms only while awaiting the call of their cases. There are three courts: two presided over by judges called, respectively, the Common Serjeant and the Recorder, together with the Lord Chief Justice of England, or such other judge of the High Court as may be designated for the month, who comes from his civil work in the Strand Law Courts to try criminal cases at the Old Bailey.

The court rooms are rather small and nearly square. Like every London court, they have oak panelled walls, and excellent illumination from above by skylights; they are arranged with a high dais—on which are the chairs and desks for the presiding judge, the sheriffs, or for any guest—and they have the usual steep upward slope of the benches for barristers on the one side and for the jury on the other. Only the solicitors' table is at the floor level. This arrangement brings all the participants in a trial more nearly together than if they were distributed over a flat floor. At the end of the room farthest from the judge is the prisoners' dock, a large square box, elevated almost to the judge's level. This the prisoner reaches by a stairway from the cells below (invisible because of the sides of the dock), accompanied by officers, and he stands throughout the trial—unless invited by the judge to be seated—completely isolated from his barrister and from his solicitor and can only communicate with his defenders by scrawling a lead pencil note and passing it to an officer. A small area of sloping benches, together with a very inadequate gallery, are the only accommodations for the public.

If the visitor happens to be a guest of the Court, he will be ushered in by a door leading to the raised dais and will sit at a desk beside the judge. His eye will first be arrested by a small heap on his desk of dried aromatic herbs and rose leaves and, while speculating as to the purpose of these, he will discover similar little piles on the desks of the presiding judge and sheriffs. He will also observe that the carpet of the dais is thickly strewn with the same litter. Vaguely it is suggested that the court room has been used over night for some kind of a horticultural exhibition and that the sweeping has been overlooked.

Later, his astonishment, however, is redoubled when enter the sheriffs and the judge each carrying a bright colored bouquet of roses or sweet peas bound up in an old-fashioned, stiff, perforated paper holder. The visitor ventures to whisper his curiosity and he is then informed that, in the former times, these herbs, and the perfume of fresh flowers, were supposed to prevent the contagion of prison fever; and that the ancient custom has survived the use of disinfectants and the modern sanitation of prisoners and cells.

The opening of court in the morning and after luncheon is a curious ceremony. The Bar and audience rise and, through a door corresponding to the one by which the visitor has reached the dais, enter the two sheriffs gowned in flowing dark blue robes trimmed with fur. Then comes the under-sheriff in a very smart black velvet knee breeches suit, white ruffled shirt, white stockings, silver buckled shoes, cocked hat under arm and sword at side. The sheriffs bow in ushering to his seat the judge, who is arrayed in wig and robe, which, in the case of the Lord Chief Justice, or one of the judges of the High Court, is of brilliant scarlet with a dark blue sash over one shoulder, or in the case of the Common Sergeant, is of sombre black.

Each member of the court carries the bouquet referred to and the whole group afford a dash of color strong in contrast with the dark setting. The judge, having seated himself in a chair—so cumbersome as to require a little track to roll it forward sufficiently close to the desk—the sheriffs dispose themselves in the seats not occupied by the judge or his guest, and, later, they quietly withdraw. They have no part in the proceedings, their only function being to usher in and out the judges, and to entertain them at luncheon—the judges being by custom their guests. The judge having taken his seat, the Bar and public do the same and the business begins. There are usually two such courts sitting at the Old Bailey—sometimes three of them.

At lunch time the sheriffs again escort the judges from their seats, and all the judges, sheriffs and under-sheriffs, and any guests they may invite, assemble in the dining-room of the court house for an excellent, substantial luncheon served by butler and footman in blue liveries with brass buttons, knee breeches and white stockings. The luncheon table looks odd with the varied costumes, the rich blues, the bright scarlets and the wigs of the party, who, no longer on duty, relax into jolly sociability.

While enjoying a cigar after luncheon with one of the under-sheriffs, the voice of the Common Serjeant or Recorder is heard at the door of the smoking room. Robed and armed with his bouquet, he smilingly inquires if there are no sheriffs to escort him into court. A hasty buckling on of sword, a snatching up of his bouquet and a little dusting of cigar ashes from his velvet knee breeches, prepares the under-sheriff for the function, and, preceded by the sheriffs in their blue gowns, his Lordship bringing up the rear, the little procession starts along the corridor and enters the door leading to the judges' dais. The under-sheriff shortly returns to finish his cigar but the guest tarries beside the judge.

An English criminal trial is quick, simple and direct. The simplicity and directness of such trials is due to the absence of irrelevant testimony and imaginative arguments; these, counsel scarcely ever attempt to introduce—so certain is their exclusion by the judge. Thus, the real object of all punishment—its deterrent effect upon others— is greatly enhanced because it is swift and sure. The public, moreover, are usually spared the scandal and demoralizing effects of prolonged, spectacular and sensational trials.

Until a short time ago any person convicted in an English court was without appeal—the rulings and sentence of a single judge were final—but this manifest injustice has lately been cured by a law granting the right of appeal."

Scotland Yard and Crime

The Metropolitan Police Service, colloquially known as "Scotland Yard," moved to new headquarters, designed in a Scottish baronial style by architect Norman Shaw, along the Embankment in 1891.

The prospective candidate for the police force was expected to prove an unblemished character, "be over twenty and under twenty-seven years of age, stand at least 5ft 9 ins. in his bare feet, and be of a strong constitution, free from any bodily complaint." Upon possessing all of the qualifications, the candidate then entered police school for at least eight weeks, where he studied from 9 am to 7:30 pm, learning the laws policemen had to obey.

Scotland Yard of the Edwardian era had become a well-oiled machine, and George Dilnot, a journalist and crime novelist, described the organization of the police force circa 1915.

"The great deterrent against crime is not vindictive punishment; the more certain you make detection, the less severe your punishment may be. The brilliant sleuth-hound work of which we read so often is a less important factor in police work than organisation. Organisation it is which holds the peace of London. It is organisation that plucks the murderer from his fancied security at the ends of the earth, that prevents the drunkard from making himself a nuisance to the public, that prevents the defective motor-bus from becoming a danger or an annoyance to the community.

Inside the building of red brick and grey stone that faces the river, and a stone's throw from the Houses of Parliament, there are men who sit planning, planning, planning. The problems of the peace of London change from day to day, from hour to hour, almost from minute to minute. Every emergency must be met, instantly, as it arises—often by diplomacy, sometimes by force. A hundred men must be thrown here, a thousand there, and trained detectives picked for special work. With swift, smooth precision, the well-oiled machinery works, and we, who only see the results, never guess at the disaster that might have befallen if a sudden strain had thrown things out of gear.

In the tangle of departments and sub-departments, bewildering to the casual observer, there is an elastic order which welds the whole together. Not a man but knows his work. The top-notch of efficiency is good enough for Scotland Yard. Its men are engaged in business pure and simple, not in making shrewd detective deductions. The lime-light which occasionally bursts upon them distorts their ways and their duties. Really, they have little love for the dramatic. Newspaper notoriety is not sought, and men cannot "work the Press," as in times gone by, to attain a fictitious reputation.

It is through well-chosen lieutenants that Sir Edward Henry works. There are four Assistant-Commissioners upon each of whom special work devolves. Sir Frederick Wodehouse, for instance, is the "Administrative Assistant-Commissioner." He deals with all matters relating to discipline, promotion, and routine so far as the uniformed force is concerned.

The Criminal Investigation Department is under Mr. Basil Thompson, a comparatively young man who came from the Prison Commission to succeed Sir Melville Macnaghten, and who has successfully experimented with some new ideas to make the path of the criminal more difficult. Mr. Frank Elliott, who was formerly at the Home Office, holds sway over the Public Carriage Office; and the Hon. F. T. Bigham, a barrister—and a son of Lord Mersey, who gained his experience as a Chief Constable of the Criminal Investigation Department—deals with and investigates the innumerable complaints and enquiries that would occur even in a police force manned by archangels. Mr. Bigham is also the Central Authority under the terms of the international agreement for the suppression of the white slave traffic.

There are six Chief Constables, mostly ex-military officers. One of these assists in the administration of the Criminal Investigation Department, the remainder control districts of four or five adjoining divisions. To adopt a military simile, they may be compared to major-generals in command of brigades, with each division representing a battalion, and the superintendents, colonels.

Only once in the whole history of the Metropolitan Police has a man risen from the ranks to the post of Chief Constable, though many, like Mr. Gentle at Brighton, and Mr. Williams at Cardiff, have become the heads of important provincial forces. The post of superintendent in London is at least equivalent in its responsibilities to the average chief-constableship of the provinces. There are metropolitan section sergeants who have as many men under their control as some chief constables of small boroughs.

The unit of the Metropolitan Police is a division which averages about a thousand men. Each is under a superintendent, with a chief-inspector as second in command. Thereafter the ranks run:

UNIFORM BRANCH.	DETECTIVE BRANCH.
Sub-divisional Inspectors	{ Divisional Detective-Inspectors. { Central Detective-Inspectors.
Inspectors	Detective-Inspectors
Station-Sergeants	First Class Detective Sergeants.
Section-Sergeants	Second Class Detective-Sergeants
Constables (reserve)	Third Class Detective-Sergeants
Constables (according to seniority)	Detective-Patrols

These are distributed among close on two hundred police stations in the metropolis, and in twenty-two divisions. Some are detailed for the special work with which London as London has nothing to do. Thus there are: the King's Household Police; divisions guarding the dockyards and military stations at Woolwich, Portsmouth, Devonport, Chatham, and Pembroke; detachments on special duty at the Admiralty and War Office and the Houses of Parliament and Government Departments; and men specially employed, as at the Royal Academy, the Army and Navy Stores, and so on. In all, there are 1,932 men so engaged. Their services are charged for by the Receiver, and the cost does not fall upon the ratepayers.

Scotland Yard is run on the lines of a big business. To the intimate observer it is strangely similar in many of its aspects to a great newspaper office, with its diverse and highly specialised duties all tending to one common end. The headquarters staff is a big one. There are superintendents in charge of the departments, men whom no emergency can ruffle—calm, methodical and alert, ready to act in the time one can make a telephone call.

There are McCarthy, of the Central Criminal Investigation Department; Quinn, of the Special Branch which concerns itself with political offences and the care of Royalty; Bassom, of the

Public Carriage Department; Gooding, of the Peel House Training School; West and White, of the Executive and Statistical Departments.

The Metropolitan Police is the only force in England which is independent of local control. The Commissioner—often wrongly described as the Chief Commissioner—is appointed by the Crown on the recommendation of the Home Secretary, and has wide, almost autocratic powers. It is an Imperial force which has duties apart from the care of London. It has divisions at the great dockyards; it is the adviser and helper of multifarious smaller zones in case of difficulty. It has charge of the river from Dartford Creek to Teddington, and its confines extend far beyond the boundaries of the London County Council.

In one year its printing and stationery bill alone amounts to over £10,000; its postage, telegrams, and telephone charges to another £13,000. Its gross cost is nearly three millions a year. The machinery of Scotland Yard misses little. How many crimes have been prevented by the knowledge of swift and almost inevitable punishment it is impossible to say, but they have been many."

Prisons

Once sentenced, the prisoner was taken from court and ushered into a small compartment in a prison van, or into a four-wheeled cab which would take them to the gaol to which they'd been assigned. The following is a harrowing description of a female prisoner, written by the 6th Viscount Mountmorres:

"She is taken to the receiving-room—a small room, with whitewashed walls and a deal table, at which sits another wardress. The only other furniture is a weighing machine and a measuring-machine. The wardress who has brought her, hands over the committal note and gives the necessary particulars as to the case, receives a receipt for her, and from that hour Emma Smith becomes No. 77.

She has to undress, and is led into an adjoining room, in which several baths with wooden partitions round them are let into the floor; the floor itself is covered with a bath-sheet. A wardress bids her enter one of the baths, and asks her whether it is hot enough. Yes, it is all right. After her bath she is anthropologically examined in the receiving-room: her weight, height, measurements, are all duly recorded, together with notes as to the colour of her hair and eyes, any peculiarities in her features, any disfigurements or marks upon her.

She notices meanwhile, upon the table, all her clothes set out, the contents of her pockets ranged side by side. Whilst she dresses in prison garb she is asked to check all these her possessions as an inventory of them is read over, which she has to sign.

The preliminaries are soon at an end; she is taken to her cell, and on the morrow she will begin the regular routine of prison life. If she be a first offender, her uniform will differ from that of other prisoners in that in the cap and on the sleeve is a white badge with a great red star upon it; otherwise it will be the regulation drab-brown shapeless dress of coarse serge, with apron and cap. The "red star" women are all kept to themselves, in work and in leisure, so that they may not become contaminated by intercourse with their more depraved sisters.

The first evening she will no doubt receive at five o'clock—supper time—a tin basin of rich cocoa, or a bowl of stirabout, and an eight-ounce loaf of bread. It is more than the regulation allowance, but she needs it after the strain and excitement of the day, though probably she has not the heart to taste it, and so the cocoa grows cold and the "butter" rises and sets in a thick white layer on the surface. She mechanically takes in the details of her surroundings with a vacant eye, as she sits staring upon the edge of her narrow bed, or walks feverishly round the confined apartment like a caged animal.

The cell is about twelve feet in length by seven feet in width, and about nine or ten feet high. The floor is either boarded or else flagged, and in the latter case it is black-leaded until you can almost see your face reflected in it. The walls are whitewashed. In the heavy door through which she entered is a small peep-hole, so that she can be kept under observation from the outside. On one side of the door is a small window of thick, opaque glass, behind which a gas-jet burns and serves to light the cell until 8.30 p.m., when all the lights are put out.

On the other side of the door is the heating apparatus, by which hot air is let into the cell. Immediately opposite the door, high up near the ceiling is a closely barred window, one pane of which opens by a lever under the prisoner's control. Beside the window is the ventilating apparatus, which exhausts the cell of foul air. The monotony of the walls is broken only by a corner bracket, on which stand the prisoner's slate, salt, comb, etc., and a small wooden bookshelf containing a Bible, prayer-book, and hymn-book. The only furniture in the room is a little wooden stool, a low table, the bed, and a set of utensils—basin, slop-pail, water-can, mug, food utensils, etc. The bed is merely a sloping plank, at present standing up on end in one corner of the cell, with a mattress hanging over it, and a couple of blankets folded on the top of it.

Next morning No. 77 has to rise at 6.30. Her cell must first be cleaned and tidied, with infinite pains, until its appearance is, if possible, even more glitteringly new than when she entered it. At 8 o'clock comes breakfast—and here a word about her diet. This will depend upon her sentence. There are four different classes of diet, as follows :—

Class I.
Breakfast at 8: Bread, 8 oz.
Dinner at 12.30: Stirabout (a kind of gruel made with oatmeal and Indian meal), 1½ pints.
Supper at 5: Bread, 8 oz.

Class II.
Breakfast: Bread, 5 oz. ; gruel, 1 pint.
Dinner: Bread, 5 oz., and either suet pudding, 6 oz.; or, potatoes, 8 oz.;
or, soup, ½ pint; - according to the day of the week.
Supper: Same as breakfast.

Class III.
Breakfast: Bread, 6 oz. ; gruel, I pint.
Dinner: Bread, 4 oz. ;potatoes, 6 oz.; suet pudding, 6 oz. : or, bread, 6 oz.; potatoes, 8 oz. ; cooked beef, 3 oz.; or, bread, 6 oz.; potatoes, 6 oz.; soup, ¾ pint.
Supper: Same as breakfast.

Class IV.

Breakfast: Bread, 6 oz ; gruel, 1 pint.
Dinner: Same as Class III., with the addition of 2 oz. more of potatoes in each case, and 1 pint of soup instead of ¾ pint on soup days, and 10 oz. of pudding in place of 6 oz. on pudding days.
Supper: Same as breakfast.

Life in prison is divided into four stages, or classes. Every prisoner on entering is in Stage I., and during the first month of her term she remains in this stage, the principal feature of which is that she works her whole time in her cell, and only leaves it for her "exercise " of one hour per day, and for her attendance at chapel.

Each day she can, by good behaviour and industry, earn eight marks; if at the end of a month she has earned the full tale of two hundred and twenty-four marks she is advanced to Stage II., when her work will be with the other prisoners in the workshops, the laundries, the kitchen, or in the general work of the prison.

At the end of her second month, if she has earned four hundred and forty eight marks, she advances to Stage III, and a further two hundred and twenty-four marks during the third month entitles her to Stage IV, and to the privilege of writing and receiving one letter, and of receiving a visit, at which three people may be present, for twenty minutes. For every further completed six hundred and seventy-two marks she may write and receive a letter, and have a visit of thirty minutes.

In addition to this, after she has got into Stage II her marks have a monetary value; that is to say, that for every completed two hundred and twenty-four marks; per month, she has a small sum, which gradually increases, credited to her to receive upon her leaving prison, until this sum totals ten shillings, the maximum which she can thus receive. In Stage II. she is credited in this way with a penny for every twenty marks, or a shilling for the whole two hundred and twenty-four.

In Stage III, her two hundred and twenty-four marks are worth eighteen pence, and a penny is earned for every twelve marks up to the two hundred and twenty-four. In Stage IV and onwards (until the maximum is reached) ten marks bring her a penny, or each completed two hundred and twenty-four two shillings.

Prison life is monotonous, of course: all routine is, and well-disciplined routine such as is found in prison is especially so. Day after day to rise at six-thirty, work till eight o'clock, breakfast at eight o'clock, then to work on till chapel, exercise for an hour by the clock, work on again till dinner at twelve-thirty, work on afterwards till supper at five o'clock, finish work and have a little well-earned quiet and leisure till lights out at eight-thirty, and go to bed looking forward to exactly the same next day—when one knows that such a life is to go on week in week out from month's end to month's end, each day as like any other as two rococo doves— then one realises the monotony, the dreariness of it.

Sunday alone differs from other days — unfortunately, not to Sunday's advantage in the eyes of prisoners: it is a long, dull day in cells, with no work and with two chapels, with nothing to do but to sit and watch the shadows cast by the window bars creeping across the floor and up the wall and on to the ceiling."

Bibliography

Emsley, Clive. *Crime and Society in England: 1750-1900*. London: Longman, 1987.

Emsley, Clive. *The Great British Bobby: A History of British Policing from 1829 to the Present*. London: Quercus, 2009.

Dilnot, George. *Scotland Yard: The Methods and Organisation of the Metropolitan Police*. London: P. Marshall & Co., 1915.

Leaming, Thomas. *A Philadelphia Lawyer in the London Courts*. New York: H. Holt, 1911.

May, Trevor. *Victorian and Edwardian Prisons*. Oxford: Shire, 2006.

Taylor, David. *Crime, Policing and Punishment in England: 1750-1914*. Basingstoke: Macmillan, 1998.

Thomas, Donald, and Henry Mayhew. *The Victorian Underworld*. New York: New York UP, 1998.

The Viscount Mountmorres. "Women Prisoners." *Lady's Realm* Sept. 1898: 691--97. *Google Books*.

Whitmore, Richard. *Victorian and Edwardian Crime and Punishment from Old Photographs*. London: B.T. Batsford, 1978.

Politics

The primary focus of Edwardian politics narrowed so tightly to Irish Home Rule, that on the eve of WWI, the topic on the minds of most socialites and politicians was the Third Home Rule Bill. This had been introduced in 1912 and traveled through the same cycle of struggle for passage, rejection by the House of Lords, and multiple readings thereafter that Parliament had seen for the past forty years. Yet, stronger and more impacting things than merely Irish Home Rule knit the fabric of the political climate. In a scant fourteen years the political landscape was dominated by the debate between Tariff Reform and Protectionism, the menace of trade unionism, the infamous 1906 election, the upsurge of the working class, the suffragist and suffragette movement, the fight to reform of the army and navy, Britain's place in the troubled world of international politics and diplomacy, and the stirrings of the welfare state.

Political Parties

The Conservative Party traced its origins to a faction, rooted in the 18th century Whig Party that coalesced around William Pitt the Younger. It was originally known as "Independent Whigs", "Friends of Mr. Pitt", or "Pittites," but after Pitt's death the term "Tory" came into use. George Canning first used the term "Conservative" in the 1820s and John Wilson Croker suggested it as a title for the party in the 1830s, but it was Sir Robert Peel who adopted the name and is credited with founding the party. After the expansion of the franchise, the party widened its appeal under the aegis of Lord Derby and Benjamin Disraeli, who supported the Reform Act of 1867, which enfranchised working class men.

In 1886, the Conservative Party formed an alliance with Lord Hartington (8th Duke of Devonshire) and Sir Joseph Chamberlain's Liberal Unionist Party, which was comprised of the Liberals who opposed their party's support for Irish Home Rule and the combined party held office for all but three of the following twenty years. The Conservatives suffered a large defeat when the party split over the issue of free trade in 1906, and in 1912, the two parties amalgamated into the Unionist party.

Leaders between 1880-1914: Benjamin Disraeli, Marquess of Salisbury, Lord Hartington, Lord Randolph Churchill, Arthur Balfour, Sir Stafford Northcote, Sir Michael Hicks Beach.

The Liberal Party grew out of the Whigs, which had its origins as an aristocratic faction in the reign of Charles II. The Whigs were in favor of reducing the power of the Crown and increasing the power of the Parliament. As early as 1839 Russell had adopted the name Liberal Party, but in reality the party was a loose coalition of Whigs in the House of Lords and Radicals in the Commons. The formal foundation of the Liberal party is traditionally traced to 1859 and the formation of Palmerston's second government, but it was after Palmerston's death that the Liberal Party reached its zenith. For the next thirty years Gladstone and Liberalism were synonymous.

The "Grand Old Man", as he became known, was Prime Minister four times and the powerful flow of his rhetoric dominated British politics even when he was out of office.

The Liberals however, languished during the 1880s and 1890s due to infighting and the coalition of the Conservatives and Liberal Unionists. They rose again after the unpopular Boer War, and were led by Herbert Henry Asquith and David Lloyd George. The Liberals pushed through much legislation in the 1906-1911 period, including the regulation of working hours, national insurance and welfare. It was at this time that a political battle over the so-called People's Budget resulted in the passage of an act ending the power of the House of Lords to block legislation. World War One splintered the group, and it quickly disintegrated after 1918.

Leaders between 1880-1914: William Gladstone, Sir Henry Campbell-Bannerman, David Lloyd George, Herbert Henry Asquith, Winston Churchill (after famously crossing the floor in 1904).

The Liberal Unionist party was created in 1886 from a split in the Liberal Party. Led by Lord Hartington and Joseph Chamberlain, the LU's formed a political alliance with the Conservatives in opposition to Irish Home Rule. The two parties formed a coalition government in 1895 but kept separate political funds and their own party organizations until a complete merger was agreed in May 1912. The political impact of the Liberal Unionist breakaway marked the end of the long nineteenth century domination by the Liberal party of the British political scene. From 1830 to 1886 the Liberals (the name the Whigs, Radicals and Peelites accepted as their political label after 1859) managed to become almost the party of permanent government with just a couple of Conservative interludes. After 1886 it was the Conservatives who enjoyed this position and they received a huge boost with their alliance with a party of disaffected Liberals.

Leaders between 1880-1914: Marquess of Hartington, Joseph Chamberlain

Commonly called the Irish Party or the Home Rule Party, the Irish Parliamentary Party was formed in 1882 by Charles Stewart Parnell, the leader of the Nationalist Party, replacing the Home Rule League, as official parliamentary party for Irish nationalist Members of Parliament until 1918. The IPP evolved out of the Home Government Association founded by Isaac Butt after he defected from the Irish Conservative Party in 1870. Its intention was to gain a limited form of freedom from Britain in order to protect and control Irish domestic affairs in the interest of the Protestant landlord class, when William E. Gladstone and his Liberal Party came to power in 1868 under his slogan "Justice for Ireland" and Irish Liberals gained 65 of the 105 Irish seats at Westminster. The party lost its hold when its ardent Catholicism frightened the Protestants, and Butt reorganized the party as the Home Rule League. But no other man is as synonymous with the IPP than Charles Stewart Parnell. Parnell resurrected it in October as the Irish National League (INL).

It combined moderate agrarianism, a Home Rule program with electoral functions, was hierarchical and autocratic in structure with Parnell wielding immense authority and direct parliamentary control. Parliamentary constitutionalism was the future path. The informal alliance between the new, tightly disciplined National League and the Catholic Church was one of the main factors for the revitalization of the national Home Rule cause after 1882. Parnell saw that the explicit endorsement of Catholicism was of vital importance to the success of this venture. At the end of 1882 the organization already had 232 branches, in 1885 increased to

592 branches. The INL grew to become a formidable political machine built in the traditional political culture of rural Ireland, for it was an alliance of tenant-farmers, shopkeepers and publicans.

The party lost its footing when the scandal of Parnell's relationship with the very married Katherine O'Shea was revealed, and despite the loyalty of his party and friends, Parnell was disgraced. He married Katherine after her divorce, but died soon after. After his death, the Irish Party put pressure on its traditional ally, the Liberal Party, which culminated in a series of Home Rule bills that tore British opinion apart. The outbreak of WWI distracted everyone from the "Irish Question," but Ireland took matters into its own hands, resulting in the Easter Rising (1916), the war of independence (1919-1921), civil war (1922-1923) and the eventual partition of Ireland into Northern Ireland (Ulster was anti-Home Rule), and the Republic of Ireland.

Leaders between 1880-1914: Charles Stewart Parnell, John Redmond, Justin McCarthy, John Dillon

The Labour Party's origins lie in the late 19th century numeric increase of the urban proletariat and the extension of the franchise to working-class males, when it became apparent that there was a need for a political party to represent the interests and needs of those groups. after the extensions of the franchise in 1867 and 1885, the Liberal Party endorsed some trade-union sponsored candidates. In addition, several small socialist groups had formed around this time with the intention of linking the movement to political policies. Among these were the Independent Labour Party, the intellectual and largely middle-class Fabian Society, the Social Democratic Federation and the Scottish Labour Party. In the 1892 General Election, held in July, three working men were elected without support from the liberals, Keir Hardie in South West Ham, John Burns in Battersea, and Havelock Wilson in Middlesbrough who faced Liberal opposition. Concurrently Hardie adopted a confrontational style and increasingly emerged as parliamentary spokesman for independent labour.

At the Trade Union Conference meeting in September a meeting of advocates of independent labour organization was called, and chaired by Hardie, an arrangements committee was established and a conference called for the following January. This conference, held in Bradford 14-16 January 1893, was the foundation conference of the Independent Labour Party. The object of the party should be `to secure the collective and communal ownership of the means of production, distribution and exchange`. The party's program called for a range of reforms, with much more stress on the social – an eight hour working day, provision for sick, disabled aged, widows and orphans and free `unsectarian` education `right up to the universities` – than on the political reforms which were standard in Radical organizations.

In the 1906 election, the party won 29 seats, during their first meeting after the election, the group's MPs decided to adopt the name "The Labour Party". Keir Hardie, who had taken a leading role in getting the party established, was elected as Chairman of the Parliamentary Labour Party. The Fabian Society provided much of the intellectual stimulus for the party.

Leaders between 1880-1914: Keir Hardie, Bruce Glasier, Philip Snowden, Ramsay MacDonald, Frederick William Jowett, William Crawford Anderson

The Irish Question

The "Irish Question" dominated British politics for the majority of the nineteenth century. No other issue tore families, friends, and otherwise friendly political opponents apart than that of Home Rule. The seeds for this conflict were sown long before the nineteenth century, stretching back to the 17th century, when Oliver Cromwell, who detested Roman Catholicism and believed that the Irish could never be trusted, sent his New Model Army and coerce the Irish into obedience. The army laid siege to the island, the most brutal being that waged on the towns of Wexford and Drogheda, where defenders of the towns were summarily executed. Cromwell also believed the best way to bring Ireland to heel in the long term, was to "export" children from Ireland to the sugar plantations in the West Indies, so that Ireland would suffer from a long term population loss, making it less of a threat to mainland Britain.

Anglo-Irish tensions were further exacerbated by the presence of the "Protestant Ascendancy," or the "Ascendancy," who were comprised of the Protestant English landowners who received large swaths of land from the Crown confiscated from Irish landowners after a series of unsuccessful revolts against English rule. English soldiers and traders became the new ruling class, as its richer members were elevated to the Irish House of Lords, and eventually controlled the Irish House of Commons. This process was facilitated and formalized in the legal system after 1691 by the passing of various Penal Laws, which discriminated against Irish Catholics and non-Anglican Protestants deemed "Dissenters."

Though the Ascendancy lost much of its overt political and social clout by the early 19th century, the "abolition of the Irish parliament was followed by economic decline in Ireland, and widespread emigration from among the ruling class to the new center of power in London, which increased the number of absentee landlords." The Potato Famine of 1848-1852 exposed the vulnerability of Irish tenant farmers, and as a consequence, the British Parliament was moved to pass a number of acts to bolster the Irish economy. But these belated Acts did little to counteract the centuries of absentee landlord abuses, nor the history of British oppression.

The life of an Irish tenant farmer was difficult. Land prices in Ireland were high—sometimes 80-100% higher than in England—and those who leased land from an absentee landlord rented out small parcels to those who paid to farm it. Each estate leased out was divided into the smallest possible parcels of land and many families who worked the land had only half-an-acre to live on. There were no rules controlling the work of those who had leased land from absentee landlords, and this lack of rules worked in conjunction with the Royal Irish Constabulary who, with the Army, enforced evictions if needed. As such, there were three systems in place which forced Irish farmers into the endless cycle of debt:

Rundale: a system whereby land rented to a person or persons was scattered throughout an estate. Therefore, it was very time consuming to travel to each parcel of land. The argument given for using this system was that everyone got a chance of getting at least some good land to farm. One man in Donegal had 42 pieces of land throughout one managed estate.

Hanging Gale: a system whereby a new tenant was allowed to delay his payment of rent for 6 to 8 months from the start of renting the land. Therefore, he was permanently in debt and had no security.

Conacre: a system whereby the landlord/manager prepared the land and then the tenant moved in. The tenant was then allowed to pay part of his rent using the crops he had grown. If there was a bad harvest, then he had no crops to pay part of his rent. Therefore, he was gambling that he would get a good harvest. In 1845 to 1847, this system was ripe for a disaster.

Dissent spilled over in the 1840s and 1850s with the rise of the Young Ireland party. They believed the only solution for Ireland was complete independence: Home Rule. After a failed attack on the government, Young Ireland's most prominent leaders, James Stephens and John O'Mahony, fled for Paris. O'Mahoney later found his way to America where he stirred up the ire of Irish-Americans to create the Fenian Brotherhood. The Fenians planned a number of rebellions and uprisings, and though initially their causes garnered much sympathy, after December 1867, when several Londoners were killed when a bomb planted by the Fenians exploded at Clerkenwell Prison, there came a wave of intense anti-Irish feeling in London and elsewhere in England.

Prior to his taking up the cudgel for Home Rule, William Ewart Gladstone's political career was somewhat distinguished but mostly ordinary. In 1867, Lord Russell retired and Gladstone became a leader of the Liberal Party, shortly thereafter becoming Prime Minister, where he remained in the office until 1874.

In the 1860s and 1870s, Gladstonian Liberalism was "characterized by a number of policies intended to improve individual liberty and loosen political and economic restraints. First was the minimization of public expenditure on the premise that the economy and society were best helped by allowing people to spend as they saw fit. Secondly, his foreign policy aimed at promoting peace to help reduce expenditures and taxation and enhance trade. Thirdly, laws that prevented people from acting freely to improve themselves were reformed."

During Gladstone's rise, there also arose Ireland's most intelligent and charismatic leader, one whom many on both sides of the political spectrum admitted could have swayed the tide of Home Rule: Charles Stewart Parnell. Born into the gentry and, surprisingly, of American stock via his mother, he rose swiftly through the ranks of politics, gaining fame during the 1870s when he refuted the claims that Fenians had been behind the murders in Manchester. His defense gained him the attention of the Irish Republican Brotherhood (IRB), a physical force Irish organization that had staged the rebellion in 1867, and Parnell began to cultivate Fenians from America and Britain. By the 1880s, Parnell had become the face of Irish Nationalism, and so popular was he that during his tour of Toronto, an associate dubbed him the "uncrowned king of Ireland."

By the time of Gladstone's Second and Third Ministries, he was aligned with the pro-Home Rule movement. Gladstone, impressed by Parnell, had become personally committed to granting Irish home rule in 1885. With his famous three-hour Irish Home Rule speech Gladstone sought to convince Parliament to "pass the Irish Government Bill 1886, and grant Home Rule to Ireland in honor rather than being compelled to do so one day in humiliation." The bill was defeated in the Commons by 30 votes. The split the Liberal (Whig) Party led to the founding of the Liberal Unionists by Lord Hartington (later the Duke of Devonshire, whose brother was murdered by Irish nationalists at Phoenix Park in 1886) and Joseph Chamberlain, who then formed a political alliance with the Conservatives in opposition to Irish Home Rule.

From then on, the "Irish Question" was fought bitterly in the House of Commons, and politicians were not afraid to resort to various deceptions such as forgeries, bribes, dissenting anonymous pamphlets, etc in support or in opposition. One of these backdoor deals is rumored to have resulted in the sudden petition for divorce by Captain O'Shea, the husband of Parnell's longtime love, Katherine, with whom he had three children.

The divorce scandal stunted Parnell's political career, and though he remained popular, his reputation was forever tarnished and he died in 1891. The fight for Home Rule marched on, and prior to the Great War, two more Home Rule bills were introduced in 1892 and 1914, only to experience a crushing defeat (though the 1914 bill was interrupted by WWI and the Easter Rising). Though the issue of Home Rule was finally settled violently and bloodily, it cast a pall over British politics and was the first sign of a weakness in the armor that was the British Empire.

The Suffrage Movement

The militant suffrage movement in Great Britain began as a Pankhurst family enterprise that, from 1903 to 1905 remained focused around Manchester, until the general election of 1905 brought matters to a head. Prior to the Pankhursts, the fight for women's suffrage in Britain was a relatively tame one. In the mid 1860s, a group of women, all pursuing a career in either medicine or education, formed a discussion group dubbed the "Kensington Society". Their initial reasons for forming the group had little to do with suffrage; the seven founding ladies merely wished for a society of like-minded women of independent means and an interest in fields not normally associated with the female sex.

It wasn't until the topic of suffrage was raised that the Kensington Society discovered their mutual dismay. In reaction, they drafted a petition asking parliament to extend to vote to women. Presenting the petition to Henry Fawcett and John Stuart Mill, a pair of MPs known for their sympathy towards women's suffrage, the Kensington Society saw their petition almost immediately shot down in Parliament. Vastly disappointed with the action, they formed the London Society for Women's Suffrage. Soon thereafter, many cities in Britain found themselves hosts to similar societies.

In 1887, seventeen of these groups formed the National Union of Women's Suffrage Societies, or NUWSS. Under the presidencies of Lydia Becker and Millicent Fawcett, the society raised awareness of the cause by holding meetings, holding marches, printing pamphlets and newsletters, and writing politicians and petitions. NUWSS also lent support to Josephine Butler's campaign against white slavery as well as Clementia Black's attempts to force the government to protect low-paid women workers. Inoffensive, efficient and ladylike, NUWSS attracted support from all walks of life—including a good number of men.

The cause chugged along in this manner until the Manchester group splintered, and the women, led by Christabel Pankhurst, grew fed up with the constitutional methods NUWSS favored. The Women's Social & Political Union (WSPU) was born.

A far cry from the genteel group from whence they came, the WSPU immediately showed its difference in the fact that it attracted women from the working and middle-classes—women who were less inhibited by the traditional trappings of "ladyhood".

Though at first fearing the stance the WSPU took would harm the cause, the NUWSS admired their courage and refused to speak out against them. However, by 1905 public interest in women's suffrage had waned, and the WSPU made a decision that would forever change the face of the suffragist movement. Christabel Pankhurst and Annie Kenny threw down the gauntlet by interrupting Sir Edward Grey's speech during a Liberal Party meeting with the cry of "Will the Liberal Government give votes to women?".

The women were soon after charged with assault and arrested. Christabel and Annie then proceeded to shock the world when, after refusing to pay the five shilling fine, they were thrown in jail. Never before had English suffragists resorted to violence to support the cause and newspapers were quick to pounce on this new movement, with the Daily Mail nicknaming the followers of militancy "suffragettes". Far from decrying this derogatory term, the WSPU adopted it with pleasure since the term separated them from the moderate actions of the NUWSS.

The WSPU moved their headquarters from Manchester to London, by 1908 the suffragettes had launched an all-out war for the cause, targeting those MPs notoriously anti-suffrage like Prime Minister H.H. Asquith and Winston Churchill. The suffragettes marched through London, interrupted speeches, assaulted policemen attempting to arrest them, chained themselves to fences, sent letter bombs and damaged property–the most infamous being their destruction of the windows of department stores and shops in Bond Street.

Viewed as unfeminine since many of the women were unmarried and had careers instead of housework, the Establishment were at a loss as to how to deal with suffragettes. They baffled the common perceptions of Victorian womanhood, and once they were released from jail, the suffragettes merely went out and repeated the same misdemeanors. By using this loophole in the justice system, the suffragettes increased their militant campaigns, including a devastating arson campaign during which attempts were made to burn the houses of anti-suffrage MPs, railway stations, golf courses, cricket fields and racecourse stands.

When the jailed suffragettes went on hunger-strikes while incarcerated, the government passed the "Cat and Mouse Act" in 1913: if a suffragette went on a hunger strike, once ill she would be released from prison and re-arrested when well again. However, by the summer of 1914, the militant campaign was exhausted by the imprisonment, exile or poor health of the WSPU's leading members (Christabel had fled to Paris in 1912 to escape arrest), and the splits within the WSPU, and the number of active members able to continue the violence was now very small. Naturally, WWI put a damper on the suffrage campaign, and both the WSPU and NUWSS focused their energies on the war effort, using their platforms to drum up support for the troops.

But ever antagonistic to the end, the WSPU took patriotism to their breast as much as they did suffrage, using their newspaper to attack those in power whom they saw as pacifists or communists. In the end, married women over the age of 30 were granted the vote in 1918, and ten years later the vote was given on equal terms as men (age 21).

Trade Unions, Working Class Power & Social Welfare

The Education Act of 1870 educated the working class, and the Third Reform Act of 1884 empowered them (well, the men at least). From this educated and enfranchised mass came trade unions. Unions had been brutally suppressed until the 1820s, but in the 1880s, new unions were militant, led by men with a socialist bent, recruited semi-skilled and unskilled labor as opposed to just skilled trades, and used their mobility to spread their ideas. They were also unafraid to go on strike, and there were three major disputes between 1894 and 1898 (the Scottish Coal Miners' in 1894, the Engineers' in 1897-98, and the South Wales Coal Miners' in 1898).

In 1901, the position of the trade unions were challenged when the Taff Vale Railway Company "successfully sued the Amalgamated Society of Railway Servants, a trades union, for damages due to losses accrued during a strike." The Company won £23,000 in damages, which proved that trade unions were not immune to the damages caused by its members, but this lawsuit only infuriated the working classes and alienated them from the Conservative Party who set up a Royal Commission in 1906 merely to discuss the situation. The Conservatives were in for an extremely rude awakening that year, for during the General Election, they lost over half their seats in the House of Commons, the Liberals—under Campbell-Bannerman—gained a clear majority, and the Labour Party considerably increased its seats.

This election also saw the downfall of the Liberal Unionist party, who experienced their own split between the moderate LU's and the more radical members allied with Joseph Chamberlain, over the debate between Free Trade vs. Tariff Reform. Chamberlain had always been strongly pro-Empire, and he saw the installment of tariffs on imported goods and subsidies on exported goods as a way to bind the Empire more tightly together and help Britain maintain its power in the face of German and American industrialization and wealth. This sounded good on paper, but for the working classes, this was a repeat of the Corn Laws of 1815-1846 (which protected homegrown grains and cereals from competition against imported grains and cereals, but ultimately led to high prices and low wages).

Chamberlain's political career reached its zenith between 1903 and 1904, when he became the face of Tariff Reform, the cause for which he stumped across England giving rousing speeches to sway electors to his side. Unfortunately, the winds of change were against him, and the Liberal Unionist Party collapsed in the months leading up to the 1906 General Election. The Pro-Tariff Reform Liberal Unionists and Conservatives in Chamberlain's hometown of Birmingham remained triumphant, but everyone else lost their seats or retreated to the Liberal or Conservative Parties from whence they came.

The Prime Minister Sir Henry Campbell-Bannerman died two years after he lead the Liberal Party to its victory and was replaced by his Chancellor of the Exchequer (what would be known as the Secretary of the Treasury in the US), Herbert Henry Asquith. Now the face of British politics had definitely changed for Asquith, and his Chancellor of the Exchequer, David Lloyd George, were both staunchly upper-middle class, non-Anglican (Asquith was raised a Congregationalist, Lloyd George a Nonconformist), and were not land owners—three attributes which placed them firmly outside of the traditional political mold. They were also progressive, though Lloyd George more so than Asquith, and with the equally fiery Winston Churchill, launched a campaign to reform British society.

Topics mentioned before, such as women's suffrage, workmen's compensation, trade unionism, old age pensions, and sweated labor, to say nothing of Home Rule, unemployment, and child welfare, aroused heated debates from the Palace of Westminster to social and political gatherings across the nation. Times were changing swiftly and violently, but no act of social reform aroused as much controversy and firestorm as the People's Budget of 1909.

The People's Budget was the brainchild of David Lloyd George and was championed by his ally, Winston Churchill, who was accused of being a traitor to his class. Lloyd George, a Welsh politician who gained fame by his vehement opposition to the Second Boer War, made social reform the linchpin of his personal political platform. Though it could be said that the Liberal Party adopted a measure of socialistic platforms to keep the Conservative Party in check, and to stem the rise of the Labour Party, Edwardian society was changing, and politicians were kicked into the twentieth century, whether they liked it or not.

After the Liberals introduced old age pensions for the sick and infirm, Lloyd George shocked both sides of the political spectrum with the budget he revealed on April 29, 1909, which proposed taxes on luxuries, liquor, tobacco, incomes, and land, and an increase in death duties (introduced in 1894) and duties on undeveloped land and minerals, a levy on unearned increment, and a supertax on incomes above £5000 (6d. on the pound). This influx of taxes would support such programs as pensions, unemployment insurance, health insurance, free school meals for children, etc, and the costs of building the dreadnoughts the Royal Navy claimed it needed to shore up defenses against Germany.

Also causing controversy was the reform of the Army under the Secretary of State for War, Richard Haldane. The physical conditions of recruits during the Boer War exposed the shameful state in which poor and working class people lived. These young men who rushed to enlist were puny, underfed, and in no shape to fight Boers under the hot South African sun. But the British Army was incredibly slow to adapt and very resistant to change, and when the war ended, they considered the matter closed. Haldane didn't, and when he was appointed Secretary of State during the Liberal landslide, he was determined to whip the Army into shape. The Territorial and Reserve Forces Act of 1907 enabled him to launch his reform: a Territorial Force and a Reserve Army—both of which formed the foundation of the British Expeditionary Forces sent to France in WWI.

This was too much for the traditional Establishment to handle, but their successes in establishing a Territorial Army, making sweated labor illegal, and Old Age Pensions made them sure of their budget, which galvanized the Liberal Party to action. They fought for the Finance Bill throughout the summer, but a blow was struck when the House of Lords vetoed the budget, and the tug-of-war resulted in another General Election in January 1910. A greater blow was struck to the House of Lords, who, though they passed the budget April 29, 1910, experienced their first real challenge of power.

So great was the battle for the People's Budget, Liberal politicians threatened to make King Edward (and after his death in May, King George) ennoble Liberal MPs so they could then sit in the House of Lords and pass the bill. This constitutional crisis did not come to pass, but 1911 saw the passing of a Parliament Act which "prevented the Lords from vetoing any public legislation that originated in and had been approved by the Commons, and imposed a maximum legislative delay of one month for "money bills" (those dealing with taxation) and two years for other types of bill."

Society was rent in two as much by this crisis as by Irish Home Rule, and the thirty odd years of "peace" between the major political parties (from which sprang The Souls, who were adamant that everyone bridge the gap between their political beliefs in order to enjoy one another's company) were over. In the four years between Edward VII's death and the outbreak of WWI, England was far, far from the bucolic "long Edwardian summer" so many post-war memoirs harkened back to with longing. In fact, much of the period was marked by strife, estrangement, and violence, as the people pushed against the marginalization created in the Nineteenth century and were determined to bring the nation into the Twentieth.

British Diplomacy and the Road to the Great War

When in 1902, Britain raised its head from its "splendid isolation" to realize it had no allies, its enemies and neutral peers had long since formed alliances and treaties that crisscrossed across Europe. One can see the thread tying various countries together in the mad declarations of war in the summer of 1914 (Austria-Hungary on Serbia, Russia on Austria-Hungary, Germany on Russia, France on Germany, etc), and Britain herself was pulled into the melee by a treaty with Belgium from the 1830s.

In 1873 Russia, Germany, and Austria-Hungary signed a pact called the "League of the Three Emperors." Since the three dominated a large swath of land and people, it was considered imperative that they look out for one another. Yet, the Emperors (Tsar Alexander II, Franz Josef, and Wilhelm I)—and Bismarck—failed to take into account their individual agendas. Russia considered the Balkan region, long under Ottoman reign, its sister since both Russia and the Balkans were made up of predominantly Slavic peoples. Austria-Hungary, however, considered the Balkans, who gave the landlocked empire warm water and regular ports and were due south to Austria and Hungary, their own.

When the Ottoman Empire collapsed in 1878 and its possessions parceled out between the leading Powers, the tension between Russia and Austria-Hungary simmered until the alliance finally broke for good in 1887. Germany and Austria-Hungary had since signed their own secret Dual Alliance, and in 1882, Italy surreptitiously joined them to form the Triple Alliance. Bismarck could not allow Russia to go and align itself with France, and he badgered Russia into a secret treaty known as the "Reinsurance Treaty" in 1887, wherein Germany promised to stay out of any conflict between Russia and Austria-Hungary.

Unfortunately, Bismarck's best laid plans went awry when Wilhelm II ascended to the throne of the German Empire after his father's premature death after eight months of rule in 1888. The arrogant and impetuous young Kaiser decided to rid himself of anything and anyone associated with his father and grandfather's reigns, and meddle in foreign affairs himself. With the Iron Chancellor dropped, the secret treaty with Russia was as well, and Bismarck's worst fears came true with Russia publicly aligned itself with France in 1892.

In the meantime, Britain felt threatened on all sides: by her traditional enemy France, by Russia, whom they feared would attempt to take India from them (this "cold war" between Russia and Britain was played out in Central Asia [Afghanistan, Persia, Turkestan, etc] and was known as the Great Game), and by the rapidly-industrialized and militarized Germany, whom they mistrusted. Britain and France nearly came to blows in 1898 with the Fashoda Incident, when a French expedition in East Africa sought to take control of the Nile River and expel Britain from Egypt. The frantic diplomats of both nations and the show of Britain's might only averted battle when it sent a flotilla of gunboats to Fashoda. As a result of this humiliation, French opinion of Britain greatly soured, and when the British declared the Second Boer War in 1899, the press in all of its enemy nations were brutal.

Britain's first friend was Japan, with whom they admittedly had little in common other than a opposition to Russian expansion in the East. The Anglo-Japanese Alliance was signed in January 1902, and in March a mutual pact was signed by France and Russia, which ultimately had the effect of keeping France out of the Russo-Japanese War of 1904-05, since that would have embroiled the French in a war with Britain. Meanwhile, this alliance had the positive affect of bringing a bit of Japan to England and a bit of England to Japan.

After this first step at ending its diplomatic isolation, it seemed natural than Britain would align itself with Germany. After all, the Kaiser was Queen Victoria's grandson and King Edward VII's nephew, and the cultural exchange between the two nations were actually quite strong. Many of Britain's top politicians assumed a German treaty would be the natural conclusion, but the King had other ideas.

Edward had loved France since he was a little boy. When the Emperor Louis-Napoleon and his lovely wife Eugenie visited England in the 1850s, the little Prince of Wales was seduced by French manners, French language, French culture, and best of all, French beauties (the perfumed and beautifully-dressed ladies in the Empress's retinue). As an adult, he was as much at home in French salons and French racetracks as he was in English drawing rooms and English race courses, and the French aristocracy were so mad about him, many became ardent Anglophiles, even going so far as to begin the custom of having afternoon tea.

Now as King he was determined to bring the two nations he loved best together, and in the spring of 1904, France and Britain signed the Entente Cordiale, thus ending almost a thousand years of enmity between them, and signaling to Germany that Britain would never be their ally.

With the Entente, France and Britain let bygones be bygones in the squabble for North Africa, but the world experienced a further shock when Britain and Russia finally laid down the weapons in their cold war and signed the Anglo-Russian Entente in 1907, thereby establishing once and for all the boundaries between India and Central Asia.

In the meantime, Germany began to meddle in the affairs of the weak Ottoman Empire, and Austria-Hungary's abrupt annexation of Bosnia-Herzegovina in 1908 nearly blew the fuse seething in the Balkans.

With the former, Germany descended upon the "Sick Man of Europe" with its engineers and bankers, and promises of loans, support, and industrialization, and with the latter, Austria had practically pounced when the other nations weren't looking. This move outraged the Ottomans, Russia and the Balkan peoples, which nearly upset German's hold over the Ottoman Empire, since remember, Austria-Hungary was their ally.

However, when Italy defeated the Ottomans in 1912, the Balkan nations realized how weak the Ottoman Empire was, and how hesitant the European powers were to meddle in their affairs, and promptly declared war. 1912 and 1913 saw the Ottoman Empire felled for good after five hundred years of rule in Eastern Europe, the Middle East, and North Africa, and the establishment of independent nations in the Balkan Peninsula (Albania, Serbia, Macedonia, and Bulgaria).

France and Germany's own bitter rivalry spilled over during this time as well, with two crises over the status of Morocco. As one of the last independent countries in Africa and situated beside France's colonial possessions in North Africa, it was a given that the French would want to add Morocco to its possessions. Germany, however, was determined to meddle, and in 1906, the Kaiser sailed away to Morocco to offer the Sultan his support in maintaining the country's independence. The dispute was calmed by a conference of the world powers and France was announced the natural protector of Morocco, but it reared its head again in 1911, when the Kaiser sent a gunboat to the port of Agadir during a rebellion against the Sultan. The result of this crisis was to allow France to annex Morocco, thereby ending its independence, in exchange for a piece of France's territory in the Congo.

All of these conflicts, practically one after another, served only to draw particular nations further together against other nations, and now we see the world on the edge of war. But Britain remained blind to the implications of this, distracted as it was by its own domestic troubles, and when Austria declared war on Serbia in July of 1914, many assumed the war would be localized and brief, or even calmed by yet another conference and treaty. Unfortunately for them, the web of alliances and agendas that entangled the Concert of Europe had been spun too deep for too long, and it took a major war to force it apart.

Bibliography

Crow, Duncan. *The Edwardian Woman.* New York: St. Martin's, 1978.

Gladstone, W. E., and James Bryce Bryce. *Handbook of Home Rule: Being Articles on the Irish Question.* London: K. Paul, Trench, 1887.

Hale, Oron J. *The Great Illusion, 1900-1914.* New York: Harper & Row, 1971.

Hattersley, Roy. *The Edwardians.* New York: St. Martin's, 2005.

Jackson, Alvin. *Home Rule: An Irish History.* London: Phoenix, 2004.

Jalland, Pat. *Women, Marriage and Politics, 1860-1914.* Oxford: Oxford UP, 1988.

Kee, Robert. *The Laurel and the Ivy: The Story of Charles Stewart Parnell and Irish Nationalism.* London: Hamish Hamilton, 1993.

MacDonagh, Michael. *The Book of Parliament.* London: Isbister and Limited 15 & 16 Tavistock Street, Covent Garden, 1897.

McGee, Owen. *The IRB: The Irish Republican Brotherhood, from the Land League to Sinn Féin.* Dublin, Ireland: Four Courts, 2005.

Nowell-Smith, Simon, ed. *Edwardian England, 1901-1914.* London: Oxford UP, 1964.

Petrie, Charles. *Scenes of Edwardian Life.* London: Eyre & Spottiswoode, 1965.

Purvis, June. *Emmeline Pankhurst: A Biography.* London: Routledge, 2002.

Toye, Richard. *Lloyd George & Churchill: Rivals for Greatness.* London: Macmillan, 2007.

Tuchman, Barbara Wertheim. The Guns of August. New York: Ballantine, 1994.

The Military

The British Army was honed by the colonial skirmishes of the Victorian Age, but the advent of the Boer War and its aftermath revealed serious deficiencies in the quality of recruits and the organization of this branch of the military. At the same time, the Navy, long considered the pride and might of Great Britain, also underwent serious reforms in the wake of Germany's naval expansion. The development of an aviation branch came late in the Edwardian era, and many were skeptical of its use as a method of offense in and of itself; nevertheless, the Royal Flying Corps and Royal Naval Air Service soon proved themselves a worthy component to the British Armed Forces in the early months of the Great War.

The Army

The year of Edward VII's coronation also heralded the end of the embarrassing, blundering, and costly Second Boer War, which was essentially a very nineteenth century war dragged into the twentieth (the war having begun in October 1899). It was embarrassing because the British resorted to inhumane tactics like "scorched earth" policies and concentration camps to wrestle the Boers into submission; it was blundering because the British Army underestimated their foes and their terrain; and it was costly, since this supposedly quick battle was dragged out into a two and a half year long war that cost Britain one hundred and fifty million pounds.

Reform of the British Army was slow and largely unpopular with both the public and politicians due to the "wishful thinking...that the sea was Britain's best defense against a foreign foe, and that the Navy could always be relied upon to ward off invasion." Change was also hampered by the myriad of traditions separating regiments, and the aristocratic privilege of the British officer. Matters came to a head due to the aforementioned Boer War and King Edward's push for the modernization of the army. A split in the Cabinet under Balfour's premiership over Chamberlain's tariff campaign prompted a reshuffling of Cabinet Ministers, and the King's nomination for the War Office was his close associate, Lord Esher.

Esher had been appointed to Lord Salisbury's (PM between 1895-1902) royal commission to investigate the organization of the army during the war, and proved a diligent "spy" for the King. Once in office, Esher promptly went to work, and his Committee on the War Office "reported with impressive speed in January 1904. Esher proposed to establish an Army Council or General Staff...scrapping the commander-in-chief...[reducing] the influence of the Crown." When the Liberals came to power in the 1906 landslide, H.B. Haldane, the new Secretary of State for War, set about making the largest reform of the British Army since the Childers Reforms of the early 1880s.

Under Haldane's reforms, the "regular troops serving in the United Kingdom, together with the army reserve, were made to form the Expeditionary Force, while the militia was converted into a Special Reserve charged with the duty of training and providing drafts for the regular units at the front." These regular units were composed of the Yeomanry and Volunteers, both of which comprised the Territorial Force of "fourteen infantry divisions and fourteen mounted brigades for Home Defense." The General Staff now only concerned themselves with strategy and training, the Staff College at Camberley was enlarged and the Staff College at Quetta, founded by Lord Kitchener, was built up. At these colleges, Staff officers were trained in business management, railway organization, and other subjects "not taken very seriously in the past."Another major change was the transformation of the University Volunteer Corps into Senior Officers' Training Corps, which would provide candidates for officers' commissions, and the transformation of the Public Schools Cadet Corps into the Junior O.T.C. For most of the First World War, officers were drawn directly from these O.T.C. units.

In *The British Army from Within*, Evelyn Charles Vivian describes the inner workings of the Edwardian Army:

"The main station in England is Aldershot, headquarters of the first Army Corps. Theoretically, in all cases of national emergency, the Aldershot Command is first to move, and the units composing it are expected to be able to mobilise for active service at twenty-four hours' notice. Next in importance are Colchester, Shorncliffe, York, and Bulford—the centre of the Salisbury Plain area under military control. In Ireland the principal stations are Dublin and the Curragh. In these stations, under normal circumstances, the furlough season begins at Christmas time and lasts up to the following March; for this period men are granted leave in batches, and drill and training for those who remain in barracks while the others take their holidays is somewhat relaxed.

Serious training begins in March, when the corporals, sergeants, and troop and section officers begin to lick their squads, sections, and troops into shape. Following on this comes company training for the infantry, squadron training for the cavalry, and battery training for the artillery, and this in turn is followed by battalion training for infantry, regimental training for cavalry, and brigade training for artillery. Somewhere during the period taken up before the beginning of regimental and battalion training, musketry has to be fitted in, and, as the ranges cannot accommodate all the men at once, this has to be done by squadrons and companies, while those not engaged in perfecting their shooting continue with their other training.

At the conclusion of the training of units— regiments, battalions, and brigades of artillery— brigade and divisional training is begun, and then manoeuvres follow, in which the troops are given opportunities of learning the working of an army corps, as well as getting practical experience of camp life under conditions as near those obtaining on active service as circumstances will admit. By the time all this has been completed, the furlough season starts again, and the round begins once more with a few more recruits to train, a few old soldiers missing from the ranks.

In addition to the regular course of training that lasts through the year and goes on from year to year, there are various " courses " to be undergone in order to keep the departmental staff of each unit up to strength. Thus, in the infantry, signallers must be specially trained, and pioneers, who do all the sanitary work of their units, must be taught their duties, while musketry instructors and drill instructors have to be selected and taught their duties. Each unit, except as regards medical service and a few things totally out of its range of activity, is self-contained and self-supporting, and thus it is necessary that it should train its own instructors and its own special men for special work, together with understudies to take their places in case of casualties.

The cavalry trains its own signallers, scouts, shoeing smiths, cooks, pioneers, and to a certain extent medical orderlies. The artillery does likewise, and in addition keeps up a staff of artificers to attend to minor needs of the guns—men capable of repairing breakages in the field, as far as this is possible. Wherever horses are concerned, too, saddlers must be trained to keep leather work in repair.

The Engineers, a body of men who seldom get the recognition their work deserves, have to train in telegraphy, bridge-building, construction and demolition of all things, from a regular defensive fortification to a field kitchen, and many other things incidental to the smooth working of an army in the field. Departmental corps, such as the Army Service, Army Ordnance, and R.A.M.C., not only train but exercise their functions in a practical way, for in peace time an army must be fed, equipped, and doctored, just the same as in war—except that in the latter case its requirements are more strenuous."

The organization of the Army was as such:

"The highest rank with which the soldier is brought in frequent contact is the commanding officer of his own regiment or battalion. This post is usually held by a *lieutenant-colonel*, as by the time an officer has attained to a full colonelcy he is either posted to the staff or passed out from the service to half-pay under the age limit.

The Lieutenant-Colonel is responsible for the efficiency of the regiment in every detail, since, as its head, he is responsible for the efficiency of the officers controlling the various departments. He is assisted in his work by the second-in-command, who is usually a *major*, and is not attached to any particular squadron or company, but is responsible for the internal working and domestic arrangements incidental to the life of his unit. These two are assisted in their work by the *adjutant*, a junior officer, sometimes captain and sometimes lieutenant, who holds his post for a stated term, and during his adjutancy is expected to qualify fully in the headquarters staff work which the conduct of a military unit involves. These three form the headquarters staff.

It must not be overlooked, however, that the *quartermaster*, who is either a lieutenant or a captain, and has won his commission from the ranks in the majority of cases, is also unattached to any particular squadron or company. He is, or should be, under the control of the second-in-command, since, as his title indicates, he is concerned with the quarters of the regiment, and with all that pertains to its domestic economy. He cannot, however, be regarded as a part of the headquarters staff; his position is unique, somewhere between commissioned and non-commissioned rank, and it is very rarely that he is accorded the position of the officer who has come to the service through Sandhurst.

To each squadron of cavalry, battery of artillery, or company of infantry is allotted a *captain or major* as officer commanding, and, in the same way as a colonel is responsible for the efficiency of his regiment, so the captain or major is responsible for the efficiency of the squadron, battery, or company under his charge.

Next in order of rank are the *[second] lieutenants and subalterns*, youngsters learning the business: the lieutenant, having won his second star... the subaltern, fresh from Sandhurst or Woolwich. Lieutenants and subalterns are given charge of a troop in the cavalry, a gun or section—according to the number of young officers available—in a battery and of a section of men in an infantry company. Nominally in command of their men, they are in practice largely dependent on their senior non-commissioned officers for the efficiency of the men under their command. An officer's real efficiency, in peace service, does not begin until he "gets his company" or squadron: in other words, until he is promoted to the rank of captain.

Next in grade of rank to the commissioned officers stands the *regimental sergeant-major*, who is termed a *warrant-officer*, since the "warrant" which he holds, in virtue of his rank, distinguishes him from non-commissioned officers. He has, usually, sixteen years or more of service; he has even more knowledge of the ways of the regiment than the commanding officer himself, and his place is with the headquarters staff, while his duties lie in the supervision and control of the noncommissioned officers and their messes and training.

From this point of rank downward the ways of the different arms of the service diverge. In the infantry, the chief non-commissioned officer of a company is the *colour-sergeant*, who is responsible both for internal economy and efficiency at drill. In the cavalry and artillery the presence of horses and the far greater amount of equipment involved divide the work that is done in the infantry by the colour-sergeant into two parts. In the cavalry each squadron, and in the artillery each battery, is controlled, so far as drill and efficiency in the field is concerned, by a *squadron sergeant-major* and a *battery sergeant-major*, respectively, while the domestic economy of the squadron or battery is managed by *squadron quartermaster-sergeant or battery quartermaster-sergeant.*

Next in order of rank come the *sergeants*, the non-commissioned equivalent to troop and section officers, but of far more actual importance than these, since parades frequently take place in the absence of the troop or section officer, while the troop or section sergeant is at all times responsible to his superiors for the efficiency of his men. The rank of sergeant is seldom attained in less than seven years, and thus the man of three stripes whom Kipling justly described in his famous phrase "as the backbone of the Army" is a man of experience and fully entitled to his post.

Next in order of rank to the sergeant is the *corporal*, whose duties lie principally in the maintenance of barrack-room discipline, though he is largely responsible for the training of squads and sections of men in field work. Often in the cavalry he is given charge of a troop temporarily, and in the artillery, though each gun is supposed to be in charge of a sergeant, it happens at times that the corporal has charge of the gun. The lowest rank of all is that of *lance-corporal.*"

The Navy

1904 marked the date of the Royal Navy's advance into the 20th century, steered by the sure hand of the First Sea Lord, Sir John "Jacky" Fisher. Fisher, born in 1841, entered the Navy as a midshipman in 1854, and rose quickly by the end of the nineteenth century. Along the way, Fisher acquired a reputation as arrogant and overbearing, causing his contemporaries to view having him about as akin to "harbouring Attila the Hun." He needed this reputation to commence with the complete overhaul of the Navy, which had only suspended flogging with the cat-o-nine-tails in 1880.

The Navy of the early Edwardian era was "antiquated and obsolete," with over a hundred ships that would be absolutely useless in the event of a naval war (especially since Germany had begun revamping its navy in the late 1890s out of fear of British blockades and encirclement). Most of these ships were scrapped and were replaced with four types of vessels: battleships, armored cruisers, destroyers, and submarines. Naval bases in the West Indies and Canada were closed, all gunboats were withdrawn, save those necessary in China and West Africa, and three Fleets were formed—Mediterranean, Atlantic, and Channel. Lastly, a Cruiser Squadron of six ships was formed for training and deployment to the West Indian and South American ports.

Fisher's most lasting and game-changing legacy was the introduction of the H.M.S. *Dreadnought*. The *Dreadnought*, a nearly 16,000 ton steel ship equipped with ten 12-inch guns, made every single ship in the Royal Navy obsolete and ushered in a new class of armored battleships. It also raised the Navy's annual budget, which Fisher had been appointed First Lord to beat down, and the tussle over expenditure on more dreadnought-class ships became a political issue during the bitter battle over Lloyd George's "People's Budget." Another Fisher legacy was the construction of submarines, of which the First Lord had long been an advocate. By the time Fisher left the Admiralty in 1910, he had "achieved the construction of sixty-one submarines."

In *The British Navy From Within*, the anonymous author describes life in the reformed Royal Navy:

"Up till till 1902 all naval and marine officers had been entered in the three definite and distinctive branches of the service: Executive, Engineers, Marines. The future Executive Officers, entered as Cadets at from 13 to 15 years of age, were sent direct to the Britannia at Dartmouth, where they underwent their schooling and early training preparatory to being sent to sea. The Engineer Students were sent to Keyham College, where they graduated as Engineer Officers ; while the Marines, Red and Blue, entered their respective corps, where they went through a long course of training preparatory to a sea life.

In 1902 the whole of this system was altered for one of common entry. Every future officer would be entered as a Cadet at the age of from 12 to 14, and would undergo two years' training; a new College was built at Osborne and an entire new system of education and training was instituted. The Cadet goes through his course of College training and is then drafted to sea in a special training cruiser. He becomes a midshipman and is eligible for ships in the fleet. Here he has charge of a boat and other responsibilities thrown upon him to teach him how to handle men.

His next step is Sub-Lieutenant, and another series of courses and College, more sea time and promotion to Lieutenant. It is from here that he becomes a specialist amongst specialists, gunnery, torpedo, or navigation claiming him for its own. If he desires, he may, having qualified in other directions, enter the Submarine Service or the Air Service. It is from these specialists that promotion to the higher ranks are chosen."

The qualifying examination included the following subjects: English, History and Geography, Arithmetic and Algebra, and Geometry. While attending the Naval College, the cadets studied Mathematics, with Geometrical Drawing, Physics and Chemistry, Mechanics and applied Mechanics, Applied Electricity, Seamanship with Gunnery in the Training Cruiser, Navigation, French or German, English Grammar and Composition, Literature, History (including naval history), Geography, Bible Study, and Drill and Physical Training. The cost of entering the naval college was expensive at £75 per annum (£25 paid each term), though the Admiralty admitted a quota of boys under reduced rate of £40 per annum.

Men entered the Navy through naval recruiting stations at the Royal Naval Barracks at Chatham, Portsmouth, and Devon, and also Oxford and London; at any Coast Guard Station, or the Royal Marine Recruiting Staff Officer in various major cities in England Scotland. A change was made in the Edwardian era to open up engineer training to "bluejackets," or enlisted sailors, and they were more along the lines of a mechanic than an ordinary seaman. Bluejacket boys were "entered between the ages of 15¼ and 16¾ for training as Seaman. Boys who have been in Prisons or Reformatories are not received."

Candidates for Engine-room Artificers had to be "competent workmen at one of the following trades, and of very good character and ability:--Engine fitters and turners, coppersmiths, boilermakers, engine smiths, pattern makers, and moulders," and were between the ages of 21 and 28. All enlisted men were required to: "possess the ability to read and write, and work the first four rules of arithmetic, simple and compound, be acquainted with the names and uses of the different parts of a marine engine and boiler, understand the use and management of the steam and water gauges and other boiler mountings, know how to ascertain the density and height of water in the boilers, and know what should be done in the event of water passing into the cylinders," among other capabilities.

"A bluejacket boy on entry is sent, in most cases, direct to the R.N. Training Ship Ganges, which is in reality the barracks at Shotley, on the east coast. At these barracks every possible convenience is provided from a bakehouse to a bathroom and from a school to a hospital. The very first thing after entry is to be kitted up, and from thence the boy passes from one course of instruction to another until he is fitted for drafting to sea. At the age of eighteen they are rated Ordinary Seamen, and at once have to start qualifying for the higher rating of Able Seamen. Having passed for Able Seaman and attained to that rating, they then pass to the gunnery and torpedo school for instruction in the higher branches of those two sciences, and also if they desire study for the higher substantive rank of Leading Seaman. As they advance at each grade they have to pass both professional and educational examinations; if a man desires to qualify for Warrant Officer then there are special courses and opportunities allowed for the same."

The Royal Flying Corps and Royal Naval Air Service

The War Office was slow to react to flight, but finally, after the formation of a sub-committee of the Committee of Imperial Defence, the government formed the Royal Flying Corps, with Military and Naval "Wings" in April 1912. Unfortunately, the War Office and the Admiralty were eternally suspicious of one another, and after growing unable to decide upon one course for the development and organization of military aviation, they split. The Royal Naval Air Service officially became a separate service in July 1914.

Both branches of air service experienced most of their change and reformation during the First World War, during which they were merged in April 1918 to become the Royal Air Force—a military branch in its own right. Because the Royal Flying Corps was considered an arm of the Army, their rankings and organization were similar: Colonel, Lieutenant-Colonel, Major,

Captain, Lieutenant, and Second Lieutenant, with the enlisted ranks being made up of sergeant-majors and sergeants (corporals and flight sergeants were added in May 1914).

Wilfred Theodore Blake discusses the early days of the RFC in his 1918 book, *The Royal Flying Corps in the War*:

"In pre-war days much talk and a good deal of thought was spent in considering the war possibilities of the aeroplane, and the general conclusion reached was that while the new arm would be of incalculable assistance as a reconnoitring force, its sphere of utility would end there, with the exception of possibly a little bombing as opportunity afforded. The very fact that the average machine could not encompass a flight of more than about three and a half hours, and had therefore a radius of action of only about 130 miles, seemed to preclude the possibility of organised bombing raids on a large scale, and aerial fighting was almost undreamt of, though experiments had been carried out at Brooklands with a light gun fixed to an aeroplane. Also the reliability of any engine used was so poor that machines were being constantly held up on that account.

As regards the actual growth of the Corps, in August, 1914, there were about one hundred officers and a thousand other ranks, with perhaps eighty serviceable machines. At the present time one is safe in saying that the total personnel would have been a very considerable addition to the original Expeditionary Force.

During the first months of war the function of the Royal Flying Corps was largely to reconnoitre for the various armies and report the position and movements of the enemy. But there is no doubt that the Corps largely helped to save the Mons army, and probably the whole of the western front during the critical period of August, 1914. If it had not been for the aeroplane scouts who brought in confirmation of the report that General Smith-Dorrien was faced by not three German Divisions as had been thought, but by three whole Army Corps, it is possible that the whole of the British Army might have been wiped out, the Germans might have reached Paris, and probably the whole aspect of the war would have been changed, and certainly not to the advantage of the Allies."

Bibliography

Barnes, R. Money. *The British Army of 1914: Its History, Uniforms & Contemporary Continental Armies.* London: Seeley, 1968.

Blake, W. T. *The Royal Flying Corps in the War.* Toronto: Cassell, 1918.

Bowman, Timothy, and Mark Connelly. *The Edwardian Army: Recruiting, Training, and Deploying the British Army 1902-1914.* Oxford: Oxford UP, 2012.

Cormack, Andrew, and Peter Cormack. *British Air Forces, 1914-18.* Oxford, U.K.: Osprey Military, 2000.

Ex-royal Navy. *The British Navy from within.* London: Hodder and Stoughton, 1914.

Farwell, Byron. *Mr. Kipling's Army.* New York: Norton, 1981.

Massie, Robert K. *Dreadnought: Britain, Germany, and the Coming of the Great War.* New York: Random House, 1991.

Petrie, Charles. *Scenes of Edwardian Life.* London: Eyre & Spottiswoode, 1965.

Villard, Henry Serrano. *Contact!: The Story of the Early Aviators.* Mineola, NY: Dover Publications, 2002.

Vivian, Evelyn Charles. *The British Army from within.* New York: George H. Doran, 1914.

Edwardian London

At the time of Queen Victoria's death, London had transformed from merely the capitol of Great Britain, to the pulse of an Empire. Inside a scant 120 square miles resided the wealthiest and the poorest, the modern and the ancient, and every strata of society from royalty down to the humblest flower girl. London was also where bankers, financiers, politicians, and Cabinet ministers directed the money and administration of a people spread across many lands and made up of many tongues and religions. During the Edwardian era, the drastic change that characterized 19th century London had slowed a bit, but the population did not, growing from 4,536,063 persons in 1901 to 4,872,700 in 1910.

Baedeker's *London* describes Edwardian London thusly: The definition of "London" had two meanings: the Administrative County of London, including the City and the districts more directly under the jurisdiction of the London County Council, and Greater London, or the district of the Metropolitan and City Police. The latter extended 12-15 miles in every direction from Charing Cross, which embraced an area of 700 sq. M., with a population estimated in 1910 at 7,537,000. London was halved by the flow of the Thames into two areas: north (Middlesex) and south (Surrey and Kent), with the former being of less importance (Southwark, Lambeth, Greenwich, etc).

The Middlesex portion of London was also halved:

I. The City and the East End, consisting of the part of London that lay to the East of the Temple, and formed the commercial and money-making quarter of the Metropolis. It embraced the Port, the Docks, the Custom House, the Bank, the Exchange, the innumerable counting-houses of merchants, money-changers, brokers, and underwriters, the General Post Office, the printing and publishing offices of The Times, the legal corporations of the Inns of Court, and the Cathedral of St. Paul's.

II. The West End, consisting of the part of London that lay to the West of the Temple, was the quarter of London that spent money, made laws, and regulated the fashions. It contained Buckingham Palace, the mansions of the aristocracy, the clubs, museums, picture galleries, theatres, army barracks, government offices, Houses of Parliament, and Westminster Abbey; and it was the special locality for parks, squares, and gardens.

Then, London was divided into areas known for particular trades or social class:

I. East End and South London

   a. Long Shore, which extends along the bank of the Thames, and is chiefly composed of quays, wharves, storehouses, and engine-factories, and inhabited by shipwrights, lightermen, sailors, and marine store dealers.

   b. Whitechapel, with its Jewish tailoring workshops.

   c. Houndsditch and the Minories, the quarters of the Jews.

   d. Bethnal Green and Spitalfields to the N., and part of Shoreditch, form a manufacturing district, once occupied to a large extent by silk-weavers, partly descended from the French Protestants (Huguenots) who took refuge in England after the Revocation of the Edict of Nantes in 1685. Furniture-making and boot-making are now the chief industries.

   e. Clerkenwell, between Islington and Hatton Garden, the district of watch-makers and metal-workers.

   f. Paternoster Row, near St. Paul's Cathedral, the focus of the book-trade.

   g. Chancery Lane and the Inns of Court, the headquarters of barristers, solicitors, and law-stationers.

   h. Wapping, Shadwell, Limehouse, Poplar, and MUlwall, all chiefly composed of quays, wharves, storehouses, and engine-factories, and inhabited by shipwrights, lightermen, sailors, and marine store dealers.

      i. Southwark and Lambeth, containing numerous potteries, glass-works, machine-factories, breweries, and hop-warehouses.

      j. Bermondsey, famous for its tanneries, glue-factories, and wool-warehouses.

      k. Rotherhithe, farther to the E., chiefly inhabited by sailors, ship-carpenters, coal-heavers, and bargemen.

      l. Deptford, with its great cattle-market.

      m. Greenwich, with its hospital, park, and observatory.

      n. Woolwich, with its arsenal and barracks.

II.   West End

      a. Mayfair, aristocratic neighborhood

      b. Belgravia, aristocratic neighborhood, but less exclusive

      c. Westminster & St James's, the administrative and royal boroughs

      d. Kensington, upper middle class, though marked by Kensington Palace

      e. Bayswater, middle class neighborhood

      f. Pimlico, part of Belgravia

      g. The Strand, theatres, restaurants, and Fleet Street

      h. Chelsea, a bit Bohemian

      i. Brompton, with the South Kensington Museums

      j. Bloomsbury, boarding houses for university students, the British Museum.

Center of the Empire

The aorta of the British Empire lay in Westminster. In it lay Buckingham Palace, Westminster Abbey, and other offices vital to the official, diplomatic, and legislative functions necessary to keeping everything running in shipshape and Bristol fashion. During the Queen's reign, Buckingham Palace was only used for state ceremonies, since Victoria preferred Windsor Castle.

When Edward VII came to the throne, he cleared Buckingham Palace of its decades of clutter and neglect and turned it into the centerpiece of his glittering court. Though the palace eventually came to symbolize the British monarchy, it was only built in the 1820s during the reign of George IV, and only made the official London residence of the monarch—as mentioned above—under Edward VII.

According to a description in 1901:

"Buckingham Palace is splendid inside, much more so than most people imagine, and can hold its own in point of magnificence with anything of its kind abroad. The vestibule, into which the Sovereign's entrance in the quadrangle opens, and the grand marble staircase with its ormolu acanthus balustrades, are very imposing; as are also the state apartments—the throne-room with its splendid ceiling, huge crystal chandelier, and emblazoned arms; the grand saloon; the state dining-room; the handsome Bow Room; the green, yellow and blue drawing-rooms; and the picture-gallery, a noble apartment in the centre of the Palace with gorgeously-gilded door-cases and with four marble chimneypieces elaborately sculptured with medallion portraits of great painters.

There is a fine collection of pictures here, and, indeed, all over the Palace, only surpassed by that at Windsor Castle, where every square foot of available wall-space is covered by them. In the Dutch and Flemish school, the Buckingham Palace collection is remarkably rich—Rembrandt, Rubens, Teniers, Ostade, Cuyp, Gerard Dow, and Van Dyck, etc. Amongst the numerous English painters represented, Wilkie is well to the front, and there are endless Royal portraits by Kneller, Lely, Lawrence, Angeli, Winterhalter, etc.

Like the Bow Room, the lower dining-hall overlooks the gardens and terrace, and is one of the cosiest apartments in the Palace. White and gold form the basis of the decorative treatment, and numerous oil-paintings hang on the walls, including portraits of Queen Anne, George III., his Queen, Caroline, King Frederick I. of Prussia, etc., and a wonderful picture by Stanfield of the opening of London Bridge in 1831 by William IV.

The grandest thing in the Palace, is perhaps the ball-room. It is nobly proportioned, lighted from above by electricity, and from the sides by handsome gilt-bronze candelabra. Its ceiling is richly decorated; the walls are panelled in crimson silk; and the floor is beautifully inlaid with oak. When a state concert is in progress, its appearance is striking in the extreme.

On either side are three tiers of seats facing those on the floor-level, all occupied by most brilliantly-attired personages, for on these occasions the most beautiful dresses and jewels are worn. At the upper end of the room is the organ (originally at the Brighton Pavilion) ; on one side of the platform is a right royal-looking harp, and on the other a fine Brard Grand, ornamented with richly gilt scroll-work."

Buckingham Palace's gardens, some forty acres in size, was the sight of splendid garden parties, which was nearly the only time the "public" (that is, those not in the highest circles of society—doctors, lawyers, scientists, etc) could meet or mingle with the Queen. The Palace was used strictly by the reigning monarch, however, and many family members resided in the block of private apartments allotted for royal guests. The Palace of St. James's was of less importance, though many state functions generally for male guests, were held here. As befitting the London home of the monarch, all major roads in the West End lead from Buckingham Palace—The Mall to Trafalgar Square, Constitution Hill to Piccadilly at Hyde Park Corner, Buckingham Palace Road to Belgravia, and Birdcage Walk into the heart of the Government.

"Whitehall" was the metonym for the area in which lay the Foreign Office, Home Office, the Houses of Parliament, the Treasury, the Admiralty, and Scotland Yard. The name derived from the old Palace of Whitehall, which burnt down in 1698.

Number 10, Downing Street, the residence of the Prime Minister, and No. 11—the office of the Chancellor of the Exchequer—were of little architectural consequence, but on the ground floor of No. 10 was the Council Chamber where the Prime Minister discussed matters of grave importance with the Cabinet. The Foreign Office was approached from Downing Street, and "inside were the great apartments—Cabinet Council room, conference rooms, reception rooms, etc.—, the Library, where every book or pamphlet bearing upon Foreign Office affairs was to be found, and suites of pleasantly situated rooms, devoted to interviews with Ambassadors, the Diplomatic Corps generally, and the Consular section of the Foreign Office. Other apartments are the sanctuaries of Chiefs of Departments, Heads of sub-divisions, and their staffs, etc., where is transacted a vast amount of real business, the routine work alone being very heavy."

A square tower facing St. James' Park marked the separation of the building of the Foreign Office from the India Office. "Here, too, there is a splendid library, whose shelves quickly reveal that this Department directs a Great Eastern Empire. Indian curios in the chief offices, and a certain air of dignified languor in the officials themselves, make the fact more apparent." Going up Downing Street was the Colonial Office, where "the Crown's authority, such as it is, over the self-governing colonies, is exercised, and Governors are nominated."

There also existed the office of the Crown Agents for the colonies, who managed the affairs of such British possessions as the West Indies, Straits Settlements, etc, and the Emigrants' Information Bureau.

The Admiralty was also in Whitehall, where naval matters were overseen, and further down the way was the War Office in Pall Mall, which handled army matters (and both sections were very jealous of one another—their respective secrecy was one of the factors that hurt the British military during the early stages of WWI). There was also Somerset House, where taxes were handled, the Wills and Probate Office, the Custom House, and the various agencies of Dominion colonies (Australia, Canada, New Zealand, etc).

Westminster Abbey was separate from the Palace of Westminster, or Houses of Parliament, but both existed on the same plot of land. Big Ben and its spires are iconic, but they were only built in 1834, after the old Palace was destroyed by fire. Inside lay the two houses—Commons and Lords—, galleries, chambers, and a restaurant for the use of members and their guests.

High Society London

The smartest and only addresses for aristocratic society were in Mayfair and Belgravia. St. James's was also a residential district, capped by the extremely smart and elegant row of terraced mansions on Carlton House Terrace, which was built over the site of the Prince Regent's Carlton House, and the London mansions of the Earl Spencer, the Earl of Ellesmere, and the Marquess of Stafford. However, it was primarily known as clubland, for this is where the great political, sporting, social, and military clubs had their residence.

A list of these clubs would take up an entire section, but these are the primary ones: Carlton, 94 Pall Mall, the premier Conservative Club; Brooks's. 60 St. James's St. (Whig/Liberal club); Army and Navy, 36 Pall Mall; Guards', 70 Pall Mall; Automobile, Pall Mall; Boodle's, 28 St. James's St. (chiefly for country gentlemen); Marlborough, 52 Pall Mall; Travellers', 106 Pall Mall (where each member must have travelled at least 1000 miles from London); and White's, 37 St. James's Street.

The most favored shopping district of aristocratic London was Bond Street. Untainted by the department stores in Knightsbridge or Brompton, Bond Street—divided into New and Old—remained dominated by exclusive shops where goods were elegant and costly, service discreet and obsequious, and where one needn't leave anything but a card with the shopkeeper once you had chosen all you desired.

Young ladies were never permitted to shop alone, and even married ladies were required to take a footman with them, who would carry packages, open doors, and man the carriage. And best yet, Bond Street refused to bow to the motorcar fashion. Well into the Edwardian era, the street was free of the tuff-tuff and petrol of the automobile—though not free of the "droppings" left behind by horses. Off Bond Street were a number of ladies' clubs—a late Victorian invention—which were perfectly placed for the well-to-do lady to drop in after a busy afternoon's shopping for a cup of tea or a hand of bridge.

In the mid-1900s, couture came to London, and when Paquin, Worth, and Doucet opened London branches (though, mostly for the wealthy Americans living in London, since many aristocratic women preferred to have their lady's maids copy the latest modes), the old, reliable court dressmakers were forced to smarten up or be left in the nineteenth century. Savile Row tailoring, however, remained the pinnacle of menswear, and even Parisian gentlemen traveled to London at least once in their life to be measured by the best London tailors. Also in Bond Street were hatters and milliners, purveyors of women's underclothing, furriers, shoemakers, opticians, and makers of waterproof goods.

The tents of High Society required these "uniforms," so to speak, in order to mark one another as members of the same tribe. Another mark was the appearance at Hyde Park during the fashionable hours for riding (8 am to 12 pm) and driving (5-7 pm), and the Sunday Church parade (1-2 pm).

Middle Class London

Middle class London was less lavish, but no less exciting than high society life. The wealthier middle class lived in Kensington and Bayswater, in nice mansions and apartment flats, and the less wealthy tended to live in St. John's Wood or around Regent's Park.

London's wealthy Jewish popular also lived in or near these areas, with Maida Vale being a particular enclave. Since the middle classes lived and played indoors, it was perhaps fitting that their areas of residence were mostly filled with houses, apartment blocks, and villas—though the great stores of Whiteley's and Harrods sprawled across large swaths of land.

Other middle-class areas were Chelsea and Bloomsbury, though both, with venerable museums in their boundaries, were considerably more bohemian in tone than the more staid areas mentioned above. The latter was home to the British Museum, whereas the former was home to the Tate Gallery and the Victoria and Albert Museum (though this was more in Brompton than in Chelsea). Chelsea was also the home of Thomas and Jane Carlyle, and a group that included Virginia Woolf's father turned their home into a museum.

Now that Woolf has been mentioned, one cannot leave out the Bloomsbury Group, who, though mostly associated with the 1920s, had its roots in the 1900s when Virginia and Vanessa Stephens purchased a house at 46 Gordon Square after the death of their father. The group gelled in or around 1910 (to quote

Virginia: "on or about December 1910, human character changed"). The Edwardian era was where they all fermented, and the dichotomies of the age were very apparent in their group.

London at Play

Edwardian London was a playground not merely for the idle rich. From theatres and halls, to parks, to restaurants and chop houses, to exhibitions, to bands, to the trooping of the colors, to sports, to great events, there was no end to amusements at the reach of just about every resident. The theatre was the most democratic amusement of all, with London boasting 30 west end theatres, about 20 suburban theatres, and about 60 regular music-halls.

The most popular of these were: Drury Lane, famed for the electrifying performances of Garrick, Kean, the Kembles, and Mrs. Siddons. The Gaiety Theatre (post-1903), where George Edwardes' "Gaiety Girls" and the frothy, romantic musical comedies became the leading attraction. The Lyceum, for popular drama; the Prince of Wales, for comedies; Haymarket, for Shakespeare with Mr. Beerbohm Tree; and the Empire and the Alhambra, both on Leicester Square, and famed for their spectacles and elaborate ballets.

Also crowding London were the numerous places to eat. The West End was where the choicest and chicest restaurants lay, mostly in the top hotels like the Savoy, the Ritz, or Claridge's, where excellent French cuisine was served. Good English cookery could be found at Simpson's-in-the-Strand, the Old Cheshire Cheese, or the chop houses in the City. Soho was where one could find cheap Italian and French restaurants, which were popular spots after the theatre, and there were also a fair number of Chinese, Indian, and German restaurants. For the less wealthy, or less discriminating, oyster shops abounded, where for a few shillings, one could down as many oysters as one could consume.

In the late Victorian era, consciousness of the poor and disadvantaged inspired the creation of parks across London. In their zeal to create these spaces, many ancient cemeteries were torn up, the graves moved elsewhere, and grass, trees, and bandstands planted in their stead. A bit morbid, but for Londoners who rarely saw greenery, much less an open space, these parks were gratefully received.

The popularity of exhibitions saw the founding of Earls Court in the Kensington area, which hosted The Empire of India Exhibition in 1896, The Victorian Era Exhibition in 1897, The Military Exhibition in 1901, Paris in London Exhibition in 1902, the International Fire Exhibition in 1903, Venice by Night in 1904 and the Imperial Austrian Exhibition in 1906. There was also the White City in Hammersmith & Fulham, where the 1908 Summer Olympics were hosted.

Sunday afternoons were key times for visiting these parks and open spaces, and Londoners of different backgrounds played cricket or football to the sound of the band playing in the bandstand.

The City

Britons of the Edwardian era, and the aristocracy in particular, referred to London as "Town." This is because The City, or the financial district, was the whole of medieval London (and its traditional boundaries were that of the wall constructed by the Romans).

The heart of the City was the Bank of England at Threadneedle Street, from which radiated seven streets, each possessing their own metonym. Of them, Lombard Street was synonymous with banking, and was similar in might to Wall Street in New York or the Bourse in Paris. Lombard was also the home of NM Rothschild & Sons, and Lombard also became synonymous with the rich and powerful English branch of the Rothschild family, though there were over thirty great banking houses on Lombard alone.

A great description of the City is found in George Sims' *Living London*:

"It is midday, and London's business is at high tide. Those whose working hours commence at eight o'clock, nine o'clock, and ten o'clock have all by this time got into the swing of the day's work. Shoppers and leisurely sightseers add to the throng. At innumerable stages, up to four, five, and six miles away, towards every point of the compass, omnibuses have filled at their conductors' cry, "Bank! Bank!" Through great stress of traffic have they come, and hither in long, uninterrupted processions do they continue to come. Of all colours are they, and so closely ranged together that they blot out of view all but the upper portions of the buildings. At the will of traffic-managing policemen, now this stream of vehicles, now that, holds the field.

...You are now in the money region, the land of stocks and shares. Close by are the Stock Exchange, the Royal Exchange, and a remarkable gathering together of banks. Here the throng, representative of the district, contains a big proportion of men who deal on exchanges or are employed in the banks. The glossy hats, the well-conditioned black coats and trousers, the expensive waist. ...Through the great glass doors you see rows of busy clerks. Across the street dart young men carrying account-books or a bag secured to their person by a heavy chain. If the thousands of busy feet do not actually tread on gold, you have a feeling that underneath are vaults and strong rooms guarding fabulous hoards.

The Lord Mayor is sovereign in the City, and upon his election to the post, he is conveyed through the streets in a State coach, accompanied by aldermen, City officials, military music, and cars emblematical of their trades. He represented, figuratively and politically, the interests of the businesses and people of the City, and was treated with as much pomp as the actual Sovereign."

The Lord Mayor took "precedence of every subject of the Crown, not excepting members of the reigning house, and holds a quasi-Royal position. By virtue of his office he is head of the City Lieutenancy, and recommends the names of persons to fill vacancies. He is ex-officio chairman of the Thames Conservancy and a trustee of St . Paul's Cathedral; he has power to close or grant the use of the Guildhall; and the Company of which he is a member has precedence over all the other City companies during his year of office. Besides the financial district, the Lord Mayor was aligned with the legal community of the Inns of Court and the Central Criminal Courts. The former was built on the site of the infamous Newgate prison, which was demolished in 1902 after seven hundred years of existence."

The East End

Last, but not least, we come to the East End. The "East End" was a catch-all phrase for numerous neighborhoods known for particular trades. In fact, there were pockets of poverty across London, and one could find a workhouse tucked even in the corner of Mayfair (there was one just off Berkeley Square). Far from being uniformly poor and downtrodden, the people of the East End ranged from working class to working poor to habitually unemployed to underemployed—essentially, just like today's lower class.

The 1890s saw the clearing of the Victorian rookeries—and also the airing of the aristocratic slum lords like Lord Colebrooke and Lady Kinloss of the Old Nichol rookery—for the construction of sanitary housing and council flats. The East End was also the site of settlement homes, in particular Toynbee Hall, all of whom were founded by civic-minded college graduates and vicars, who strove to improve the lives of the poor while living among them (as opposed to dispensing charity and returning to one's mansion). The settlement house movement caught fire across Britain and came to America—and Jane Addams' Hull House in Chicago remains one of the most famous settlement houses in the United States.

Arthur Beavan described a typical East End neighborhood in the early 1900s. "The houses are chiefly one story, or at the most two stories high; the shops, small, and such as minister solely to the necessities of life. Should the back-street happen to have no regular shops, there is still business done. Numerous parlour-windows demonstrate the nature of the retail-trade carried on within; some, by means of a couple of "new-laid " eggs, as many loaves, and samples of sweetstuff; others by a tailor's card portraying the latest thing in coats and trousers; or a brass plate on door indicates the abode of a dressmaker capable of designing the " latest fashion" in costumes or Court dresses; the main characteristic throughout being that everything that can possibly be discoloured or mildewed, is so.

Lodgings for single men abound; ladies apparently being not desirable. A great many of these streets are, like those described by Dickens, faded and tumble-down, with two irregular rows of tall meagre houses generally let out into lodgings where all kinds of small trades are plied, mostly by foreigners. The doors of these tenements are seldom closed, and a row of much-used bells denoting the various floors, suggest that the lodgers wait upon themselves. The shops in the neighbourhood cater chiefly for French and Germans; there are Gallic restaurants, and Teutonic restaurations, where dinners a la carte or a prix fixe can be had of fair quality and at astonishingly low prices. Besides this, there are the usual London eating-houses and coffee-shops where plates of meat at threepence, coffee at a halfpenny a cup, and halfpenny slices of pudding are largely sold.

The overcrowding of the Metropolis is perhaps the most pressing social problem of the day, and the most difficult to cope with. The poorer classes must live near their place of employment, being unable to afford even the smallest and cheapest railway-fare; while the value of land anywhere near the centres of business is so great, and the demolition of small houses thereon to make room for big warehouses so continuous, that the filthiest and most meagre lodgings are filled to overflowing, though let for rents that absorb nearly all the scanty earnings of the tenants.

Overcrowding is also due to the fact, that whereas the increase or population is estimated at from fifty to sixty thousand per annum, the number of new tenements is comparatively small, or, at any rate, disproportionate. For example, in Kensington, one of the wealthiest parishes in the world, one quarter of the population live two or more persons in a room. In Soho, ten per cent. live, on an average, four to one apartment. In Whitechapel, the average is ten to a room—a density of about 225 persons to each acre. In Spitalfields, 4575 houses are let out in single rooms, of which 1400 are occupied by four to eleven persons each.

Distinct from the "regular-wage" earning community, there is an immense class in London, whose earnings are entirely precarious, some being, in unfavourable weather, cut off altogether.

First and foremost of these is the hard-working costermonger (under which denomination I include hawkers and stall-keepers), familiarized to West-enders by the clever impersonations of Mr. Albert Chevalier. The stock-in-trade of the present-day coster is contained in a barrow, owned or hired, to which he is sometimes able to harness a donkey; but when he attains this height of prosperity, he, as a rule, calls himself a "general dealer." At night, the well-to-do coster, converting his barrow into a stall, lights it up with naphtha, the poorer one having to be content with the humble candle, as in the earlier times.

Besides fruit and the commoner vegetables, all kinds of cheap foreign fruit and tomatoes are sold by them, and, in their season, mackerel, herrings, cauliflowers, asparagus, melons, strawberries, cherries, holly, cut flowers, and growing plants. Costers, as a class, have made much progress of late years. Their name used to be a term of contempt, and the bearers of it noted for roughness, but the efforts of Lord Shaftesbury and others on their behalf, have worked a wondrous improvement in their language and ways.

Amongst women, the most hardly-earned wages are those of tailoresses. Other occupations for women—somewhat better paid—are the shelling of walnuts and peas on the confines of fruit and vegetable markets, paper-bag-making, sack-making, fur-pulling, choking to the lungs and blinding to the eyes; and the raking-over of refuse heaps in dust-yards, sorting out bits of string, flannel, cardboard, and rag, anything in fact that can be converted into paper or shoddy cloth. But the most disgusting occupation for females, though not so uncertain, is the preparation of animal entrails for manufacture into sausage-skins; the greasy, slimy lengths of intestines are scraped until denuded of fat, etc., then turned inside out and thoroughly cleansed, again washed, and finally twisted up and dressed with salt for the market, the stench of the operation being nauseating.

Curiously-earned livelihoods are endless in variety: among them, that of the maker and vendor of fly-papers, with his cry of "Catch 'em alive, blue-bottles and flies." Then there are the miscellaneous vocations (of which one man may be engaged in several), such as "calling" people early in the morning, achieved by tapping at the windows with a rod until the sleeper wakes; oiling people's gates for a halfpenny a time; picking up the scattered oats, chopped hay, etc., found lying about cab-stands, and selling it to cabmen at a very cheap rate.

A few collect newspaper-contents-bills, and sell a quantity for a halfpenny to unfortunate sleepers-out, who use them as a protection from the damp air and cold flags. Then there are cab-runners —men who run after luggage-laden cabs to earn a copper by carrying the luggage into the house; and "cab-glimmers," who open and shut cab-doors, and with their hand protect the lady's dress from the wheel as she gets in and out of the cab. The collecting of cigar-ends is another industry of the streets; these are sold to florists at from 6d. to 10d. per pound to fumigate plants with."

Bibliography

Beavan, Arthur H., and Hanslip Fletcher. *Imperial London*. London: J.M. Dent & Co., 1901.

Hannavy, John. *The Victorians and Edwardians at Play*. Oxford: Shire, 2009.

Kennedy, Carol. *Mayfair: A Social History*. London: Hutchinson, 1986.

Palmer, Alan. *The East End: Four Centuries of London Life*. New Brunswick, NJ: Rutgers UP, 2000.

Schneer, Jonathan. *London 1900: The Imperial Metropolis*. New Haven: Yale UP, 1999.

Wilson, A. E. *Edwardian Theatre*. London: Barker, 1951.

London and Its Environs; Handbook for Travellers. Leipzig: K. Baedeker, 1911.

The Countryside

Due to various governmental changes since the 1970s, the map of England today looks somewhat different from its Edwardian counterpart. Some counties have disappeared, some have decreased in size, and some have been invented from large metropolitan areas. Nevertheless, the basic character of the countryside remains despite—or perhaps in spite of—the myriad of ways people, technology, and warfare has affected it.

These shires—which could be very loosely defined as "states"—were created as administrative areas, which is why so many older peerages are named for a particular county (*e.g.*, Duke of Devonshire) or why courtesy titles (which are usually the original peerage from which an ancestor was raised to a higher rank) are named after towns or cities that the newly-ennobled influenced.

Life in the Edwardian Countryside
The English have always loved their countryside, and as stated before, roots in the country were of vital importance: it represented—literally—the strength, the wealth, and the political might of the elite. During the Edwardian era, the countryside ironically witnessed the exodus of underemployed and largely impoverished workers and farmers for factories in cities and the influx of artists, poets, and the well-to-do inspired by its beauty and simplicity.

The agricultural depression of the last twenty years of the 19th century had hit the land and its workers hard, but those that had survived setbacks reaped the benefits of the land's recovery. Yet, despite the technological advances and the "rural exodus" of laborers and workers, old village customs and traditions experienced a brief resurgence of popularity, no doubt fueled by the uneasy aristocrats and artists who felt the decline of land meant the decline of Britannia.

Edwardian farmers reaped the benefits of a newly-recovered economy. Though some skepticism of better times remained, on the whole, freeholders and tenant farmers alike had a good prospect of making a profit from their labors. Their optimism was characterized in the increasing adoption of new and expensive farming technologies like steam operated equipment, seed drills, threshing machines, and tractors. Into the market also came fancy artificial fertilizers and feedstuffs for livestock.

Another addition was the new generation of farmer, some of whom had little to no experience in agriculture, who had a fresher view of the situation. They, combined with the new innovations and improvements, took Edwardian farming to a new level. Most farmers of the period had what was known as a "mixed farm"— land allotted for crops and land allotted for livestock. They grew wheat, barley, root crops, and hay ("cereals"), on the former, and raised cattle and sheep on the latter. Few farmers devoted themselves to one crop, or to one animal, though some farms in the Fens were known for their excellent potatoes.

Many farms were of a modest scale, with more than half if the 340,000 farms of more than five acres being smaller than fifty acres, and only 37% between fifty and three hundred acres in size. 90% of the farmers working the land were tenant farmers—that is, they rented their farms from great landowners and paid the rents from what they earned from the sale of their produce and livestock.

A typical farm was managed by the family, with employees ranging from carters to shepherds to day laborers—many of them relatives. Unlike their predecessors, Edwardian farmers were likely to be educated, having benefited from the 1870 educational act and the founding of colleges for agriculture. Our Edwardian farmer now had technical know-how of soils, animals, and crops, and could use these skills to solve problems on the farm that his father or grandfather before him would have left to fate.

The beginning of the agricultural year was October 11, or "Old Michaelmas". The farm was plowed to break up the cereal harvest and prepared for the sowing of winter corn. After this was the task of clearing ditches, trimming hedges, and cutting the first of the roots, which would last into January. This was followed by the cultivating, rolling, and harrowing for the spring. Hay was farmed in the summer, and plowing the summer fallow took place. Throughout this, the cattle and sheep were prepared for their destination, though the prices of wool had fallen in the Victorian era and had yet to fully recover.

Since most farmers were, as stated before, tenant farmers, they took ample part in the festivities and entertainments of the local area. Most villages possessed a cricket green, there were various societies got up by citizens—the most popular being theatrical societies—, and no one needed an excuse for a county ball or dance. Also, like in other areas of Edwardian society, farmers began to organize into trade unions, which influenced the political persuasions of Parliamentary candidates.

However, prosperity for farmers did not automatically equal prosperity for the great landowners. During the agricultural depression, many landowners lowered the rents or extended longer grace periods for their tenants, thereby decreasing their annual profits. As a result, many were forced to sell large tracts of their land to speculators and would-be landowners. The decline in number of rural laborers, both skilled and unskilled, made finding new tenants difficult, and it grew increasingly common for whole estates to be leased or sold to *nouveaux riches* who fancied playing "Squire" and turned good farmland into shooting or hunting territory.

Though the agricultural depression lifted during the early years of Edward VII's reign, but the well-to-do did not cease their country pursuits, and the Edwardian era was also the last hurrah of the great country house party. The birth of the motorcar—and creation of roads on which to drive—revitalized the inns and shops virtually abandoned once the railway made travel cheap, fast, and easy. Once more, irony via new technology rears its head: the very technological advances that made work in the city attractive to the children of farmers also made the country attractive to the social elite. Society periodicals of the mid-Edwardian era lamented to sharp decrease in number of those taking part in the Season once everyone adopted the motorcar, as many chose to motor between country houses and Town during the months were it was previously de rigueur to live in London.

This mobility brought about the creation of the automobile tour. Armed with a luncheon hamper, a spare tire, and a map, motorists would set off on a drive around a particular section of the countryside, visiting sites and architecture that had mostly fallen into obscurity (villagers were frequently perplexed by the excitement an old Roman ruin aroused in these visitors). Very soon, bookstores abounded with travelogues and handbooks detailing the hows, whens, and whats of motor touring, and it became the craze to jump into one's automobile and drive to the remotest areas of the earth. This led to the long-held notion that the automobile was a rich man's plaything and that motoring was a sport (cheaper cars, which were available to the middle classes, democratized the motorcar, but kept the sport accessible only to the rich).

Others who found inspiration in obscure Roman ruins, verdant pastures, and wildlife were artists, poets, and writers. One particular movement had a "back to our roots" zeitgeist—the Arts & Crafts Movement, which was a reaction against the artificial, the imitation, and the gaudiness born from the Industrial Revolution.

William Morris was the founder of this movement, and "students" of his ideas, such as garden designer Gertrude Jekyll, architect Edwin Lutyens, and designer Charles Rennie Mackintosh, went on to create interiors and exteriors that were shocking to most of Edwardian society. Proponents of Arts & Crafts considered proportion, space, simplicity, and harmony more important than displaying one's wealth through crowded rooms, heavy imitation furniture, and neo-Gothic mansions. They also valued England's historic craftsmanship, and held exhibitions to display typesetting, embroidery, and other decorative arts that had been superseded by machines rather than hands. The movement had also spread to Ireland and Scotland, and in the former, was an impetus in preserving Irish culture and crafts.

Life in the Edwardian countryside presented another of those dichotomies so characteristic of the era. As the elite and well-to-do fought to maintain and revive old arts, pastimes, and customs (and in the case of Ireland, used them to strengthen nationalist movements), the rural population rejected their traditional place in society. They not only desired a better life, but were avid adopters of the technology the Arts & Crafts movement abhorred.

Far from viewing the countryside with the starry-eyed romanticism of artists, farmers and villagers and craftsmen and women now viewed their work as earning them the right to own their land and to have a voice in politics, and soon society was forced to oblige.

Major Cities

London was the heart of Britain and the Empire, but there were many other major cities that played a definite role in Edwardian society. Manchester in particular was the heart of northern England, England's industries, and its political agitations. This city, more than any other city in England, characterized the shift in power from the traditional landed gentry and aristocracy to the might of industry. The growth of Manchester from a northern market town into an industrial and financial powerhouse was rather like the transformation of New York from Dutch village to five boroughs.

As the hub of the Industrial Revolution, the primary industry was cotton. Cotton was transported from Liverpool to the mills, and from these mills sprang bleach works, textile design firms, and foundries. So important to the industry was Manchester and the surrounding area, it was soon dubbed "Cottonopolis." The rapid growth of the city was helped by advances in transportation—river navigation, railways, and omnibus services—and the multitude of people moving to Manchester for work.

Manchester was also the natural hub for radicalism and reform, and the Manchester Guardian soon carved out a place in the nation's papers for its hard-line stance against the status quo. By the Edwardian era, Manchester was one of the largest regions in the world, and its industry had expanded to engineering and chemical fields. Yet, despite all of this growth and prosperity, Manchester's citizens did not escape crippling poverty. The city had its slums and crime and despair just like London, and for all the rags-to-riches industrialists running factories and mills, marginalization and income disparity was even more acute amongst workers.

However, these workers were more vituperative than in London, and the 1890s witnessed the birth of the Labour Party. There were pockets of Conservative strongholds in the Edwardian era, but during the election of 1906, old-time MPs soon realized no seats were safe from social revolution.

Other important English cities of the Edwardian era were:

- Liverpool, the principle seaport of England, which burst into importance when the sea link between it and America was established in the 1840s. Manufactured items were exported—cotton from Manchester, and coal from Wales—and American raw cotton, grain, and breadstuffs, Irish cattle and butter, and Canadian timber were imported.

- Folkestone, a thriving and fashionable seaside resort on the southern coast.
- Blackpool, a seaside resort in Lancashire geared towards the working class and factory workers.
- Bristol, a very important trading town. Manufactured of chocolate, soap, leather, and glass. Later a hob of British aviation.
- Birmingham, the chief center of England and the most important industrial town after Manchester.
- Coventry, major city in the West Midlands and center of bicycle and motorcar manufacturing.
- Sheffield, another principal manufacturing town known for its cutlery, steel, and iron goods.

Bibliography

Briggs, Asa. *Victorian Cities*. New York: Harper & Row, 1965.

Brown, Jonathan. *The Edwardian Farm*. Oxford: Shire Publications, 2010.

Howitt, William. *The Rural Life of England*. Shannon: Irish UP, 1972.

Hylton, Stuart. *A History of Manchester*. Chichester: Phillimore, 2003.

Langlands, Alex, Ruth Goodman, and Peter Ginn. *Edwardian Farm: Rural Life at the Turn of the Century*. London: Pavilion, 2010.

Pearsall, Ronald. *Edwardian Life and Leisure*. New York: St. Martin's, 1974.

Part III: Society

Edwardian Society

The Aristocracy

The British aristocracy is divided into two components: the peerage and the landed gentry. The peerage is, as the name states, made up of peers—dukes, marquesses, earls, viscounts, and barons—and the landed gentry made up of baronets, knights, and gentlemen of no title, but of noble blood (think Mr. Darcy of *Pride and Prejudice*).

To outsiders, this gradation of social rank could be confusing: why was Mr. Darcy a gentleman, but Mr. Collins was not? Simply stated, it was because of land. Since suffrage was long tied to land ownership, and land ownership tied to inheritance or wealth, a landowner was almost always a gentleman, and a gentleman was almost always a landowner.

Because of this social truth, the first move made by the *nouveaux riche* of the late Victorian and Edwardian eras was to purchase property in the country. Anglo-Jewish magnates such as the Rothschilds and Sir Julius Wernher became just as known for their lavish country estates as they were for their wealth. Wealthy Americans, such as Bradley Martin and Andrew Carnegie, also sought to legitimize their social status with a house in the English (or Scottish) countryside—to say nothing of the manor houses built on Long Island, along the Hudson River, and in Newport.

The late Victorian and Edwardian eras were also the epoch of *Country Life* magazine, which celebrated the country pursuits and simple, bucolic life of this class. More than a decade later, British officers prized the copies of *Country Life* sent to the trenches, passing them on to one another in order to savor the stately homes, fetes, and sports they left behind. In issues of society magazines like *The Tatler* or *The Bystander*, there were also pages of advertisements listing country estates for sale or to let, thus revealing both the demand for one's own place in the country and how hard up many traditional aristocrats actually were.

This combination of private wealth and land ownership kept political power in the hands of landowners, as it was considered a gentleman's duty to represent the interests of the public and their right as wealthy, well-born, and educated. This public duty and the duty to tend to the land is why the most important tenet of the aristocracy was that a gentleman did not work. Young gentlemen were steeped in the glories of their special calling to rule from their early schooling at Eton or Harrow (Winchester, Charterhouse and Rugby were also acceptable), and it was further cemented by their time at Oxford or Cambridge, or, if desirous of an army or navy career, Sandhurst and Dartmouth, where they were automatically trained as officers.

The aristocratic lady was usually less educated than their male counterparts, but their upbringing focused on the social niceties and necessities for their future roles as political and social hostesses. Unlike the American heiresses who swooped in and filched their potential suitors, the English lady was taught to run an aristocratic household, how to deal with servants and tradesmen, and how to advance her husband's career in whichever field he so chose. Because she was bred to compliment her husband and to further the goals of her own family, young debutantes were guided only towards suitable prospects. If her family were High Tories, the only eligible men she would meet were also High Tory. If she were from a diplomatic family, marriage to another diplomat or a Foreign Office official was a foregone conclusion. Everything about her upbringing was designed to rule on some level, and shyness or shirking of duties was not tolerated.

The responsibilities of the landed gentry were on a smaller scale, but were of no less importance. In fact, county families, by dint of their year-round residence, frequently possessed greater power and influence than the local aristocratic family, who typically moved between London and their various country estates throughout the year. These were the magistrates or justices of the peace, the squires, the Masters of the Hunt, and the MPs. The women ran the village charities, visited schools and the poor, and organized country entertainments such as church bazaars and flower shows. Granted, the wife of a mere knight or Mr. would accede precedence to the local peeress, but in the eyes of the village, Mrs. ___ was just as important as the Countess of ___.

Both pieces of the aristocracy worked in tandem to rule and reign society from the top down. They considered it their birthright and duty to lead and lead by example, though the basis of their might began to erode during the Edwardian era. Yet, the singular characteristics of the peerage and landed gentry remained a benchmark for the formation of English society, and no amount of Labour MPs or aristocratic bankruptcies could shake this.

The Peerage

The British peerage retained its influence in its simplicity and uniformity. Unlike the European peerage, which basically handed titles to each offspring, thereby diluting the exclusiveness of a title, land and titles remained mostly bound together and created a sturdier foundation for building and retaining wealth and influence.

At the top of the peerage is a *duke*. The title was first introduced by Edward III in 1337 when he created the Black Prince the first English duke. A Duke is called "Duke" or "Your Grace" by social equals, but only "Your Grace" by commoners. His eldest son bore his courtesy title, his younger sons were known as "Lord Firstname Lastname," and his daughters as "Lady Firstname Lastname."

Next is a *marquess/marquis*: This was introduced in 1387 by Richard II. A Marquess is called "My Lord" by both social equals and commoners. His eldest son also bore his courtesy title, and like a duke's other children, his younger sons are "Lord Firstname Lastname" and his daughters "Lady Firstname Lastname."

The title of *earl* was Latin for comes or comte/count in French. Before the creation of a duke, this was the highest degree of rank and dignity in the British peerage. An earl is called "My Lord" by social equals and commoners, the eldest son bore his father's courtesy title, but though the daughters are "Lady Firstname Lastname," the other sons are "Honorable Firstname Lastname."

The *viscount* is the fourth degree of rank and dignity in the British peerage, and was introduced by Henry VI in 1440. A viscount is called "My Lord" by social equals and commoners. All of his children are "Honourable Firstname Lastname."

The *baron* is the lowest rank in the British peerage. A baron is called "My Lord," and all children are "Honorable Firstname Lastname."

Though a *baronet* is a hereditary rank instituted by James I in 1612, it is lower than the peerage but higher than all knights, those of the Order of the Garter the lone exception.

In matters of precedence, women took theirs from the rank and dignity of their fathers, and all unmarried sisters in any family held the same degree, which is the degree that their eldest brother held (or would hold) amongst men. For example, when the half-brother of Ottoline Morrell (née Cavendish-Bentinck) became the 6th Duke of Portland, she was granted the courtesy title of a duke's daughter, thereby becoming *Lady* Ottoline.

The Middle Classes

The middle class was stratified along a host of lines, ranging from income and profession, one's family background, where one lived, and where one was educated.

According to Alastair Service in his book *Edwardian Interiors*, the lower middle classes ranged from "clerks and shop assistants earning between £90 and £170 a year, up through several other subtle levels and occupations. Senior foremen in factories, commercial travellers, practitioners of some arts or crafts, members of some professions such as most school-teachers or surveyors, small business men—all these were grouped in the higher levels of the lower middle class and earned between £150 and £600 per annum."

The Upper middle classes were "mostly speaking English within shades of a nationwide 'educated' accent, except in the north of England, Scotland and Wales"...their occupations might be in "suitable businesses or in professions such as law or medicine, or they might be landowners. Their incomes, to maintain an ostensibly upper middle-class way of life in Edwardian times, had to be around or at least £800 and above" depending on financial success.

Each level of this class was jealous of their position, very aware that one false move—a bankruptcy, an unwanted pregnancy, a redundancy, an accident—could plunge them into poverty, or worse, a lower rung on the social ladder. The anxieties of the Edwardian middle class are apparent in E.M. Forster's best-known novels, *A Room with a View* and *Howard's End*. Both deal with three layers of the middle class: the leisured upper middle class is represented in Cecil Vyse and the Schlegel siblings, the fastidious and climbing lower middle class by the Honeychurch family and the Wilcoxes, and the uncertain lower-lower middle class by George Emerson and Leonard Bast (and Bast hangs on the lowest rung: a clerk).

The contrast between country life and London life for the middle classes is also evident in these books, particularly in *Howards End*. The ownership of a London residence and a country house is a source of pride for Henry Wilcox, and the potential loss of Howard's End to Margaret Schlegel awakens his fear of losing both his foothold in the upper regions of the middle class and a possession.

The livelihood of the middle class was dependent upon, as stated before, income and profession, one's family background, where one lived, and where one was educated. Most of the middle class lived in cities where they worked, but they also lived in the newly created suburbs or in the spacious Garden Cities created along the aesthetics of the Arts and Crafts Movement. Some—daringly—even lived in apartment flats.

For the most part, the middle classes, barred by lack of wealth, connection, or background from most of the London Season, created their own little society within their homes: dances with gramophones or pianists rather than expensive orchestras; dramatic and operatic societies, golf, cricket, and tennis; intellectual games; and reading books by the latest writers (the middle classes were more apt to read "radical" novels than the upper and aristocratic classes).

In general, the middle class man did not attend exclusive public schools like Eton or Charterhouse, nor was he likely to go up to Oxford or Cambridge for his advanced education. Many were first educated by governesses, and then sent to kindergarten at five or six. After that, the young middle class boy attended a private or grammar school, which were often run from large private houses in the country and proclaimed to teach the sons of "Gentlemen". The gradations in middle class society rear its head once again, for in Middle Class speak, a gentleman was a man of the professional class or a businessman, and anyone in "Trade" was excluded from this designation. The son of a builder could get into these types of school, but the son of a prosperous grocer could not.

When schooling ended, these sons of the Middle Class would enter their father's line of business, or earn their stripes as an apprentice with their father's friend, before being allowed to take up a management position in their father's company. If, however, this young man showed a marked aptitude for some other profession, such as architecture or law, their father rifled through his vast business connections to give his son a boost.

Middle class young ladies were bred to be wives, but they were fortunate in that they were allowed education and work before— or perhaps in lieu of—marriage. They, like their brothers, were educated by governesses and a kindergarten teacher, and also attended one of the numerous girls' schools founded in the 1870s and 1880s. If destined to be a typist in the City, these young ladies attended secretarial schools or took business courses, but the wider world of employment was open to them as well.

In addition, it was the Middle Class young lady who breached the masculine enclaves of Oxford and Cambridge to attend Somerville or Girton, and were taken on as equals in such places as Manchester University. The Middle Class young lady was also the pioneer in the medical profession and the teaching profession, and were from whence the formidable headmistresses of girls' schools derived.

Overall, the Edwardian middle classes were not the repressed and extremely moral types associated the Victorian era. They were less wealthy and less powerful than the aristocracy was, and a little insular in outlook, but they were surprisingly more progressive in many areas in which the aristocracy feared to tread.

The Working Class and the Poor

The lives of the Edwardian working class and poor were widely documented by Socialists, journalists, and novelists of the day. During the Victorian era, religious leaders and literature influenced the growth of social activism for the benefit of the poor.

Though the mindset of many was that poverty was the fault of the impoverished—hence the formation the workhouse—and wealth the sign of blessing, many wealthy Britons were moved to devote their time and money to helping the underclass. Philanthropy became a sort of business, and by the end of the nineteenth century, there were scores upon scores of organizations and charities created to help a variety of indigent people, ranging from unwed mothers, to sailors' widows and children, to the blind—and many were based in London alone.

Mandatory schooling and a gradually increase in men's suffrage went hand-in-hand in creating a generation of poor who saw charity as merely the salving of an aristocrat's conscience and not genuine action to help the less fortunate. The legalization of trade unions in the 1870s gave the underclass a voice, and by the Edwardian era, the working classes had transformed from the pathetic to the political. It is here that the Labour Party was birthed, and the socialist agitation that unnerved the ruling classes.

A great majority of the working class lived, worked, and played in Britain's major cities. The best account for life in London is Charles Booth's *Life and Labour of the People in London* , whose nearly 30 volumes published between 1886 and 1903 provided an incredibly rich and detailed portrait of life for the working classes and poor of late Victorian and Edwardian London. While living in England, American author Jack London followed the example of Jacob Riis's celebrated book of underclass New York, *How the Other Half Lives*, by penning *The People of the Abyss*, his own first-hand account of life in London's East End. London's book was well-received, but it was one of many books that fed the "better half's" insatiable desire for a glimpse of poverty.

Best-seller lists of the late 1890s revealed a fad for fiction written from the perspective of the grimy, dull-eyed poor, and Stephen Crane's *Maggie: A Girl of the Streets* was popular on both side of the Atlantic. Well-to-do readers gloried in these books, and the more sordid, the better—perhaps to convince themselves that these ill-bred and derelict people could never rise above their station to challenge the social order.

In general, the lives of the working class bore a superficial resemblance to sensational novels and newspaper articles. These men and women, many of whom found work ranging from temporary labor, sweatshops, and manufacturing, to waiting on tables in good restaurants, millinery, and respectable street trades, took pride in their labors, and caught the zeitgeist of the period: change, reform, and militancy.

Their education was meager in comparison to the classes above them, and they resided in slums rather than elegant flats and country estates, nor were they as adequately fed and shod as wealthier people. However, they did wrest control over their destiny and rather than being passive acceptors of poor relief and charity, many working class men and women found their own voices and formed their own societies for the betterment of their class.

The Servant Class

Contrary to the images in period dramas, the life of a domestic servant was dreary, wearying, dirty, and often thankless. The domestic servant knew their place, and was proud to serve the grandest of houses, but their tenure in service was largely left up to a combination of their temperament and the temperament of their masters and mistresses.

However, the turn of the century saw the rise of the "Servant Problem," wherein households found it difficult to obtain and retain their staff. This was due to the increase in factories, entry-level white collar positions in department stores, and education. Male servants also became increasingly expensive to keep, and after the passing of the Workmen's Compensation Act of 1906, employers were required to pay insurance on their staff.

Despite the sprightliness of TV's fictional servants, all other details are rather accurate. In a smaller household of perhaps five or six servants, it was easier to rise in the ranks. A typical "tweeny"—a young girl of eleven or twelve assigned to the "in between" tasks of cleaning, setting fires, and assisting Cook—could rise to housemaid by age fourteen. If she so chose, she could find a position in another household, where she could be hired on as parlourmaid and waitress. After toiling there for a few years, she would take her experience to a larger household, where she could be head housemaid at aged eighteen, and should the daughter of the house take a liking to her, become this young lady's personal maid.

Once the young lady married (say, seven years later, aged twenty-one), our former tweeny, now twenty-five, had the option of going with the newly married young lady as her personal lady's maid. Or perhaps the ambitious maid set her eye on becoming a housekeeper. If the married young lady did not marry a titled gentleman or a gentleman with a country estate, our maid could double her duties as lady's maid and pseudo-housekeeper in the London residence, thus earning twice the experience necessary for further ascension up the domestic ranks.

Perhaps her mistress attends a country house party and takes her lady's maid, whose brisk manner catches the eye of the housekeeper anxious to retire. Our lady's maid/housekeeper is then "poached" by the lady of the house, and with a "Mrs." in front of her surname and the keys to the house, the lowly eleven year old tweeny has now become a housekeeper of a grand estate. The trajectory for a male servant was rather the same, though they had less steps to take, should they rise from hallboy to footman to butler.

The First World War effectively ended the affordability of domestic servants, and only the wealthiest of households could afford just a fraction of the immense staff employed before the war. Domestic servants in the post-war era now demanded better pay and treatment, and many women, having experienced a taste of freedom in the munitions factories (and male servants jaded by the shared experience of the trenches with their masters—and seeing many of them maimed or killed), were less likely to blindly accept the yoke of being in service. In the country, domestic service did continue to dominate the employment opportunities for farm girls and boys, but the exodus of would-be servants from this field began in the early 1900s, and the lifestyle of the leisured class changed drastically to suit this decline in available employees.

The Peerage at Work

In the 1880s, falling rents, an agricultural depression, and taxation all conspired against the lavish lifestyles of England's aristocracy, and ten years later, articles appeared in leading journals and magazines, detailing the entry of the peerage into *trade*.
The old verse—

Lord Stafford mines for coal and salt,
The Duke of Norfolk deals in malt,
The Douglas in red herrings;
But gartered name and noble brand

Are powerless to the notes of hand
Of Rothschild and the Barings

had lost a bit of its bite by the Edwardian era, for the boundaries of Trade and Aristocracy began to overlap, with self-made men rapidly appearing in Debrett's and longtime denizens of Debrett's rapidly appearing on the Stock Exchange.

Though many of the great landholders made their fortune from minerals such as coal (the Earl of Derby sold his wholesale, though Lord Londonderry sold it at retail), others—such as the 3rd Marquess of Bute, who owned the only vineyard in Britain, and the Earl of Harrington, who opened a fruit store in London—were more creative with their money-making schemes. Other inventive peers included Lord Sudeley, who owned a flourishing jam business, Lord Mulgrave, who turned Mulgrave Castle into a boys' school charging 220 guineas a year, and Lord De La Warr, who developed his own property in Sussex to found the seaside resort, Bexhill-on-Sea.

Aristocratic ladies also struck out into business, combining their adherence to philanthropy with the pursuit of profit. The Duchess of Abercorn ran a successful creamery on her Irish estate, Lady Molesworth established a jam factory at Walters Hall, near Minster-on-sea, the Hon. Frances Wolseley founded a school for women gardeners at Glynde, Sussex, Lady Augusta Orr-Ewing owned a hotel with popular golf links in Scotland, and Miss Edith Kerr established a servants' registry in London.

The most prominent peeress in Trade was Daisy Warwick, who opened a needlework shop in Bond Street boldly called "Countess of Warwick". The socialist peeress also founded an agricultural school for women at Studley Castle. There, for £80 to £100 for three terms of thirteen weeks' residence in the year, young ladies were equipped with the necessary training to become superintendents of the dairy, the garden, and the conservatories. The hardest working aristocrat was Lady Duff Gordon, whose fashion house Lucille set many trends over the course of the Edwardian era.

So influential were businessmen and industry titans of the late Victorian era, many newly-created peers were rumored to have purchased their titles, and those deriving from the brewing industry were so numerous they were dubbed the "Beerage".

Bankers like the Baring family and the Rothschilds were also ennobled for their contributions to society, and South African Randlords were, if not elevated to the peerage, at least given baronetcies.

Other ways in which peers and aristocrats could make money were to be appointed directors and presidents of companies and financial firms. This was lucrative in a time where a new trust or firm could raise money from investors and brokers on the prestige of its Board of Directors.

An article in Jerome K. Jerome's *To-Day* noted acerbically: "There is a peer who is a director of twenty-one companies, a barrister who sits upon the board of eighteen, [and] a half-pay officer, who once observed that he did not come to the City to play marbles, who is on the board of eleven companies. Nor is there any attempt to keep to any particular class of business. All is fish that comes to their net. One man I know is director of four telegraph companies, of eight railway companies, of trusts, insurance companies, land companies. His income from directors' fees alone must be over £4,000 a year."

The rise of the ennobled businessman or woman did much to bolster aristocratic coffers, and to the relief of many, the Edwardian era eventually recovered from the agricultural depression. Interestingly enough, many critics of the day credited the survival of the British aristocracy to their flexibility, and no doubt their bold move into the "workforce" reflected this survival instinct.

Bibliography

Crook, J. Mordaunt. *The Rise of the Nouveaux Riches: Style and Status in Victorian and Edwardian Architecture*. London: John Murray, 1999.

Dyhouse, Carol. *Girls Growing up in Late Victorian and Edwardian England*. London: Routledge, 1981.

Hesilrige, Arthur G. M. *Debrett's Peerage: Baronetage, Knightage and Companionage*. London: Dean & Son, 1926.

Horn, Pamela. *Ladies of the Manor: Wives and Daughters in Country-house Society 1830 - 1918*. Stroud: Sutton, 1997.

Horn, Pamela. *Life Below Stairs the Real Life of Servants, the Edwardian Era to 1939*. Amberley: Stroud, 2012.

Horn, Pamela. *The Victorian and Edwardian Schoolchild*. Gloucester, UK: Alan Sutton, 1989.

Service, Alastair. *Edwardian Interiors: Inside the Homes of the Poor, the Average, and the Wealthy*. London: Barrie & Jenkins, 1982.

Education

The Education Act of 1870 ensured that "every child would have a school place available to it in a building of reasonable quality and with a certified head teacher." For the first time ever, children of the working and lower-middle classes had access to education that was easily available, taught on a regular basis and at a certain standard, and best of all, free.

T.H.S. Escott's *Social Transformations of the Victorian* Age reiterates this monumental transformation in society: "[T]he 1870 Act at once partially enabled the child of the poorest parents to mount through the elementary schools, to the secondary schools of the Kingdom and thence to those seats of learning at which the picked youth of the country enjoy the choicest opportunities of mental culture, or are qualified for the highest posts in after life to which English ambition can aspire."

In these schools—never called "public school," a term reserved for the endowed boarding schools like Eton or Rugby—the typical subjects taught were English grammar, geography, history, mathematics, science, Latin, modern languages, and domestic economy. Granted, girls were unlikely to be taught the subjects deemed by society as "masculine," and were steered towards "feminine" subjects such as needlework and cooking; however, the curriculum was rigorous and thorough.

The early days of the Act were not smooth and carefree. It came up against two foes: religious institutions, who had traditionally been at the forefront of children's education, and were upset at their loss of power, and poor parents, who relied upon the income their children could produce, and were loath to force their children to keep up regular attendance. To mitigate the reaction of the former, board schools were deliberately non-sectarian, and for the latter, a new act passed in 1876 to make attendance compulsory for every child at least age 10, and thereafter aged 13 unless he or she could pass a special leaving examination.

The Act of 1880 finally made school compulsory for all children, with the minimum leaving age gradually raised, to eleven in 1893, and twelve in 1899, and in 1893, all Board schools were free. The 1890s and 1900s saw the transformation of public education from a privilege grudgingly given to those who could pay for it into a right for every child. London in particular was at the forefront of this change, as the curriculum and scope widened to include music lessons, trips to museums, etiquette lessons, dancing, theatrical amusements, and games. The reforms were predictably met with skepticism and suspicion, since the education of the lower class was not really supposed to foster their imaginations or reasoning skills, but the school system marched on, intent upon building up the nation through the mind and body.

The progress of girls' education in the late Victorian and Edwardian eras was remarkable. For much of history, women, whether noble or of yeoman stock, were barred from more "strenuous" education than sewing, cleaning, and cooking. Even allowing the average woman to read and write more than the Bible and her name, respectively, was viewed with horror, and basic mathematics were likely to only be taught to a merchant's daughter or wife.

A highly educated woman was an anomaly, and even ladies were strongly against the education of their daughters: Lady Mary Wortley Montagu complained bitterly that "there is hardly a creature in the world more despicable and more liable to universal ridicule than that of a learned woman," while "folly is reckoned so much our proper sphere, we are sooner pardoned any excesses of that than the least pretensions to reading and good sense."

Eighteenth century feminist Hannah More deplored craze for turning out "accomplished daughters" amongst the lower-middle classes (aping the aristocracy), asserting that "a young lady may excel in speaking French and Italian, may repeat a few passages from a volume of extracts, play like a professor, and sing like a siren" and yet be very badly educated, if her mind remains untrained. Nevertheless, she, and other female supporters of women's education, remained marginalized, and attempts throughout the first half of the 19th century to give girls as rigorous an education as boys were intermittent and done on a small scale.

This changed in 1848 with the inauguration of Queen's College in London, which had formerly been the Governess's Benevolent Institution (est. 1843), under the aegis of Queen Victoria's Maids-of-Honour. Girls of the upper classes had long been educated by Swiss and German governesses due to the poor education of English young women, and it was determined to equip young women thrown by circumstance into the (limited) workforce with the education necessary to teach children. The most famous of these early women's colleges was Cheltenham Ladies' College (est. 1853), which, under Dorothea Beale, became the prototype for advanced education.

By the 1860s, the best ladies colleges were brought in close connection with Oxford and Cambridge, and the introduction of entrance examinations and the opening of other universities to women students led to the formation of women's universities in their own right. Lady Margaret Hall was founded in 1878, Somerville College in 1879, Miss Beale founded St. Hilda's in 1885, and St Hugh's was founded in 1886 (all at Oxford). At Cambridge, Girton College was founded in 1872, and Newnham College in 1871.

Women students were permitted to study courses, sit examinations, and have their results recorded from 1881, but they were not allowed to take degrees at Oxford and Cambridge until 1920 and 1921, respectively. However, despite these advances in education, their function still served the purpose of delineating masculine and feminine spheres.

Women who graduated from college were likely to only become teachers at Board schools (and paid less than their male counterparts!) or at their own alma maters, or were expected to use their intelligence to educate their own children when they married. However, in the Edwardian era, educated ladies found public office open to them and to their liking, and though the vote and a seat in Parliament were denied to them, women could hold office on a lower scale—School Boards, Poor Law Guardians, Inspectors, City Councils, etc.

Nevertheless, education for the lower classes and for women widened and deepened their career horizons. The growth of the Empire lay not merely on the shoulders of its soldiers and seamen, but on its vast network of Civil Service officials, and one can even pinpoint the growth of the middle class not merely to the Industrial Revolution, but to the open examinations that allowed the intelligent son of a grocer to become a clerk in the Civil Service or in the Indian Public Works Department.

The law and medical fields were also wide open to lower class men (and some women), both of which boosted a determined person up the social ladder. The army and navy were still ruled by class—though the navy was less hidebound by privilege than the army—but a young boy of middling birth could enter the ranks as a seaman or private and under the right circumstances, rise to the rank of Admiral or Brigadier by the end of his career.

In the upper class and the aristocracy, the education of girls and boys diverged at quite an early age. Up until a boy was seven or eight, he shared a governess or tutor with his sister, where both were taught the rudiments of reading, writing, and arithmetic. After this, he was sent away to preparatory school, where he was prepared to enter Eton, Harrow, Winchester, or any other top public school at age 12 or 13. His sister, however, was stuck with the governess until she was 16 or 17, and her curriculum consisted only of Hannah More's dreaded "accomplishments".

Some young ladies, depending on the attitude of their parents, read widely on a number of subjects, but the typical lady was much, much less education than her middle-class counterpart. In the meantime, her brother left public school for a college at Oxford or Cambridge at 18, and remained there until about 20 or 21, thereupon his career was decided for him: enter the army or navy (or attend Sandhurst or Dartmouth, where he was study to become a high grade officer), enter the Diplomatic services, or take the Bar. A young peer was less likely to choose a profession, since the running of his estates and his duties in the House of Lords were his profession.

So, throughout all of this, you see that the passage of the 1870 Education Act (and subsequent acts) leveled the playing field for Edwardian society. The social discrepancies did not disappear, but mobility was easier to achieve. Also, this was the era of women's education, which also played a major role in the growth and spread of the suffragist/ette movement. Those at the top (the gentlemen at least) were still bred to remain at the top and lead the nation, but they no longer had their foot on the necks of the underclass, and from this change sprang the Liberal Party reforms and the Labour Party, as well as the legitimization of trades unions.

Bibliography

Dyhouse, Carol. *Girls Growing up in Late Victorian and Edwardian England*. London/Boston: Routledge, 1981.

Gathorne-Hardy, Jonathan. *The Public School Phenomenon: 597-1977*. London: Hodder and Stoughton, 1977.

Horn, Pamela. *The Victorian and Edwardian Schoolchild*. Gloucester, UK: Alan Sutton, 1989.

Robinson, Jane. *Bluestockings: The Remarkable Story of the First Women to Fight for an Education*. London: Viking, 2009.

Stephen, Barbara. *Girton College 1869-1932*. Cambridge: Cambridge Univ Pr, 2010.

The Social Round

English society was and remains a country-based society, and during the reign of Charles I, a trip to London after six to eight months or more on an estate was considered a treat. The status of London as the center of all that was licentious, amusing, and lavish became fact during the Restoration. Soon Town Houses appeared in the West End, pleasure gardens were erected in open spaces, theatres filled, and play became serious business.

During the reign of Queen Anne, the season was rather short. According to G. M. Trevelyan's *English Social History*, "The London season was over by the first week in June when people of fashion dispersed to their country homes or adjourned to Bath. A longer residence in town would have ruined many families who had strained a point to bring their daughters to the London marriage market."

As the eighteenth century wore on, the growth in power of politicians and courtiers around the Hanoverian dynasty formed the nucleus of the Season's function and purpose: London, the focal point of the burgeoning British Empire, was the place to see and be seen, and more pleasures sprang up around this exclusive group of aristocrats. Mothers anxious to marry their daughters recognized the convening of society provided ample opportunities to place them on display, and statesmen and courtiers—the eligible marriage partners—were also in need of entertainment.

For the most of the eighteenth century, the Season was exclusive to the few hundred aristocratic families of England. Everyone knew one another, or knew of one another, and outsiders were rarely permitted entry. Because of this assurance of rank and blood, Society lived, ate, and played in public. They had no need to hide their rituals from the general public because no merchant or shopkeeper would ever have the opportunity to mingle with them or ape their mores and manners. This changed during the Industrial Revolution, which saw the growth of the middle class and the creation of non-landed millionaires practically overnight.

When the prosperous middle class clamored for a voice in politics, and more horrifying, a place in the social round, the reaction of the aristocracy was to close ranks. Their amusements and entertainments now took place behind closed doors, where the middle classes, who hoped to copy the way they dressed, spoke, ate, and played in effort to acquire "gentility" could not see them. After all, should these nouveaux riches acquire the habits deemed aristocratic, one could not tell a gentleman and a greengrocer's son apart.

The middle class then turned to the example set by Queen Victoria and her large family. During the early decades of her reign, Queen Victoria shrewdly used "social media"—illustrated newspapers, magazines, photography, official portraits, and public sightings—to recreate the mystique and awe of the Royal Family lost under the reign of Mad King George and his profligate sons. The Royal Family and its doings were now accessible to the curious middle and lower classes, but on Victoria's terms. However, the secluded aristocracy grew bored with middle-class respectability, and though there were some rebels (the fast and beautiful Duchess of Manchester aroused the ire of Queen Victoria in the 1850s), they had to wait until the Prince of Wales came of age to indulge in the raucous amusements and lavish display of the past.

Yet, throughout these changes, and even into the Edwardian era, when society had expanded to include the wealthy financiers and plutocrats despised eighty years before, the importance of the Season continued to lay in its role of uniting the country's leading families for social, political, and marital contacts.

The London Season
Court festivities and functions had always had an influence on the season, but when Queen Victoria came to the throne, the London season became fixed upon the social calendar.

The meeting of Parliament in February marked its beginning, it was at its fullest during Whitsuntide (or Pentecost) saw it at its fullest, and the onset of the summer heat in July marked its ending. Many key events of the Season, particularly the sporting events, were well in place before the Victorian era, but never did they all function in tandem.

During the early years of Queen Victoria's married life, state functions followed one another at a rapid pace, with fancy dress balls, banquets, and dramatic representations at Windsor Castle filling her days. The Derby and Ascot, with its State procession, were the great sporting events of the London Season, and the opera at Covent Garden and plays at the principal London theatres, were other highlights.

After Victoria's seclusion after the death of Prince Albert, the social calendar she had ushered in was supported by the Prince and Princess of Wales (and his siblings and their spouses to a lesser degree) and the aristocracy.

The official opening of the Season was the Private View at the Royal Academy in May. The Royal Academy was formed in 1769 when a group of artists asked George III to give his blessing to an academy that would teach painting and exhibit it. Prior to this, art was the sole province of the wealthy and the royal: there were no public art galleries, artists worked at the discretion of their patrons, and only the privileged could get in to see a private or royal collection. The first show took place in a hired room in Pall Mall and contained only 136 pictures. One hundred years later, when the Royal Academy moved to Burlington House, there were 4,500 works submitted.

From an American viewpoint in 1910:

"It is not private and there isn't any view, so far as pictures are concerned. On the previous days the noble rooms opening one out of another seem practically empty, and a dense silence prevails. Greetings between the newspaper men are few and carried on in whispers. Each of those present is confronted with serious work, and he edges along the colored walls, notebook in one hand and pencil in the other, with a catalogue tucked under his arm, writing down the points for his article in on today's paper.

The man privileged to enter Burlington House on press day enjoys the real Private View of that year's pictures. He crosses the broad courtyard of Burlington House quite unimpeded by any vehicle, climbs the broad, deserted stairs, where the dignified attendant in uniform clips the right-hand corner from his card of admission, and hands him a large-leaved copy of the catalogue, for which he does not pay—and after that he owns the building.

Vastly different is the sight on Saturday. The courtyard is packed with buzzing automobiles, splendid carriages, and so on down the list of equipages until we reach the humble hansom cab. The police in attendance are busy speeding the parting motor to make room for the next. Wide as the stairs are, the dense procession must mount slowly. At the top there is no more clipping of tickets, for the cards are taken up and flung into a waste-basket. The rooms are packed like gigantic sardine boxes, and a roar resembling that of Babel echoes down from the roof, for everyone is laughing and talking, and the silent, unnoticed pictures enjoy a private view of the world's celebrities."

Next in importance was the opening night of Covent Garden's opera season. An enduring vision of this night can be seen in the opening scenes of My Fair Lady, where Eliza Doolittle tries to sell her last bunches of flowers—for Covent Garden was London's key flower market—to the toffs waiting out the rain. The Royal Opera House had undergone multiple renovations, mostly related to fires, and it was where the choicest operas, ballets, and orchestras performed.

The patroness of Coven Garden was Lady de Grey, who plucked Nellie Melba from relative obscurity to become the prima donna of Edwardian opera. It was considered de rigueur to attend the opera in full evening dress, with ladies in their most glittering tiaras. Lady de Grey also brought the Ballet Russes to London. She saw them perform their erotic, unsettling ballet in 1907, and was determined to get them to England. She had an uphill battle against prejudices, since ballet was considered either part of music hall entertainment or a backdrop to the opera. The Ballet Russes were art unto themselves, and when they finally made their debut at Covent Garden in 1911, audiences were electrified.

After the month of May, the great social events revolved around sport—Ascot, Derby, Henley, Cowes, and Goodwood—but sandwiched in between them were luncheons, military reviews, dinners, dances, flower shows, concerts, matinees, afternoon "At Homes," polo, tennis, court balls and concerts, rides in Hyde Park, four-in-hand meets, cricket matches, House of Common teas, and evening fetes. Charitable events, such as bazaars, subscription dinners, fundraisers, and appearances, also filled the season to the brim.

Of the greatest sporting events of the season, the Derby was the most democratic. Perhaps it is the result of its founding as a lark by an aristocrat rather than founded by a royal, but when Derby Day came in early June, the sun shone brightly on the heads of prostitutes, costermongers, dukes, sailors, and princes alike. In the 1850s, Charles Dickens noted the gigantic amount of food available at the refreshment saloon: 2400 tumblers, 1200 wine glasses, 3000 plates and dishes...130 legs of lamb, 65 saddles of lamb, 20 rounds of beef, 500 spring chickens, 350 pigeon pies, and a large quantity of quartern loaves and ham for sandwiches.

Queen Victoria visited Derby once in 1840, but it was her son, the Prince of Wales, who found the race to his liking. He attended every year and entered horses from his stud, and when his own Persimmon won the Derby in 1896, cries of "Good Old Teddy!" could be heard from the diverse crowd. The most infamous Derby Day was in 1913, when suffragette Emily Davison threw herself in front of the King's horse, and when the horse of C. Bowyer Ismay, brother of Titanic's J. Bruce Ismay, was mysteriously disqualified after winning the race.

The aristocratic Ascot came next. Inaugurated by Queen Anne in 1711, whose plate of 100 guineas were very high stakes for the time, this event was grand and showy, where the men wore grey morning dress and a silk topper and the women wore their best summer frocks and most elaborate hats. The Royal Procession to the Royal Enclosure, to which only the choicest of aristocrats were invited, capped the event. Viscount Churchill, whose job it was to select those suitable for invitation, dropped applications into three baskets marked Certainly, Perhaps, and Certainly Not.

In the mid-nineteenth century, Ascot was the least raffish of all racecourses, and the middle classes, equipped with their own lovely carriages, also came to see and be seen. It was said the best horses were shown at Ascot, and the prettiest women, and the magnetism of the race was so strong, eighteen days after the Armistice was signed in 1918, bookies were already asking what horses would be raced in 1919. Edward VII left his mark on Ascot as well: the famous Black Ascot of 1910 was in his honor after his death in May.

The Henley Royal Regatta was a leisurely "river carnival" on the Thames. It was at heart a rowing race first staged in 1839 for amateur oarsmen, but soon became another fixture on the social calendar. Bungalows and houses hugging the Thames were let to spectators, and the evenings were capped by boat parties and punts, the air filled with military brass bands, and illuminated by Chinese lanterns. Dress code was strict: men in collars, ties, and jackets—though garishly-colored socks and ties were the mode—and women in crisp summer frocks and hats and parasols.

Boating clubs had their own exclusive enclosures, which kept the middle class spectators out. Since the regatta was open to non-British rowing teams, the event was known for its American element, and the Stars and Stripes were seen regularly fluttering from house boats along the river. Henley was also perfect for courting, for young men and women were permitted to man their own punts for punting parties and picnics. One can almost picture the romantic scene that could kindle a proposal of marriage.

Next on the social calendar was Goodwood. This race was founded in 1801 when the 3rd Duke of Richmond and Gordon gave members of the Goodwood Hunt permission to run a number of two-mile heats. The following year saw the first public Goodwood race-meeting, when sixteen races were run in three days for the £1001 prize-money. The Duke once hosted the Prince of Wales for the week of "Glorious Goodwood", and other aristocrats followed in his wake to set up their own house parties. The relative inaccessibility of Goodwood made the race somewhat exclusive, though the advent of the motorcar changed this. The complexity of the racecourse made winning a feat to brag about, but Goodwood never achieved the mass popular of Ascot and the Derby.

Cowes Week in August was the last hurrah for the London season. The regatta was founded in the 1820s by George IV (the former Prince Regent), but it became popular when Queen Victoria and Prince Albert sought a home away from the stresses of court life and purchased Osborne House on the Isle of Wight in 1845. The Royal family spent a lengthy period of time on the Isle of Wight each year, so it was no surprise that Society followed them there during the summer. The Royal Yacht Squadron was a natural extension of Britain's might on the seas, and Cowes was less a time for amusement than it was for showing off the latest yachts and ships in England's arsenal via maneuvers and races. Later on the 19th century, the conflict between the Prince of Wales and his nephew Kaiser Wilhelm manifested itself in a bitter rivalry over whose boat was the largest, swiftest, and most up-to-date.

This rivalry was also the cause of a humiliating scene: the Kaiser and Prince of Wales ignored the Queen's signal for supper in order to finish their race, and when they finally arrived at Osborne, the Kaiser laughed at his grandmother's disapproval as the Prince of Wales hid behind a pillar. Finally, when the Kaiser arrived with his latest and most advanced version of his yacht Meteor, the Prince of Wales retired from competing with his bombastic nephew and sold his yacht. Then as now, the purchasing and upkeep of a yacht was enormously expensive, and once more see an influx of wealthy Americans.

In fact, Cowes is where Lord Randolph Churchill first spied the darkly attractive Jennie Jerome in 1873 and immediately proposed marriage. No doubt it was with this romantic occasion in mind that she declared in her 1908 memoirs, "Ever since those early days Cowes has always had so great an attraction for me that, notwithstanding its gradual deterioration, I have rarely missed a yearly visit."

On the twelfth of August—the Glorious Twelfth—the Season was officially at an end and society abandoned London for country pursuits.

The Social Calendar
JANUARY
Race meetings are held at Newmarket, Gatwick, Windsor and elsewhere
Pheasant shooting closes at the end of the month

FEBRUARY
Sandown Park races in Surrey
Quorn Hunt in Leicestershire
The Waterloo Cup–the premiere event of the hare-coursing year

MARCH
The Grand National, the most valuable National Hunt horse race in the world

APRIL
Parliament adjourns for Whitsuntide
Oxford versus Cambridge boat race
Opening of The "Oval" for Summer season (cricket)
Primrose Day (April 19th), anniversary of the death of Benjamin
Disraeli, 1st Earl of Beaconsfield
Races at Epsom and Sandown

MAY
Private View at the Royal Academy, the traditional starting signal
of the London season
Court drawing rooms (Moved to June, and in the evening, in
Edward VII's reign)
First night of Covent Garden's opera season
Royal Horticultural Society's Great Flower Show

JUNE
The Derby
The Fourth of June at Eton
Crystal Palace Horse Show
Ascot Week
Fete & gymkhana at the Ranelagh Club

JULY
Cricket matches at Lord's; Harrow vs. Eton, Oxford vs. Cambridge
Henley Regatta
Goodwood race-meeting

AUGUST
Cowes week on Isle of Wight
Glorious Twelfth, grouse hunting on the moors of Scotland
Stag-hunting season begins in Devon

SEPTEMBER
Partridge season begins
Scottish social season in Edinburgh
Cubbing begins with the Beadle Hounds
Races at Doncaster

OCTOBER
Cubbing in Ireland
Aristocratic weddings in London

NOVEMBER
Hunting season begins
Country Ball season

DECEMBER
Christmas in the country
Boxing Day (Dec. 26)
Twelfth Night celebrations (Twelve days of Christmas: Dec 25-Jan 6)

Bibliography
Barstow, Phyllida. *The English Country House Party.* Wellingborough: Equation, 1989.
Leslie, Anita. The *Marlborough House Set.* New York, NY: Doubleday, 1973
Pascoe, Charles Eyre. London *of To-day. An Illustrated Handbook for the Season.* Boston: Roberts Bros., 1902.
Plumptre, George. *The Fast Set: The World of Edwardian Racing.* London: A. Deutsch, 1985
Sproule, Anna. *The Social Calendar.* Poole, Dorset: Blandford, 1978.
Stanley, Louis T. *The London Season.* Boston: Houghton Mifflin, 1956.

Sports & Entertainment

During the Victorian and Edwardian eras, sports became serious business. There was the tug-of-war between professionals and amateurs, the agenda of sports in boys' and girls' public schools, new fads that swept the nation, the reemergence of the Olympic Games, and the participation of women.

The theory of "Muscular Christianity," wherein physical activity and health were merged with morality, which in turn was credited for the might of British imperialism was the primary influence upon the era—and could be pinpointed as one of the forces which lead countless young men to rush off to war in 1914. Nevertheless, during the early twentieth century, sport had become commonplace in everyone's lives, so commonplace in fact, that those who did not participate were looked upon as oddities.

The downside, so to speak, to the popularity of sports, was that men and women from lower classes became just as proficient as those who honed their skills in public school or at house parties. They met the demands for public sporting events and tournaments, but because they were not well off, they expected to be paid for their talents.

Sport in Society

The English public school was heart of sporting life. From the moment boys of 12 or 13 entered Winchester or Eton, they were expected to prove their ability on the cricket fields, at football, rowing, tennis, and a host of games indigenous to the school. The boy who did not play sports would find it difficult to make friends because everyone was so focused on physical prowess, he would be left out of the cultural fabric of the school. There was also the notion that if boys spent their waking hours playing and studying, there would be no time or inclination for immorality. This line of reasoning tipped the scales in support of sports at girls' schools in the 1870s, when commonly held beliefs warned that excessive physical activity would ruin female reproductive organs and would make them masculine. Many headmistresses still struggled with allowing their girls to play sports up until the 1890s, but cultural forces of the decade toppled that reluctance.

Overall, sport rapidly infiltrated every element of society. First was the craze for bicycles. They were very popular in France in the 1880s, and this spread to England by the latter half of the decade. In the 1890s, bicycles declined in price, and the bicycle tour became a common sight in the English countryside. The bicycle also broke down the system of chaperonage that kept unmarried young ladies away from unmarried young men. After all, it would be difficult for a mother or elderly chaperone to keep up with a group of furiously pedaling ladies and gentlemen.

Other crazes included tennis (lawn and court), which also gave rise to professional tournaments, and golf, which had come down from Scotland in the 1860s and grew in popularity after Prime Minister Balfour, a Scot who detested traditional sports like shooting and fox hunting, spent his leisure hours on the green. There was also jiu-jitsu, popularized by the Japanese athletes brought over during the brief bartitsu fad, table tennis/ping-pong, and billiards.

Cricket and Association Football

The schism between the well-to-do "amateur" sportsman and "professional" sportsman was most prominent in cricket and association football (soccer). In earlier days, both played together on the same local teams, and the high profile matches were those played between Eton and Harrow, and Oxford and Cambridge, at the Lord's Cricket Oval in London. You would be right to assume that these events became yet another fashionable segment of the London Season and was not very amenable to the rowdier elements.

The tide changed when Australia beat England four consecutive times during a Test Match tour—which until then, had been financed by private cricket clubs or benefactors—and the Metropolitan Cricket Club took responsibility for future test matches. Since every town and village had its cricket club, and colliers, churches, institutes, factories, and schools their own teams, there was a plethora of excellent cricket players to fill these major cricket clubs.

The same happened with association football, and it is in the 1880s when the major football clubs still in existence today were formed. Professionalism was legalized in 1885, but the disparities in wealth between the clubs lead to poaching of good players from poor clubs, and a law was passed in 1901 by the F.A. that no player could be signed for more than £10 and paid no more than £208 a year, before bonuses dependent upon the outcome of a match.

Traditional Sports

Fox hunting and shooting were the sole province of the wealthy. For one thing, both required land, specialized staff, and expensive animals. Fox hunting also required money to keep up the Hunt, and many a bankrupt Hunt Master was forced to sell his entire stable and kennel to someone who could afford to run the hunt. Hunting could also be exclusive, and the best hunting areas were in Melton Mowbray—famous for its Stilton cheese and pork pies—and in Ireland.

Children learned to ride as early as six or seven, and were allowed to join the hunt—on their ponies and cobs—also at a young age. Girls, educated at home, spent the majority of their formative years in the saddle, and oddly enough, etiquette permitted them to ride astride until aged sixteen.

The hunting season in Leicestershire began with the first meet of the Quorn on the first Monday in November. Others began a little later, and on different days. Most packs were maintained by a subscription, and though anyone could join the hunt for one or two days, frequent visitors were advised to contribute to the support of the hounds. Expenses for hunting could mount up: hiring horses cost at least £20 a month for each horse, plus stable bills, which could amount to 25 shillings per horse, as well as the salaries of the stud groom and second horseman. The best hunters could cost hundreds of pounds to purchase.

Then there was the purchase of saddles, tack, and hunting gear—for men: shirt, tie, gloves, boots, spurs, whip, top hat, and jacket (red, or "pink" only for the hunt staff). For women: riding habit (Busvines the best) comprised of jacket, apron or safety skirt, and breeches, blouse, cravat, boots, gloves, hat (either top hat or bowler shaped) with veil, and hunting crop.

Shooting

Shooting—pheasant, grouse, partridge, woodcock, snipe, or even big game in Africa or Asia—was the sport of excess. Edward VII and his son George V were the big guns of the era, and thousands of birds were shot down at individual shooting parties. So excessive were these events, even George V was to admit the sport had gone too far when during one party, nearly 10,000 partridges had been felled by the guns.

Shooting parties were held in the autumn, after the "Glorious Twelfth" of August, and were even more expensive than regular house parties. As seen with the number of birds felled by the Kings, the men invited to shoot game expected thousands of birds available to be "beat" by the beaters. Game—and partridges and pheasants in particular—was reared by a keeper months in advance of the shooting season. If the birds were eaten by predator or suffered from a disease, that year's season was ruined. Hence, an excellent and experienced gamekeeper was an expensive treasure for the avid shooter.

Adding to the expense were the cost of guns, the best of which could run up to £60-70. Those on a more modest budget could find good guns for about £15-20. On the days of the shoot, the host and his guests were each accompanied by gamekeepers, loaders, a boy to carry cartridges, and beaters, the majority of whom derived from laborers on the estate. The etiquette of the shooting party was strict, as seen in *Manners and Rules of Good Society*:

> At the close of a visit game is offered to those of the shooters to whom it is known that it will be acceptable. The head game-keeper is usually instructed to put up a couple of brace of pheasants and a hare. But in some houses even this custom is not followed, and the whole of the game killed, with the exception of what is required for the house, finds its way into the market, both the local market and the London market.

> The first three weeks of September gives a hostess little anxiety on the score of finding amusement for the ladies of the party, as so many aids out of doors are at her command at this season of the year. This is a great advantage, as although some few ladies possessing great strength of nerve have taken up shooting as an amusement and pastime and acquit

themselves surprisingly well in this manly sport. Yet ladies in general are not inclined for so dangerous a game, and find entertainment in strictly feminine pursuits, while even those intrepid ladies who have learnt how to use their little gun would never be permitted to make one or two of a big shooting party, even were they so inclined.

Occasionally, when the birds are wild and sport is slack, a sort of picnic luncheon is held in the vicinity of a keeper's lodge, under the shade of some wide-spreading trees. [The] ladies join the party, but keen sportsmen despise this playing at shooting, and resent the interruption caused by the company of ladies at luncheon, and prefer to take it in the rough and smoke the while.

Thus ladies generally have luncheon in the house at the regulation luncheon hour, and are not rejoined by the gentlemen until the day's shooting is over, between five and six o'clock. Every day of the week is not thus given up to shooting, and there are few owners of manors who would care to provide five days' consecutive sport for their guests, and two days' hard shooting is probably followed by what is called an idle day.

Sportswomen

Though it was rare for women to take part in the higher profile sports such as cricket or shooting, they were present in just about every other sport available. In girls' schools, students were mad for basketball and field hockey, and when older, they rode horses, sailed small yachts or catboats, swam, drove four-in-hands, punted along the Thames, stalked deer in Scotland, played the aforementioned golf and tennis, and later, drove and raced motorcars and flew airplanes.

This was the age of the Sportswoman, and publishers of books and periodicals quickly flooded the market with guides, magazines, articles, and newspaper columns on how to play these sports. New magazines like the *Ladies' Field* sat beside traditional male sports' periodicals like *The Sporting Times*, and even the most traditional ladies' magazines like the *Queen* and *The Lady* bowed to the trend and added regular columns written by imminent sportswomen.

Olympics

The emphasis on sports contributed to the reemergence of the Olympic Games in 1896. Held in Athens as a nod to the last Olympic Games in 776, the ten days were devoted to fencing, weightlifting, gymnastics, tennis, shooting, marathons, cycling, and yachting. Like today, it was a time of solidarity and competition, and by the dawn of WWI, the world witnessed six Olympic meetings in St Louis, Stockholm, London, Paris, and Athens.

The 1908 Olympics, held in London, was organized almost single-handedly by William Grenfell, Baron Desborough. At 6'5, Lord Desborough towered above men of the Edwardian era. He was the ultimate sportsman, excelling in rowing, mountaineering, swimming, fishing and big-game hunting, as well as fencing, cricket, and lawn tennis. He was also president of president of the Oxford University Boat Club, the Athletic Club, the Bartitsu Club, the Amateur Fencing Association, Marylebone Cricket Club, and the Lawn Tennis Association.

Having participated in the 1906 Olympics as a member of the British Fencing team, Lord Desborough proposed for the next Olympic Games to be held in London after the eruption of Mount Vesuvius in 1906 made Rome impractical. After accepting the IOC's invitation for London to host the Olympics, Lord Desborough had eighteen months to organize the event. Lord Desborough's social and political connections enabled him to persuade the organizers of the Franco-British Exhibition, who were to open at the White City, Shepherd's Bush in 1908, to also build a stadium in the area.

This stadium was to hold 60,000-70,000 spectators, and lacking any government funding, Desborough put up £2,000 of his own money towards its construction. He also campaigned hard for donations all the way up to the opening of the games, delivering "139 speeches at luncheons and banquets and other social functions." The games were not without controversy, but the lasting image is of Italian marathon runner Dorando Pietri, who collapsed several times on the way to the finish line, and was helped to cross it—in first place—by two Olympic officials. Pietri was disqualified after the second-place finisher protested, but

Pietri's perseverance, coupled with the show of international solidarity in helping him win, made him a celebrity.

Motoring and Aviation

At the beginning of Edward VII's nine year reign, the motorcar was simply a status symbol that only the very rich could afford to purchase and maintain. The horse, generally cheaper and familiar to the population, continued to dominate everyday travel and transportation, but by 1910, equine transport had become almost obsolete.

The manufacture of motorcars originated in France and Germany in the 1880s, where Continental inventors experimented with the internal combustion engine. Engineers such as Edmund Benz, Gottlieb Daimler, Nikolaus Otto, Wilhelm Maybach, and Alphonse Beau de Rochas developed and patented a variety of engines during the 1860s through 1880s. The promise of the motorcar did not bear fruition until the mid-1880s, when Edmund Benz designed a "four-stroke engine that was used in his automobiles, which were developed in 1885, patented in 1886, and became the first automobiles in production." Gottlieb Daimler, a German engineer, patented his own version in 1885, and further production of engines for self-propelled vehicles continued into the early-1890s.

The modern automobile was built in France by Panhard et Levassor in 1890. This model had its engine in the front under a bonnet (hood), a chassis (body) much like the chassis of today, a sliding gear transmission, clutch and pedal breaks and a foot accelerator. Panhard had serious competition from Peugeot, also French, and a growing number of European and American manufacturers during the first half of the 1890s.

Meanwhile, Britain's development of comparable technology was paralyzed by the Red Flag Act of 1865. Its crippling clause– "Any vehicle on the public highway, other than a horse-drawn vehicle, must be preceded by a man carrying a red flag in day and a red lantern at night, to warn oncoming traffic of the vehicle behind him."–had been placed into affect by the railroads, who wished to halt the rising popularity of the steam-cars in the 1850s.

Because of the presence of the flag-carrying man, the speed limit was restricted to four to five miles per hour, a crawling pace that was bound to discourage any sporting gentleman. In 1895, the Honorable Evelyn Ellis brought his French-made 4 hp Panhard machine to England in defiance of the act. When it was repealed in 1896 and the speed limit increased to fourteen miles per hour, new motor enthusiasts commemorated the repeal of the hated Red Flag Act with a London to Brighton run on November 14th of that year.

While the original English motorists were typically wealthy sportsman, it wasn't until Edward VII took up motoring (with relish) that the motorcar began to gain precedence over the horse and carriage with the Marlborough House Set. The King owned several automobiles, all painted in his own royal claret color, which he took for speedy drives up and down country roads. He was an impatient and excited driver, loudly encouraging his chauffeur to pass everything and everyone on the road, regardless of their speed, size and status.

It was a very frequent occurrence for a waggon lumbering down a road to Sandringham to be upset due to the careless speed of the King of England. However, he always politely proclaimed oncoming traffic of his imminent arrival with the honk of his four-key hornet horn, which the superintendent of the royal cars, who sat in front, had to play as the king's car zoomed along.

Surprisingly, he refused to allow his wife, Queen Alexandra, to own a motor of her own. It was only after Alexandra borrowed motors from friends, much to the anxiety of the Court, that Edward was eventually persuaded to allow her an automobile of her own. Alexandra was the original backseat driver, growing notorious for prodding her driver violently in the back with her parasol, shouting directions and "helpful" orders whenever a dog, or child, or anything else crossed their way.

The Queen's ownership of a motorcar made the machine imminently respectable, and many women took to the sport with as much alacrity as their male counterparts. The Baroness Campbell von Laurentz for example, took up motoring in 1900 and soon began to travel widely, contributing articles to such publications as *Car Illustrated*, *Autocar*, *Ladies' Field*, and *Heart and Home*. The baroness, indefatigable in her love for the sport, was also an inventor, designing her own solution to the problem of transporting luggage in a car that provided accommodation to passengers alone that plagued all early motorists. She designed two square fiber boxes to fit on the luggage grid at the rear. They went on the grid with "a piece of canvas underneath and over the top, a tailored cover in proofed canvas, leather-bound."

Following in the footsteps of the baroness were Mrs. Bernard Weguelin, Mrs. Claude Watney and Miss Mee of Chichester Cathedral, who, in 1905, became the first lady to pass "the examination in driving and general proficiency set by the Royal Automobile Club for the owners of cars." Dorothy Levitt, who began her motoring career as secretary to Selwyn Edge of the Napier Motor, eventually broke ladies' speed records between 1903 and 1908, and became the leading "motorina," even penned a handbook for women: *The Woman and the Car: A chatty little handbook for all women who motor or who want to motor.*

Due to the absence of hoods or windscreens, motoring called for special clothing. Fabrics such as tweed and cloth were out, for the wind whipped them out into balloons. Loose topcoats in leather, or special motoring coats from Burberry or Aquascutum acted as protection from weather and cold, with the stipulation that the coats should button closely around the wrist. For women, long fur-lined leather or cloth coats for winter and long linen or alpaca dust coats for summer were preferred.

Oil smuts could be a problem so women wore flat hats tied on with large, thick veils. For men, double-breasted reefer jackets, buttoned high with small turn down collars, wind cuffs with straps, trousers bound tightly around the ankles, and yachting cap and gloves. For the winter, leather coats, helmets and fur-lined coats and twill holland or silk dust coats were recommended. During a bout of rain, experts advised the adoption of a garment shaped like a bell tent, from which the rain would run. Goggles were also a must.

Socially, the motorcar increased the amount of time spent on leisure activities. No longer were weekend parties hasty, hectic affairs as the motorcar allowed parties to speed from London to the countryside for what hostesses fondly called "Saturday-to-Mondays". Affairs were carried about more easily, as a wife or husband was now able to drive to a quick rendezvous with a lover in an inn or tavern and back before their unsuspecting spouse could comment upon their absence. General travel was made easier not only by the motorcar, but also by the increased network of tramways that made the countryside more available to Londoners, while railroads, ever vigilant, ran seaside excursions.

Enthusiastic motorists added another form of leisure to the motorcar in the guise of touring. Countless books were published between the years 1896 and 1914, recounting motor tours in both remote and accessible places like the Hebrides and France, as well as in places uncharted by the motorcar, such as Tunisia, China or Siberia. This new form of holidaying was incorporated into the itineraries of trusted travel agents such as Thomas Cook & Son among others, who provided maps of possible touring routes as well as the locations of petrol stations.

Soon, the 1900s became the era of speed. The first motorcar race was held in 1894, and was quickly followed by the establishment of Grand Prix from Le Mans, France to Daytona Beach, Florida, where, in 1904, Willie K. Vanderbilt, Jr. clocked up to 92 mph in his 90 hp Mercedes. The Peking-Paris race of 1907 was won by the journalist Barzini, the Prince Borghese, and the mechanic Ettore Guizzardi, who drove an Italian model called the Itala. Despite the success of British drivers in the early races, the sport was impossible on the British Isles since racing on public roads was illegal.

This caused British drivers to race on the Continent or in Ireland (i.e. the Gordon Bennett race of 1903). Hugh Locke-King, a wealthy landowner, was aided by a group of wealthy friends to propose the construction of a racing course. The result was Brooklands track, a huge oval circuit with banked corners. Work was completed in 1907, and the world had its first purpose built race-track. Other nations would soon follow suit.

The motorcar also introduced a new lexicon of terminology into the English language. One kept one's car not in a garage, which was French and therefore rather naughty, but in a *motor stable*. A driver was not yet called a chauffeur, but a *mechanic*, for he often doubled as an actual mechanic as most motoring gentlemen found it beneath them to tinker beneath the bonnet. It also altered the patterns of servants and functions of the home, which had remained unchanged for centuries. Stablehands and coachmen were either pensioned off or taught to drive, while mews were either converted into motor stables or into small, attractive residences, and horses were sold and carriages dismantled.

As with everything, there was a dark side to the motorcar. A dark, expensive side. Early motoring demanded both time and money–Money because motoring was an expensive occupation, while time was needed for running repairs, not only for a succession of tyre punctures, but for the continual mechanical faults of varying severity. A motorist who drove on a daily basis could spend at least an hour a day cleaning, oiling and adjusting. Tyres cost £25. 15s a pair and were always bursting. Because there were few instruments to maintain the car, the first sign of the engine overheating was the smell of burning paint. Pistons were easily ruined and some more powerful cars guzzled as much oil as petrol.

While the price of petrol varied enormously from a copper or two to 1s.3d a gallon (depending on the greed of the garage proprietor), filling stations were few and far between, causing drivers to depend on a steady supply on hand, especially as there were few others on the road to assist a stranded motorist.

Until 1903, there had been no numbers or licenses. From henceforth every car was required to carry a registration number. By the end of the year, 8,500 motors were licensed in Britain (the registration number A1 allocated to Earl Russell), which proved that the motorcar in Britain was no passing craze of the idle rich. At the beginning of Edward's reign, London transportation was exactly as Dickens knew it; that is, the horse provided the locomotion as it had for centuries.

However, motorbuses were first licensed by the police authorities in 1904, and by 1910, they had displaced 22,000 horses and 2,200 horse omnibuses. A few displaced drivers continued their trade, becoming known as "pirates" because of their cut-rate prices, and continued to run as late as 1916. Motorcabs, informally known as "taxis" were introduced to London in 1907 after the General Motor-cab Company placed one hundred vehicles on the road. By the end of 1907 there were 723 taxis in London, a figure that quadrupled the in the next year. By 1910, there were 4,941 taxis, though there remained on the streets, 1,200 hansom cabs (affectionately called "gondolas of the street" by Disraeli) and 2,500 horse-drawn four-wheelers.

The motorcar revolution was seen as similar to the railway revolution. Nevertheless, there was one main difference: the railway had been an instrument of democracy, while the car represented the private ostentation at its most arrogant, the final triumph of the haves over the have-nots. The ultimate in Edwardian status symbol was the 1911 Rolls Royce "Silver Ghost", which cost £1,154, more than what most people earned in ten years.

Aviation was "discovered" by the general public around the time of Monsieur Bleriot's flight across the Atlantic in July 1909. Prior to this dazzling conquest of the air, the mechanics of flight and aeronautics occupied the minds and hands of the more scientific minded and those with the love for speed.

For the first half of the Edwardian era, flight enthusiasts were taken with ballooning, and according to journalist Annesley Kenealy, in a 1904 article in *The Lady's Realm*, "ballooning is the newest sport of the smart, balloon parties are the latest social departure, and membership of the Aero Club was sought alike by *chic* woman and scientific man."

The Aero Club arranged "delightful balloon trips for members and their guests, starting from picturesque Ranelagh, or the inaccessible Crystal Palace. Ladies are chivalrously admitted to all the privileges of the Aero Club, save the use of the Club house, which forms part of the Automobile Club premises at 119, Piccadilly. Rumour hath it that the Aeroists themselves would not deprive their soaring sisters of the privilege of their Club house were it not for the well-known monastic tendencies of the Automobile Club, which relegate the woman motorist to some sort of Car Cloisters, and deny her entrance Piccadilly, either mobilist.

Few women have so far developed a taste for sky-sailing. But all who take a trial trip in the clouds become confirmed "balloonatics," for there is no other sensation at all like it. No other pursuit or sport is quite so delightful as floating sky-high in a new atmosphere, discovering all sorts of lovely new scenery and cloud effects, and gazing down with a sense of superiority on the fussy small world below, which looks like a pitiful little Noah's Ark farmyard set out for the amusement of grown-up Liliputians.

The main objects of the Aero Club are to encourage all branches of aeronautics, and to organise cloud excursions for the benefit of members who care to take part in these fascinating trips. The Club at present owns a membership of nearly three hundred, has an aerial stud of three balloons, and intends to largely increase its sailing stable as its list of members grows. All congresses, races, contests, and exhibitions of aeronautic subjects and machines are held under its auspices; the Club also acquires grounds from which ascents may be made, and arranges for all the paraphernalia needed to inflate balloons with hydrogen gas, etc. Doubtless all sorts of delightful aerial tournaments will be held under its aegis within the next few years.

A picturesque feature of this Club consists in the training of carrier pigeons to act as messengers between the clouds and the earth. In wartime such ballooning pigeons would serve a very useful purpose in carrying cipher messages to beleaguered towns and far-off troops. Indeed, ballooning, with its hundred sporting and pleasurable possibilities, is only in its tender infancy. And perhaps this is why it is so interesting, for who does not enjoy conquering a totally new world in this blase twentieth century, whose boast is that everything is played out?

Ballooning, anyway, is not blast nor played out. It is fresh and young and fascinating; and the writer recommends it from personal experience as an ideal and alluring pastime. The Hon. Lady Shelley is a member of the Aero Club, and is ardently interested in ballooning. She is a daughter of Lord Llangattock, and sister of the famous motor racer, the Hon. C. S. Rolls, and is herself a keen motorist. Mrs. Templer, another lady aeroist, is particularly interested in military ballooning. Her husband, Lieutenant-Colonel Templer, has for many years commanded the War Office Balloon Factory, and has had most thrilling adventures in the air in India and many other parts of the world. He took charge of the balloon manoeuvres during the South African War, and the adoption of military ballooning and the progress made in this direction in the British Army is entirely due to Colonel Templer.

If you want to go a-sailing heavenwards, the first step is to find your balloon—not always an easy matter. There is only one private balloon-owner in the United Kingdom, Mr. Leslie Bucknall, the ardent aeronaut, who keeps balloons as other men keep hunters. *Vivienne I.* has gone to the St. Louis Exhibition, and *Vivienne III.* is just brand-new, and has only lately taken her maiden trip. Mr. Bucknall baptizes his balloons after his pretty little daughter Vivienne, who delights in ballooning, but so far has only been allowed to take her flight in a "captive."

If you belong to the Aero Club you may buy the pleasure of a prolonged balloon sail for the very small sum of two guineas, ascending at your "own risk," and with no claim on the Club for any personal damage or injury resulting from the excursion. Of course, the possibility of accident is slight, but this is a necessary self-protective clause for the Club.

All who explore the aeronautic world find it full of charm and novelty. The Aero and Automobile Clubs have combined to invent a new and exhilarating sport —the chase by motor-cars of a series of balloons, cars and sky-craft starting within five minutes of one another. A forty mile chase at top speed on a motorcar of a fast-flying balloon, and the difficulty of catching it, is a new form of hunting. And more exciting sport cannot be easily imagined."

A more exciting sport was imagined—aviation—, and the 1910s saw a dizzying array of new pilots, new aeroplane designs, and new contests and competitions, the most famous (and lucrative) being those hosted by the *Daily Mail*. The famous tabloid had first announced a competition in 1906, where a prize of £10,000 was to be awarded to the first pilot to fly from London to Manchester. In April 1910, Claude Grahame-White and Louis Paulhan took up the challenge, but a series of misfortunes overtook Grahame-White's flight, and Paulhan won the prize. The next major Daily Mail race was held in 1911, and the challenge was the swiftest flight around Great Britain—a distance of about 1,000 miles. Another Frenchman—Jean Louis Conneau, flying under the name "André Beaumont"—won this £10,000 prize.

Far-seeing politicians such as Winston Churchill saw the use of flight in military defense, and the British government opened up bids for aeroplane construction. The Royal Flying Corps was founded in 1912 and the Royal Naval Air Service was created on the eve of WWI. However, the guns of August were far away, and the concerns of aviation divided itself between those who used flight for sport and amusement, and those focused on aeronautical advances. With the former, passenger flights were added to the general spectacles performed at the major English aerodromes—of which Hendon was most popular, situated a few miles out of London. For two pounds, two shillings, an experienced aviator would take a passenger twice around the aerodrome. Four pounds, four shillings would take the passenger on four circuits of the aerodrome. Twenty-six pounds, five shillings would take a passenger on a round trip of about 38 miles, from Hendon to Brooklands.

As with many of the Edwardian era's new advances, Englishwomen entered the field of aviation—though not in as great a number as their French and American counterparts. Many, if not all, of the first lady aviatrices gained an interest in flight after conquering the automobile: Dorothy Levitt attempted to obtain her pilot's license in 1909, and spoke a few times on her experiences. It was Hilda Hewett, however, who became a pioneer aviatrix. Hewett, wife of an esteemed English novelist, was a keen bicycle and automobile enthusiast, and was immediately enchanted by aviation after traveling to an air meeting at Blackpool in 1909. There she met French engineer Gustave Blondeau, who fostered her newfound hobby. In 1910, the two became business partners and opened an aviation school at Brooklands. Hewlett also became the first woman to earn a pilot's license in 1911—certificate No.122 from the Royal Aero Club. Later, Hewlett and Blondeau began manufacturing aircraft, and when the company was dissolved in 1920, it had supplied countless aeroplanes to the Royal Flying Corps over the course of the First World War.

The Theatre, Music, and Holidays

When in 1914, Eliza Doolittle (played by Mrs. Patrick Campbell) uttered the word "Bloody" on stage, it aroused gasps of outrage, but there were no cries for the Lord Chamberlain to shut it down, and night after night, audiences packed the house even more firmly.

By then, primed by the lavish revues of the music hall and musical comedy, the decadence of the Ballet Russes, the pomp of Beerbohm Tree's and Ellen Terry's interpretations of Shakespeare, the lightly witty plays of J.M. Barrie, and the "rough" social plays of

Shaw, Ibsen, and Maugham, audiences had long come to expect shock and spectacle.

The tide had turned in 1903, when the new Gaiety Theatre reopened after its demolition and relocation during improvements to the Strand. The old Gaiety had been an antiquated hall, but now, under the aegis of George Edwardes, it was the home of frothy and fantastic musical comedy, underpinned by the delectable row of chorus girls known as "Gaiety Girls." One by one, they were snatched up by the crème of the aristocracy, and Denise Orme, Sylvia Storey, and Olive May, were soon transformed into the Baroness Churston, the Countess Poulett, and the Countess of Drogheda.

Light opera made stars of Gabrielle Ray, Zena Dare, and Lily Elsie, the last of whom was pushed into the stratosphere when she starred in The Merry Widow, which ran from June 1907 to July 1909. Edward VII saw it four times, and when it made its final bow, audiences besieged the Gaiety all day long, with some staking out their place in line as early as 5:30 AM.

The music hall, which had grown a bit creaky and suspect in the last decade of the nineteenth century, was revived in huge, gorgeously decorated theatres like the Alhambra and the Coliseum. Stars could earn more than £1000 a week, and venerable actresses like Sarah Bernhardt and Ellen Terry raked in money performing one-act plays as part of the general program. Tease and titillation became part of the music hall: Gaby Deslys made her name singing naughty French songs, Maud Allan bared her arms and legs in her infamous role as Salome, and Australian swimmer Annette Kellerman did a swimming and diving act in skin-tight bathing costume. Male impersonators were also very popular, and Vesta Tilley was so adored, she set men's fashions.

There was a brief lull around the early 1910s, when musical comedies and halls had stagnated, but the transition of Victorian burlesque into the modern revue with *Hullo, Ragtime!* in 1912 and *Hullo, Tango!* in 1913 brought it back into vogue. As evident by their names, these two revues tapped into the craze for ragtime and its dances.

Serious theatre was found at the Haymarket, St. James's, and Drury Lane. All had the approval of royalty, and also possessed a venerable reputation for quality plays performed by quality actors.

Henry Irving, the Victorian era's greatest dramatic actor, died in 1901, and the mantle was quickly assumed by Beerbohm Tree, who ran His Majesty's Theatre. Tree's staging of Shakespeare became legendary, and his affordable seats, free programs, and no cloakroom charges made him popular with theatre goers from all tiers of society.

The brightest star during the Edwardian era was J.M. Barrie. His whimsical and warm-hearted plays brought cheer to every viewer, and oddly enough, Beerbohm Tree thought Barrie was mad when he read Peter Pan in 1904. Fortunately, American impresario Charles Frohman disagreed, and staged the play to great success at the Duke of York's, and later in America with the popular actress, Maude Adams.

The theatre allowed one to escape for a few hours, but Edwardians could also physically escape to the various seaside resorts along England's coast. The aristocracy preferred the French Riviera or Edward VII's favorite destination, Biarritz, but Brighton, Lyme Regis, Scarborough, or Margate were just as good—if not better, in the minds of more xenophobic—for upper and middle class Britons.

Clare Leighton was born to two authors, and described the family's annual exodus from their home in St. John's Wood to a summer home in East Anglia in her memoirs, *Tempestuous Petticoat:*

"The migrations started a week or two before we actually took the journey by train, for there was so much to be packed. Countless linen chests and trunks appeared on our landings, and in odd corners of all the rooms....though the trunks stood waiting, there was one unpleasant ritual to perform before the packing could take place. My mother's furs must be put away for the summer. Her ermine stole and muff, her sable stole and her skunk-trimmed velvet coat must be protected in pepper from the ravages of moths....Once the furs were safely protected against moths, my mother was free to put her mind to the packing for the annual exodus....everything that lay about [her] study was tossed into these trunks...even my father's easel and painting materials had to be strapped together and packed. The only thing of importance we did not take was the gramophone.

It was a good-sized gathering when it assembled for the migration. First there were the heads of the tribe, my father and mother...then of course, there were we three children. Walmy [Mrs. Walmisley, Mrs. Leighton's secretary]...And then came the staff, the nurse and undernurse."

The Leightons initially rented a furnished home in Lowestoft, but later purchased a home overlooking the North Sea. Their stay during the summer months was mimicked by countless families, and for the most part, seaside resorts rarely varied in appearance. All had promenades stretching to the beach, a stand for bands and minstrel players, bathing huts where one changed into bathing costume, open-air restaurants, and cricket grounds.

In Scotland, cricket grounds were exchanged for golf links, though many in England did offer this option. These summer excursions were not limited to the well-to-do. In fact, the growth of the railway was fostered by lines heading straight to seaside resorts (many hotels were owned by the railway companies), and third class tickets could take a factory worker or mill hand to Blackpool, or Southport, or Redcar with ease. In fact, so profitable were seaside resorts, Lord De La Warr created his own resort in Kent (Bexhill-on-Sea), and the directorships of many hotel and resort syndicates boasted illustrious names.

For the more adventurous, it was just as easy and inexpensive to get away from England. Thomas Cook & Son so perfected the art of travel, one could stay in a little oasis of "England" whether you were in Cairo or Constantinople. This, plus the combination of Baedeker or Murray guidebook, cheap railway fare, and fast "ocean greyhounds", enabled the English to experience foreign travel at a premium.

Depending on income, Edwardian travelers had the choice of lavish hotel, respectable boarding house or pensione, or rented house or villa. Servants were cheap and plentiful, and food was good (guidebooks like Baedeker were meticulous in their recommendation of good restaurants and eateries). In fact, so cosseted were English travelers, it was rare to experience any difficulties or surprises over the course of their journey.

The social elite tended to follow in the King's footsteps: Biarritz, Carlsbad or Marienbad, and Paris, or foreign courts

(Berlin, St. Petersburg, Rome). Florence and Venice were most popular with artists and Cairo with those interested in antiquities or recovering their health, while the more adventurous went to Bombay or Peking. Sporting tours were highly popular with men—tiger shoots in India, moose hunting in America, or Big Game in Africa—where one's prowess was tied to the size of the prize.

To return to domestic entertainments, the most enduring focused on music and art. Music accompanied almost every pastime, whether it be a dance, a musicale, or merely a pint in a pub. Opera singers of the time, such as Nellie Melba and Enrico Caruso, were treated like deities, and could command exorbitant sums for private performances. Musical accomplishments were also encouraged in both young men and women, though for the latter more so than the former, and marriage-minded mamas knew the reaction of men to the alabaster arms of their daughters as they played a piano solo at an At Home performance.

The middle classes formed musical societies, where they revived ancient instruments like the lyre, or even adopted newfangled ones like the ukulele. In the days before the radio, the only way to hear the latest tunes, usually from the stage, were on sheet or the gramophone, and soon every well-to-do home had its own record player.

Bibliography

Edes, Mary Elisabeth, Dudley Frasier, and James Laver, eds. *The Age of Extravagance: An Edwardian Reader*. New York: Rinehart, 1954.

Dyhouse, Carol. *Girls Growing up in Late Victorian and Edwardian England*. London: Routledge, 1981.

Jenkins, Rebecca. *The First London Olympics, 1908*. London: Piatkus, 2008.

Lebow, Eileen F. *Before Amelia: Women Pilots in the Early Days of Aviation*. Washington, D.C.: Brassey's, 2002.

Lord Montagu of Beaulieu, and F. Wilson McComb. *Behind the Wheel: The Magic and Manners of Early Motoring*. New York: Paddington, 1977.

Macqueen-Pope, W. *Carriages at Eleven: The Story of the Edwardian Theatre*. Port Washington, NY: Kennikat, 1970.

Tames, Richard. *The Victorian and Edwardian Sportsman*. Princes Risborough: Shire, 2007.

Shopping

The four mile radius around Charing Cross was the West End's shopping haven. Until the 1920s, when the combination of artificial fabrics and working-class girls with wartime salaries to burn resulted in a booming ready-to-wear (or off-the-peg) market, clothing was a clear marker of the haves and the have-nots.

Thus, the West End catered to the wealthy and well-to-do—though the growth of department stores (old style Swan & Edgar at Piccadilly Circus, and new style Selfridges at Oxford Street), encroached upon the old world elegance of shops devoted to one particular item. These shops, situated around Bond Street, Regent Street, Piccadilly, Oxford Street, Knightsbridge, Buckingham Palace Road, Kensington High Street, and Westbourne Grove, provided everything for the well-to-do, from gloves and hats and walking sticks, to carpets and cutlery, to jewelry and hosiery.

Frances Sheafer Waxman, in a slim guidebook intended for American visitors to London, writes: "The district which includes Oxford Circus, Regent Street, New and Old Bond Street and Oxford Street is the popular tourist shopping territory. The establishments which line these streets vary considerably in the character and quality of their merchandise. The Regent Street and Bond Street shops are more exclusive and consequently more expensive.

About Oxford Circus, things are cheaper, except at Jay's, which is now considered by 'smart' English people as a little old-fashioned, but always reliable. Londoners go there for expensive dress blouses, and also for their mourning outfits. There are of course in London, as also in Paris, certain dressmaking houses, whose names are as familiar to women interested in clothes as their own. Redfern, for example, needs no introduction to an American woman.

In the Regency era, Bond Street was the sole province of men's goods, but it expanded in the Victorian era, with Old Bond Street being the home of longtime men's tailors, hatmakers, and bootmakers, and New Bond Street more geared towards women shoppers, with their own shops as well as tea rooms. Bond Street held tightly to its aristocratic pedigree and was the only street onto which nothing but foot and carriage traffic were allowed.

A shopping trip to London was considered an all-day pursuit, and tea rooms and ladies clubs sprang up to accommodate lady shoppers--the former allowing ladies to break the taboo of dining in public and without a male escort, and the latter giving ladies a place to relax, play cards, write letters, and even smoke, just like in a gentleman's club. The best time to shop, according to Waxman, was in June, when one could receive the best bargains just as the Season came to a close.

The aforementioned department stores, with their ready-made frocks, were largely the province of the upper middle classes, but English ladies were just as tempted by its bargains and advertisements. Wealthy Americans, accustomed to stopping Macy's or Wanamaker's, made them somewhat fashionable. As a result, Harrods and Selfridges went all out in lavishness and luxury to attract the tentative aristocratic clientele unaccustomed to great shopping emporiums.

Though the wealthy visited Paris to replenish their wardrobes, the average aristocratic lady relied upon old-fashioned court dressmakers and the needles of their lady's maids to keep their wardrobes up to date. Soon, however, Parisian couture houses opened up London branches to take advantage of Americans in residence, and they no doubt encouraged their titled friends to step inside the ateliers of Lanvin, Worth, and Poiret. Ironically, English tailoring was so revered, French gentlemen traveled to London to replenish their wardrobes whilst English ladies traveled to Paris.

Co-Operative Stores

Waxman continues: "All England takes a sort of national pride in the London co-operative stores, which are quite unique and peculiar to that big city. They were founded originally to force down the "high cost of living," although their existence considerably antedates the now general agitation against this modern bugaboo. According to their social positions and affiliations, English men and women belong to the Army and Navy, the Junior Army and Navy, or the two Civil Service societies.

Since these organizations exist solely to keep prices down, their stores do actually sell at a smaller profit than the big shops can afford to allow themselves. A trifling yearly subscription is demanded of all would-be purchasers, who must, however, be vouched for by members or shareholders. This regulation, while it is no doubt wise, is irksome to the stranger who cannot consequently make purchases at any of the stores except through a member friend. When, however, they are accessible, these are good places to go for outdoor garments, polo coats, men's ulsters, etc. They also sell very durable woolen underwear and stockings."

In *The Very Best English Goods*, a facsimile of the 1907 catalogue for The Army and Navy Co-Operative Society, it is explained that The Army and Navy Stores were founded in 1871, when "a group of army and naval officers decided that wine was too expensive. A bottle of good port cost two shillings; they would reduce the cost of living by ordering it by the case at wholesale prices." The Civil Services Stores were founded six years previously by a group of clerks in the General Post Office who "clubbed together to buy a chest of tea."

Membership was restricted to "officers and non-commissioned officers, their families, and friends introduced by them; also officials of various service organizations and clubs." The subscription was five shillings for the first year and half-a-crown (2/6) annually. Shareholders participated in profits and management, and "enjoyed special privileges in the carriage of goods." Deliveries to London and its suburbs were free to all members, and vans left the premises at Victoria Street every hour between 8:30 am and 6:30 pm.. Best yet, the Army & Navy Stores took care of everything a colonial in the far-flung reaches of India or African colonies could imagine, and in 1901, branches opened in Bombay, Calcutta, Delhi, and Karachi.

How to Shop

Unlike in America, the English did not "window shop"—nor did the salesperson expect the customer who entered the shop to leave without purchasing something. Exchanges or returns were also frowned upon, as many unsuspecting Americans were surprised to learn.

Thus, when Harry Gordon Selfridge opened his eponymous "American style" department store, the lack of hard-selling, the abolishment of the odious shop walker—a "suave frock-coated gentlemen who walk up and down the aisles terrorizing any inattentive shop girl and always at a customer's elbow, murmuring 'Your next pleasure, madam?'"—and the spaciousness shook the London shopping establishment.

Waxman again: "[Selfridges'] aisles are wide, its displays are coherently isolated. It is entirely possible to find there what you are looking for, without delving through piles of irrelevant things in which you have no interest. Also the article which has perhaps caught your eye in a window setting is to be had from the general stock. You are permitted, even encouraged, to exchange any article which may not have been found entirely satisfactory on a home inspection, and this last privilege is, or has been until lately, unheard of in the native London shops."

"One peculiarity of British business customs the American shopper should know, and that is that the shopping-day does not begin in England as early as it does in alert America. London shops are seldom in good selling order before half-past ten. Wednesday is a day to avoid shopping. That being matinee day at the theaters, many cheap excursion trains are run in from the country, bringing crowds of "trippers" to the shows and the shops. On Saturday after one o'clock most of the shops are closed, though some of them substitute Thursday as their weekly half-holiday."

Luncheon & Tea Rooms
To cater to shoppers, many of whom came down from the country for the day, tea rooms and luncheon rooms were opened on the premises of most high end department stores and shops. Marshall & Snelgrove's, Selfridges, Swan & Edgar's, Peter Robinson's, Harrods', Shoolbreds', Gamage's, and the Co-Operative Society stores, provided these conveniences to "attract and keep customers." The fare was of the best quality and often cheaper than actual free-standing tea rooms like Fuller's or Rumplemayer.

Where to Shop

Ladies Dressmakers & Tailors	Kate Reily – 11-12 Dover Street
	Redfern – 26 Conduit Street

	Lucile – 23 Hanover Square
Gentlemen's Tailors	Poole – 37-39 Savile Row
	Hill Bros. – 3-4 Old Bond Street
	Herbert Johnson – 38 New Bond Street
Millinery	Henry Heath, Ltd. – 105-109 Oxford Street
	Maison Nouvelle – 240 Oxford Street
	Madame Leoty – 22 Old Bond Street
Hats	Henry Heath, Ltd. 105-109 Oxford Street
	Truefitt – 16 Old Bond Street and 20-21 Burlington Arcade
Shoes	Hoby & Gullick – 24 Pall Mall (gentlemen)
	Hook, Knowles, & Co. – 65-66 New Bond Street (ladies)
Lingerie	Josephine Sykes – 280 Regent Street (corsets)
Hosiery	Dr. Jaeger's Co. Ltd – 126 Regent Street

Food

The aristocracy did not shop for food, thus relying upon their cook's good eye and honesty for the quality of their table.

For special occasions, however, such as motoring picnics, or luncheons at the Derby or during Henley, they did order special hampers from top department stores like Harrods, the Stores, or specialty shops like Fortnum & Mason. A luncheon hamper from The Army & Navy could be ordered for two persons all the way to catering for twelve persons. For six persons, at a cost of five pounds, three shillings, and twopence, the hamper contained:

- linen, plate, glass, cutlery, etc
- a bottle of sherry, three bottles of claret, a bottle of brandy or whisky, half a dozen bottles of seltzer and an equal amount of soda water, six bottles of champagne
- boiled salmon or lobster, veal and ham pie, roast lamb and mint sauce, roast fowls, rolled tongue, cut ham, salad and dressing, bread, rolls, butter, cheese, cake, pastry, and condiments.

"Homesick Americans hungry for home cookery," as the ad declared, could find American provisions at Robert Jackson & Co. at 172 Piccadilly. Filling the shelves of this shop, which also boasted of a royal warrant from King Edward VII himself, were such American "delicacies" as Boston baked beans, gumbo, maple syrup, popcorn, tomato soup, grits, and tomato catsup.

In general, the average household was supplied by London's principle food markets. Many were established long before the Edwardian era, but "in the nineteenth century, under various Acts of Parliament, the whole market system of London was reorganised." These markets were divided into three classes: those serving the whole country as centers for the distribution of food, those distributing food for the London markets, and the general retail markets. The first class were controlled by corporations--the London Central Meat, Poultry and Provision at Smithfield, the Metropolitan Cattle Market at Islington, the Foreign Cattle Market at Deptford, the Covent Garden Market (vegetables and fruits), the Potato Depot of the Great Northern Railway at King's Cross, and the Billingsgate fish market.

East London was supplied by the markets in Spitalfields and Columbia, and the Borough Market supplied South London. The wares at these markets, mostly fruits and vegetables, were sold direct to costermongers and greengrocers. Costermongers in the West End and the City frequently hawked fish from Billingsgate and fruits and vegetables from Covent Garden. It was from their barrows, "laden with the spoils of orchards and gardens in

England, in France, and in America, fruits of tropical orange groves and banana plantations, nuts which have ripened under the hot sun of South America," that the cook or housekeeper-cook purchased the provisions for the households in which they worked.

To purchase provisions at retail, shoppers traveled to Leadenhall, which was a "collection of shops for the sale of provisions," and to Farringdon for fruit and vegetables. The poorer classes bought from the costermongers and hawkers at "unofficial" markets of Portman Market in Church Street, Lissom Grove, and Newport Market in Newport Street, or as they perambulated about the area. Leadenhall supplied most of London's poultry, and was patronized by local hotel and dining room caterers, as well as "thrifty City clerks and housekeepers" who lived within distance of the market.

Horses and Carriages

During the Edwardian era, the equine hubbub had dispersed a bit towards other horse repositories such as Aldridge's in Upper St. Martin's Lane–which, incidentally, was founded thirteen years before Tattersall's, in 1753–, the Royal City Horse and Carriage Repository (Barbican) and "Aldersgate in the City, and Ward's Repository in Edgware Road".

However, despite their presence, the removal of the Jockey Club its own premises, and the move to Albert Gate after the landlord, the Marquis of Westminster, refused to renew the lease on account of the scandalous bets exchanged between bookies and race enthusiasts, Tattersall's remained and remains the top horse repository in England.

R. Parke Buckley describes the market in 1903:

"The scene at the Albert Gate establishment on Monday is one worth going far to witness. The dramatis persona is remarkably interesting, and forms a unique opportunity for the study of character. Here may be seen various types of would-be purchasers, from the be-gaitered, straw-chewing, diminutive man with "horse" plainly written all over him from his cap to his shoes, to the stylishly-dressed nobleman in quest of a thousand-guinea pair of carriage horses, the country parson in search of a pony for a governess car, or a smart cavalry man on the look-out for a clever polo pony: men about town, famous jockeys and equally famous trainers, actors and actresses, members of the Stock Exchange and other important city organisations; and not infrequently novelists whose names are household words may be met with in search of local colour for a new novel.

The well-known oblong building with its glass-covered roof witnesses the sale of considerably over ten thousand horses annually. In the surrounding galleries every description of vehicle is standing for sale, governess cars, shooting wagons, landaus, victorias and coaches—a veritable carriage museum. As each potential purchaser of horse-flesh enters the yard, he dives into the office and provides himself with the broad-sheet sale catalogue, which is printed on almost similar lines to that issued by the firm on the occasion of the historic sale by them of the Prince of Wales' horses at the Hyde Park "Corner" in 1786, a copy of which hangs in a frame in the office. The Prince was, to all intents and purposes, hounded off the turf in connection with the suspicious running of his horse Escape. It may be mentioned that he, when King, actively devoted himself to racing again in 1826.

Punctually at 11.30 the auctioneer ascends the rostrum. "No. 1" is exhibited on a large board by an attendant in the gallery, the animal to be sold is led out from one of the numerous stables, the keen buyers line up, and the horse is galloped up and down through the throng of expert scrutinisers. In a few seconds a horsey-looking would-be buyer steps out of the crowd, takes a lightning glance at the animal's teeth, runs his hand over his legs and nods to the auctioneer. Bids are fired at the wielder of the hammer like shots from a Maxim gun, but to the casual observer it is a mystery how the auctioneer manages to catch the bids as they take the form of mysterious nods and winks.

The quick eyes of the seller, always on the alert, continually roam over the assembled crowd and quickly discern the slightest inclination of the head or covert twitching of an eyelid. Horses find new owners in the course of a few minutes; no time is cut to waste, for usually about two hundred lots require to be disposed of before six o'clock.

The offices of Tattersall's are exceedingly interesting, as the walls of the rooms and corridors are covered with old prints, engravings, paintings and photographs of famous racehorses, collected by the different generations during the last 137 years. This is undoubtedly the finest collection in the world, and it is uncertain if £100,000 would purchase them. In a conspicuous position over the stairs is a large photograph of the sensational sale of Flying Fox, who fetched the record price of 37,500 guineas. His Majesty the King attended this sale at Kingsclere, and in the photograph the majority of the sporting aristocracy may be recognised.

At frequent periods on the turf, owing to the death of some famous owner, valuable studs of racehorses are in the ordinary course of events brought under the hammer, and to Messrs. Tattersall is deputed the enormous responsibility of disposing of these racers to the best possible advantage. The general public, although such a large percentage of them take a more than passing interest in the sport of kings, have but little idea of the £. s. d. of racing, and when they read in the papers that some famous racehorse has been disposed of at auction by Messrs. Tattersall for ten, twenty, or even thirty thousand guineas, they are naturally astonished.

The inflated prices now paid for celebrated horse-flesh are due to many causes. In years gone by £2,000 was almost an unheard of sum to pay for a horse, even though he had first-class performances to his credit. When the Marquis of Hastings paid £12,000 for Kangaroo, who afterwards, by-the-by, turned out worthless, and ended his days in the shafts of a cab, the entire sporting world was staggered by the enormous amount of the purchase price, and reflections were made as to the sanity of the purchaser.

Nowadays, at Messrs. Tattersall's celebrated sales at Doncaster in September, thousand-guinea yearlings are almost as plentiful as blackberries, and during the past few years £5,000 has frequently been reached for a blue-blooded baby racer. This is not to be wondered at in view of the fact that stud fees in some instances are as high as four hundred guineas, and the cost of a brood mare may run into many thousands of pounds.

The splendid mare, Sceptre, who during the past year accomplished the most extraordinary record of winning the One Thousand Guineas, Two Thousand Guineas, Oaks and St. Leger, in addition to other races—netting for her owner, Mr. R. S. Sievier, the respectable fortune of £25,000——was sold by Messrs. Tattersall to him at the break-up of the late Duke of Westminster's stud for 10,000 guineas, which was a record price for a yearling."

Bibliography

Adburgham, Alison. *Shops and Shopping 1800 – 1914; Where, and in What Manner the Well-dressed English-woman Bought Her Clothes.* London: Allen & Unwin, 1967.

Adburgham, Alison. *The Very Best English Goods.* New York: Praeger, 1969.

A Pictorial and Descriptive Guide to London and Its Environs. London: Ward, Lock &, 1909.

Buckley, R. Parke. "Tattersall's: The Romantic Story of 'the Stock Exchange of Horse-Flesh'." The London Magazine. Vol 10. London. 1903.

Douglas-Irvine, Helen. *History of London.* London: Constable & Co., 1912.

Pritchard, Rosalind. *London and Londoners.* New York: A. Wessels, 1900.

Rutland, Arthur. "Round London's Big Markets." *Living London.* Ed. George R. Sims. Vol. 2. London: Cassell, 1902.

"Selfridges Store the Talk of London" Notions and Fancy Goods volume 43 (1909)

Waxman, Frances Sheafer. *A Shopping Guide to Paris and London.* New York: McBride, Nast & Co., 1912.

Travel

Four words summed up transportation in Edwardian England: Tube, train, tram, bus, and car, with ocean liners and steamships carrying Britons to faraway places. By the turn of the century, the migration of rural dwellers to cities and towns swelled the boundaries, and with the growth of suburbs, there came a need for cheap and fast travel. The growth of the Empire also created a need to transport troops, tourists, emigrants, and goods to far-flung places around the globe, and the speed and luxury of the steamship was also indicative of the nation's might.

Local Travel

The train, or railway in Brit-speak, has long been considered the symbol of the Industrial Revolution. For much of history, the only way to travel from point A to point B was by horse or by foot, both of which were slow and dependent upon the health of a horse or one's own self. The advent of the railway not only opened the country up to people who until then, expected to live and die in the same village, and travel no further than the nearest town, but it opened up the market for goods and services previously localized to one area.

Aristocratic memoirs of the day mentioned the transport of exotic fruits grown in the hothouse on their country estate to their London townhouse, and shops like Harrods or Peter Robinson or Jay's expanded their empire via mail orders. By the Edwardian era, the train had become commonplace, but the increase in mobility had already changed the way society looked from the bottom up, as the poor and working class were no longer reliant upon what occupations they could find in their village, and tradesmen and farmers were no longer dependent upon middle men. In a way, being able to pay for train fare, whether it was merely a third class ticket, was indicative of the growing autonomy of the lower orders, as they had freedom from the whims of those in power.

The Tube, or London Underground, had its roots in the 1840s, when it became the "world's oldest subway tunnel." Five decades later saw the opening of the City and South London, and Waterloo and City Railways, in 1890 and 1898 respectively. Oddly enough, the public was rather apathetic to this new mode of transportation, but the tide changed dramatically when in 1900, the Prince of Wales inaugurated the Central London Railway, which ran practically the entire length of London and charged only twopence between any two stations.

Quickly dubbed "The Twopenny Tube" by the Daily Mail, the railway had stations at Shepherd's Bush, Holland Park, Notting Hill Gate, Queen's Road, Lancaster Gate, Marble Arch, Bond Street, Oxford Circus, Tottenham Court Road, British Museum, Chancery Lane, Post Office, and Bank. By the end of 1900, the railway had carried 14,916,922 passengers, and by the death of Edward VII, the line stretched across the entire breadth of London and serviced nearly double that in 1900.

The tram, or tramway, was introduced in the 1850s by an American by the (apt) name of Train, and like all new inventions, were viewed with suspicion and dislike. Train laid his first tracks in Birkenhead (near Liverpool), and tried to introduce the tram to London where their use was met with resistance and classism, as residents of the West End called them the "poor man's street railway." Compounding the unsuitability of the tramway was that it was run by horse until the 1880s. You can imagine the tangle of traffic from horse-drawn carriages, horse-drawn omnibuses, and horse-drawn tramways.

By 1900, after years of experimenting with non-horse power, electricity moved to the forefront. The first electric tram was in Blackpool in 1883, and fittingly, working and lower middle class districts were quick to adopt this mode of travel. The use of the tram never quite reached the well-to-do classes the way the Tube did, but they were very elegant and comfortable in the Edwardian era, being fully upholstered, with curtained windows or fitted with shutters.

Because of their strong ties to the lower echelons of the workforce (i.e. white collar professionals), tramways linked suburb to suburb, thereby allowing suburban dwellers ease of travel in the days before the cost of the motorcar decreased. It soon became common for a family to pack a picnic lunch and travel by tram to a seaside resort for short holiday.

The omnibus, later shortened to 'bus, was introduced in the 1820s as a horse-drawn vehicle (of course) intended to convey large numbers of passengers and loosen the congestion in the streets of London and other major cities. Steam and electricity were used in the ensuing decades, but the adoption of the internal combustion engine in the 1890s coincided with the "respectability" of this mode of transport. Until then, ladies were hampered by a host of do's and don'ts for public transportation, and for those without the benefit of the private carriage, it was a wonder any woman was able to travel outside of her house.

Before the introduction of the engine, omnibuses were cramped, dirty, and of varying quality. Passengers were squeezed together in upholstered seats with floors covered with straw, and the closed windows were suffocating. Since the motor 'bus heralded swifter transport, there were now more routes and smaller intervals between 'buses, which in turn lead to bus companies to spruce up their equipment. There were no more windows, the seats were spacious, and it was even respectable for a lady to sit in the top seats.

During the early years of Edward VII's reign, the motorcar was considered a rich man's toy—and the median cost to purchase and keep up this new toy bore this out. The first automobiles were developed in Germany and France, since English law–the Red Flag Act of 1865: "Any vehicle on the public highway, other than a horse-drawn vehicle, must be preceded by a man carrying a red flag in day and a red lantern at night, to warn oncoming traffic of the vehicle behind him."–was influenced by the railway companies, who wished to halt the rising popularity of the steam-cars in the 1850s.

After this act was abolished in 1895, sportsmen and kings took up the vehicle with alacrity, and like the railway did for the working class, the motorcar did for the rich (though while the railway had been an instrument of democracy, the car represented the private ostentation at its most lavish, the final triumph of the haves over the have-nots). At the end of the Edwardian era, there were several thousand motorcars on the road, though it did not become affordable for any but the most well-to-do until the 1920s (Henry Ford's Model T revolutionized the American automobile market in 1908, but English classism reared its head to keep the market exclusive).

More than anything, the Edwardian era was the age of the Ocean Liner. These sleek and luxurious steamships reached their pinnacle in the 1900s, and were only matched in decadence by the great liners of the 1930s. The construction of "Ocean Greyhounds" pulled the focus of the ship towards luxury and comfort on the high seas, as well as speed. Now steamships were equipped with staterooms, lounge areas, amenities such as pools and libraries and gyms, and costly decor.

For the top ocean liner companies, such as Cunard, White Star, Hamburg-Amerika, and so on, competed for transatlantic travel (as well as steerage passengers headed from Europe for America) and the Blue Riband–a prize awarded to the fastest steamship across the Atlantic. By the 1910s, the average duration of a crossing was 6-9 days. The Titanic, built by the White Star Line, was amazing, but the true rivalry for supremacy was between Cunard (UK) and Norddeutscher Lloyd (German), who regularly battled for being supremacy in the ocean, until the RMS Mauretania won the Blue Riband in 1909 and held onto that title until 1929.

Transatlantic Travel

The wealthy and well-born have always had their Grand Tours and foreign processions, but the Age of Steam and Electricity, if not the explosion of colossal wealth born from these two elements, made traveling for leisure a class-wide pastime. Thomas Cook opened travel to middle-class Britons, and Baedeker's guide-books brought sophistication. However, it was the ties between the major cities of the United States and the courts of Europe (I hypothesize that the siege laid by the American heiress on European nobles created these links), and between the British Empire, which created a Society on a scale never seen before. By the end of the Edwardian era in 1914, it was common for Americans, Britons, and Europeans to live in a continuous state of Social Seasons! And all of this was facilitated by the ocean steamship.

The roots of the steamship reaches back to the 16th century, when there arose a growing need for a power other than the "fickle wind" or "laboring oar." However, this demand did not reach fruition until the early 19th century, when shipping magnates grabbed any steam-powered invention in search of one which would push them and their ships ahead of the competition.

Success came about in the 1820s, when the first steamers plied their trade between Dublin and Holyhead, and Dover and Calais.

The first vessel to cross the Atlantic was the Savannah, a ship which crossed old and new technologies, being fitted with a steam-engine and paddle-wheels, but also sails. It left New York on March 29, 1819 and arrived in Savannah, Georgia April 8th. The ship then left the Georgia port May 20th–with no passengers, as people probably feared the journey–for Liverpool, which it reached June 30th, a sailing time of 29 days and 11 hours. Needless to say, this successful trip sparked the beginning of the transatlantic trip, as well as travel to England's far-flung colonies by steam.

The 1890s saw the construction of "Ocean Greyhounds," which pulled the focus towards luxury and comfort on the high seas, as well as speed. Now steamships were equipped with staterooms, lounge areas, amenities such as pools and libraries and gyms, and costly decor. For the top ocean liner companies, such as Cunard, White Star, Hamburg-Amerika, and so on, competed for transatlantic travel (as well as steerage passengers headed from Europe for America) and the Blue Ribbon–a prize awarded to the fastest steamship across the Atlantic. By the 1910s, the average duration of a crossing was 6-9 days.

With so much passenger traffic from New York to Liverpool, Southampton to Cape Town, Le Havre to Genoa, Marseilles to Bombay, Singapore to Sydney, Tokyo to San Francisco, and all the way back again, order was definitely needed, and a number of guide books written specifically for ocean travel flooded the book market. Cook's guides were old standbys, as were Bradshaw's Routes, but a number of individuals produced charming and thoroughly-written books concerning traveling aboard a steamship , and what to do upon reaching one's destination.

The best season for traveling across the Atlantic towards Europe was between April and November, which were, naturally, the months during which the social seasons were at their height. Though neither passports nor visas were necessary during this era, a passport was required for travel in Russia (and one was liable to be turned away if Jewish), and it was customary for lodgers in Prussia to submit their identification papers and their object for residing in Berlin, however temporary. Otherwise, travelers had to worry only about their luggage, their through-tickets, and customs when arriving in Europe.

The top steamship lines, all of which were fully equipped with luxurious first and second class accommodations. elegant restaurants and dining areas, and a number of amenities such as swimming pools and gymnasiums, were Cunard, White Star, Hamburg-America, North German Lloyd, and the Holland-America line. Lesser, but equally comfortable lines were American, Leyland, and Red Star. For first class travelers sailing from New York, suites and cabins on the top steamship lines could range from $75-300 (about $1800-7100 in 2010), while the same accommodations on the second tier of steamships could run between $40-125 (~$950-3000 in 2010). Lower fares would of course be found during the off-seasons: westbound between November 1st and April 30th; eastbound between October 1st and March 31st.

Once the steamship was chosen, and the berths paid for, passengers were advised to visit their ship the day before sailing, unless one was familiar with the line. This made travel much easier, as one could inspect the rooms, and befriend one's steward or stewardess before the crush of fellow passengers in order to secure a nice bath time and have your steamer-chair (cost: $1) placed in a choice area on the deck.

Sailing day was next, and the docks were full of well-wishers, newspaper reporters, steamship employees, and passengers. It could be a chaotic time, but those who took the time—and money—to ease their entry aboard sailed right ahead to their rooms. Inside there might possibly be telegrams waiting, or flowers and fruit baskets sent from friends—though to combat sea-sickness, passengers were advised to tell their friends not to send food aboard. The trunks marked "Not Wanted" were sent to the hold, and the unmarked luggage, save tags with the stateroom number, was promptly unpacked and put away by the steward(ess).

Clothing for steamship travel was supposed to be simple and sturdy, to keep one warm and to cause as little fuss as possible in case of accident. A list of essential attire for a woman included one tailor made suit, one pair of thick silk or woolen tights, four sets of combination undergarments, shirtwaists, a sweater, a woolen wrapper for going to the bath, a dressy bodice for dinner, a pair of shoes with rubber soles or heels, and three pairs of pajamas. A man required a black coat for dinner, with the necessary shirts for evening attire, an old suit, woolen underclothing, a generous supply of handkerchiefs and socks, several pairs of pajamas, a bathrobe and slippers, and the requisite ties and collars.

Life at sea could vary in enjoyment, depending on one's temperament, experience at sea, and congenial passengers, though amusements could be limited. Most steamers carried an excellent library, from which books could be obtained by applying to the steward in charge. Many boasted of ample deck room, where all sorts of athletic games were devised, and shuffleboard and the ring-toss were popular amusements. Card playing was another pastime, with bridge-whist being favored—and passengers were advised to look out for card-sharps plying their trade. The ship's concert was always a feature of on the last day of a transatlantic voyage, during which money was collected for different institutions, both American and foreign, erected for the benefit of sailors. On German ships the concert was replaced by the captain's dinner, during which the first-class dining saloon was lavishly decorated and the menu top-notch.

The bane of shipboard life was sea-sickness. There being no cure of the ailment (and there still is not), passengers took precautions before the date of departure. A variety of cures were: cotton in the ears, a pinch of bicarbonate of soda, powdered charcoal after each meal, and sniffing ammonia each morning. Drinking plenty of hot water was another cure, as well as a diet of well-masticated beef for the first three days at sea.

Remedies of a more reliable bent were exercise, careful eating, and drinking either Vichy or Arpenta water, or a mild purgative. Mothersill's Seasick Remedy, a powder in gelatine capsules, was vouchsafed by Bishop Taylor-Smith, Chaplain General of the British forces, Lord Northcliffe, doctors, bankers, scientists, and all manner of influential people, and The Shredded Wheat Company advertised Triscuits as "the perfect Toast, the 'traveler's delight,' a satisfying, sustaining food on land or on sea." .

After six to nine days at sea, depending on the speed of the ship, the end of the journey was neigh. Perhaps new friends were made, or relationships broken by the forced proximity, perhaps one's destination was anticipated or dreaded, or one spent the entire time in misery, laid up with seasickness or another unfortunate ailment. Whatever one's experience aboard, the hassle of travel was far from over once the ship docked, with customs, luggage, and through tickets to take care worry over.

Foreign countries had different customs procedures, with the English being very lenient (spirits, tobacco, silver plate, copyrighted books, and music being the only things asked for), to very strict (as in France, Russia, Egypt and Constantinople). Train tickets could be booked in advance, speeding up the process of customs, and if traveling to the Continent, one was advised to mark the itinerary of the trip quite clearly (though, Thomas Cook was trusted because of the company's efficiency in arranging extended travel).

The popularity of motor tours created a need for automobile accommodations, and arrangements for taking a motorcar abroad (the packing [$30-75] and freight included), was between $200-300, all of which could be handled by American Express. England required no duties for automobiles entering their ports, but in France and Germany, the cost was $12. Once the duty was paid in France, a seal would be attached to a conspicuous part of the car; the machine was then said to be *plombé*. On leaving the country, the seal was removed by an official and the duty was refunded. This was expensive, but not as expensive as hiring a car overseas, which could be priced as high as $500 per day!

For many—particularly newly wealthy Americans barred from the nation's most exclusive circles—the cost was worth it if one could rub elbows with royalty and aristocratic luminaries and thumb your nose at those who snubbed you back at home. Others found that it strengthened the bond between upper class societies, mirroring the familial ties between the royal families of Britain and Europe.

Ultimately, the lines could blur between nationalities, forming a social group based on wealth and class rather than country of origin, which then diluted the importance of one social circle or another. Transatlantic society was now broken up into sets dependent upon one's interests and friends. So independent did this make Society, the ever important London season was in danger of losing its place in the annual social round.

Nevertheless, the meeting of and socializing with others of a like mind and background solidified the significance of the well-born and well-placed. Moreover, this constant moving about sparked the rise of photojournalism and society columns, which fed the need of the less fortunate public to feast on the adventures, exploits, and activities of their "social betters" prior to the advent of Hollywood cinema stars (the first of which was Florence Lawrence, the Biograph Girl). At what price, we all know now, but at the time, in the words of Mrs. Hwfa Williams, "It Was Such Fun!"

Abroad

Up to the mid-nineteenth century the great leisure center of Europe were the German spas. However, when gambling was outlawed, the pendulum swung towards France and Monaco. The greater ease and inexpensive fares offered by both railways and ocean liners enabled society to hare off to Monte for a bit of gambling, to a tiger hunt in Bengal, or hunting on Baron de Hirsch's estate in Austria. By the end of the London season, most, if not all, of society, having eaten its way through autumn to August required a place where their system could recuperate.

That notorious gourmand, King Edward, when Prince of Wales, encouraged the trend for rich, heavy sauces, multiple courses *a la russe*, and snacking at all times of day and night. This was all washed down with copious amounts of wines and champagne (pink was his favorite). He also made late-summer jaunts to Baden-Baden (*pictured above*), Marienbad or Carlsbad fashionable, where he and other gourmands were placed on a strict regime that combined diet, exercise and the taking of the waters.

The German spas were also a great place for the person with a slightly sullied reputation to mingle with people they wouldn't necessarily have been able to meet in Paris, Vienna or London. A young lady of fortune or without fortune viewed Ems, Homburg and Marienbad as the ideal terrain for post-Season husband-hunting. The general atmosphere of "here today, gone tomorrow" encouraged liaisons and friendships otherwise avoided. And even the king wasn't exempt from the somewhat permissible atmosphere of the spas: ladies of dubious antecedents and reputations regularly propositioned Edward through his equerry

Sir Fredrick Ponsonby, who tells in his memoirs of a particularly aggressive lady of easy virtue who, when the King turned her down, then offered herself to him!

After Christmas, the travelers would return to the Continent and throw themselves into the South of France Season, which lasted until mid-May. The Riviera stretched from Marseilles to Monte Carlo, and many books extolled the sunshine, dry warmth and gorgeous scenery as an ideal setting for those suffering poor health. While consumptives and hypochondriacs toddled to Cannes and Nice, those with money to burn (and sometimes with pockets to let) dashed to Monte Carlo and its world-famous casino where the ordinary gambling unit was a *mille*, worth about 40 pounds.

In its season, Monte Carlo attracted the super-rich Americans traveling over in yachts, widows both wealthy and on the prowl, and so many Russian princes and Grand Dukes that it seemed the court of St. Petersburg was replicated many miles (or versts to the Russians) away. A few, such as Alice Keppel, Edward's *maitresse-en-tete*, preferred Biarritz, a small French city founded by Empress Eugenie, where the English influence was very strong.

Towards the end of the 19th century a few sporting enthusiasts discovered skiing in Scandinavia and brought it south, causing the Alpine resorts of Wengen, Gstaad, Davos and Adelboden—all located in Switzerland—to take off. By the mid-1900s, winter sports became so popular they were to have become incorporated into the aborted 1916 Olympics.

But all good things must come to an end. After the hustle and bustle of Monte Carlo and the German spas, society returned to England with lighter pockets and trimmer waistlines, only to begin the social round again, sparking a continuous cycle of gluttony and excess counteracted with a period of diet and restriction.

Bibliography

Beavan, Arthur H. *Tube, Train, Tram, and Car; or Up-to-date Locomotion.* London: G. Routledge & Sons, 1903.

Brinnin, John Malcolm. *The Sway of the Grand Saloon: A Social History of the North Atlantic.* New York: Delacorte, 1971.

Brook-Shepherd, Gordon. *Uncle of Europe: The Social and Diplomatic Life of Edward VII.* New York: Harcourt Brace Jovanovich, 1976.

Fielding, Xan. *The Money Spinner: Monte Carlo and Its Fabled Casino.* Boston: Little, Brown, 1977.

Layton, J. Kent. *The Edwardian Superliners: A Trio of Trios.* Stroud: Amberley, 2010.

Miller, William H. *Floating Palaces: The Great Atlantic Liners.* Stroud, Gloucestershire: Amberley, 2010.

Miller, William H. *The Fabulous Interiors of the Great Ocean Liners: In Historic Photographs.* New York London: Dover, 1985.

Etiquette

Social Calls

To the Edwardians, everything had its place, and most importantly, *everyone*. For a society now transformed by the influx of wealth-sans-birth, a set rules were created to show who was in, and to keep others out. Prior to the Victorian era, Britain's ruling class of the eighteenth and early nineteenth centuries were composed of scarcely more than three or four hundred families, whose wealth and power stemmed virtually, with no exceptions, from land.

By the end of the nineteenth century, these three or four hundred families had expanded tenfold and Society was alternately termed the "Upper Ten Thousand." The main contributor to this drastic change were the increasing numbers of self-made millionaires and the declining values of land. The Reform Act of 1832, which abolished "rotten boroughs" and enabled the middle-classes and nouveaux riche the opportunity to rise in status as an MP, further contributed to the expansion of society. Thus, the newly elected MP and his family, energetically climbing the social ladder, needed guidance for behavior.

After the ascension of Queen Victoria, "gentility" was the accepted norm for social behavior not only for the middle-classes, but also the upper-classes. Outside of a few rebels (either left over from the wild Regency era, like Lady Blessington, or foreigners, like Louisa von Alten, 7th Duchess of Manchester), the first two or three decades of the Victorian era cultivated propriety and exclusiveness. To contain society against the social climbers, the card-and-call system was created. This system provided assurance that if your domestic and sexual reputation were unassailable, and your income above a certain level, you were permitted entry into a group of acquaintants with whom you could mix freely without feelings of social unease or constraint.

According to Lady Colin Campbell, one could not "invite people to your home, however often you may have met them elsewhere, until you have first called upon them in a formal manner and they have returned the visit." The first step in the call-and-card system was to obtain calling cards. Previous generations brandished important-looking, ostentatious cards of very stiff, very highly-glazed vellum, with their names written in a series of flourishes. By the 1890s, cards had grown plainer, the gentleman's name smaller than the lady's, with name and address printed in an ordinary style. Married couples often had their names together on one card:

Mr. and Mrs. Johnson

4 Elkham Place

While unmarried daughters had their names place beneath that of their mother's:

Mrs. Benson
Miss Benson

The Cedars,
Parminster
E

The method of calls varied, depending upon the occasion, but the typical call—the "calls general"—entailed the leaving of cards in the home of a prospective acquaintance. After an introduction was been made through a mutual friend, a formal visit was expected to be returned within three or four days. After receiving any particular hospitality such as a dinner or ball, it was necessary to call, or merely to leave cards at the door, within the few following days. The hours for calling were strictly confined between three and six o'clock p.m. For an acquaintance to call before luncheon would be the grossest presumption.

In regard to the calling cards, a lady left her own and two of her husband's, one intended for the gentleman of the house and the other for the lady (meaning, the lady of the house would be given cards from both the caller and the caller's husband). When leaving her husband's cards, they would be placed on the hall table, and should the lady of the house be absent when one called, one corner of the card was to be turned down, which signified that one has called personally. The formal "morning" call was the follow-up to the card. Together, they indicated that a state of friendship existed between the two parties concerned, ready to be built upon as might seem convenient or pleasurable. However, if a call was followed by a card, it was a snub and obviously indicated that the lady had reached too high above her.

If a lady progressed past the stage of leaving cards and was invited to an "At Home," the pressure had increased. Not only was she on display for the hostess, but most likely, the hostess's own social circle, which meant she had to please and impress everyone. Furthermore, she had only fifteen minutes in which to do it. When she arrived at the house, she gave her card to her footman, who then handed it in at the door. If the mistress was willing to receive guests, the lady would enter the house and be led to the drawing room, where she would be introduced and promptly seated in the nearest vacant chair to her hostess.

The question uppermost in the minds of the hostess and her friends was whether the newcomer make people feel awkward. Things that could create awkwardness included a lack of required family background, a lack of wealth (though a good background made up for poverty), a lack of assurance, lack of an acceptable moral reputation, and most important, the lack of ability to conform to the group's social demands.

To be truly accepted into the new circle, the lady had to prove that she lacked nothing in all five respects; to fail one prerequisite would mark oneself as a red-flag that the quiet drawing-room could suddenly fall into chaos. However, since her very presence indicated a modicum of acceptance, there as another hurdle to leap over: was her voice pleasant, how did she speak (did she say "father," rather than the correct "my father")? Did she gush, wear the right clothing for the occasion? Did she flutter and keep gestures to a minimum, and above all, did she carry herself with a poise the proclaims her a potential member of the circle as of right?

If the lady impressed the hostess and her friends, further calls were made and returned, and soon, the hostess's card became a familiar sight in the lady's card-basket as she was slowly absorbed into the circle. The hostess's friends also initiated card-and-call moves of their own. The one invitation to tea was followed by another. Perhaps an invitation to a ball. A visit in an opera box. Then—triumph—there was an invitation to a dinner party.

Etiquette from *Manners and Rules of Good Society: or, Solecisms to be Avoided* (1913)

Bowing

"As regards the recognition of friends or acquaintances, it is the privilege of a lady to take the initiative, by being the first to bow. A gentleman should not raise his hat to a lady until she has accorded him this mark of recognition, although the act of bowing is a simultaneous action on the part of both lady and gentleman, as a lady would hardly bestow a bow upon a gentleman not prepared to return it.

The bow between intimate acquaintances takes the character, when given by a lady, of a familiar nod in place of a stiff bow.

When a gentleman returns the bow of a lady he should do so by distinctly taking his hat off and as quickly replacing it, not merely raising it slightly, as formerly, and if he is an intimate acquaintance or friend, he should act in a similar manner.

In France and on the Continent generally, the rule of bowing is reversed, and the gentleman is the first to bow to the lady, instead of the lady to the gentleman.

Between ladies but slightly acquainted, the one of highest rank should be the first to bow to the other; between ladies of equal rank it is immaterial which of the two bows first.

A lady should not bow to persons only known to her by sight, although she may frequently have seen them in the company of her friends.

A lady should bow to a gentleman, either a friend or acquaintance, even when he is walking with either a lady or gentleman, with whom she is unacquainted.

Gentlemen do not raise their hats in recognition of each other, but simply nod, when not walking with ladies, save when a vast difference exists in rank or age.

When a gentleman meets another—a friend of his— walking with a lady or ladies, with whom he himself is unacquainted, he should raise his hat and look straight before him, not at the lady or ladies.

A lady should not bow to another who, being a stranger to her, has addressed a few remarks to her at an afternoon party, as the fact of meeting at the house of a mutual friend does not constitute an acquaintanceship, and does not authorise a future bowing acquaintance.

Ladies, as a rule, are not too ready to bow to those whom they have merely conversed with in a casual way. In the first place, they are not quite certain of being remembered, and nothing is more disconcerting and disagreeable than to bow to a person who does not return it through forgetfulness of the one who has given it, or through shortsightedness, or through actual intention.

A bowing acquaintance is a difficult and tiresome one to maintain for any length of time, when opportunities do not arise for increasing it. The irksomeness of keeping it up is principally experienced by persons meeting day after day in the Park or on public promenades, riding, driving, or walking, more especially when it is tacitly understood that the acquaintance should not develop into a further acquaintance. It would be considered discourteous to discontinue a bowing acquaintance which has once been commenced.

To know a gentleman by sight through having frequently seen him at balls and parties, does not give a lady the right to bow to him, even though she may have stood beside him for some twenty minutes or so on a crowded staircase, and may have received some slight civility from him.

A lady who has received a little service from a stranger would gladly acknowledge it at any subsequent meeting by a pleasant bow, but as bowing to a gentleman argues an acquaintance with him, and as in such cases as these an acquaintance does not exist, etiquette provides no compromise in the matter. Therefore, if a young lady takes her own line, and rather than appear ungracious bows to a gentleman who has not been introduced to her either directly or indirectly, it is a breach of etiquette on her part; and as to do an unconventional thing is not desirable, the innumerable little services which ladies receive in general society are not further acknowledged beyond the thanks expressed at the moment of their being received.

Bows vary materially: there is the friendly bow, the distant bow, the ceremonious bow, the deferential bow, the familiar bow, the reluctant bow, and so on, according to the feelings that actuate individuals in their intercourse with each other.

When a bowing acquaintance only exists between ladies and gentlemen, and they meet perhaps two or three times during the day, and are not sufficiently intimate to speak, they do not usually bow more than once, when thus meeting in park or promenade.

Shaking Hands

It depends upon whom a lady is introduced to, or upon who is introduced to her, whether she should or should not shake hands. She should not shake hands on being casually introduced to a person altogether a stranger to her; but yet there are so many occasions when it is both proper and correct to shake hands on being introduced, that ^he rule on this head is a very elastic one. For instance, a host and hostess should shake hands with every stranger introduced to them at their house.

A lady should shake hands on being introduced to the relations of her intended husband.

A lady should shake hands on being introduced to the friend of an intimate friend.

When a lady has entered into conversation to any extent with some one to whom she has been introduced, and finds she has much in common with her, she should shake hands on taking leave; but if she has only exchanged a few commonplace sentences, a bow would be all that is necessary.

A lady usually takes the initiative with regard to shaking hands as with bowing; but in reality it is a spontaneous movement, made by both lady and gentleman at the same moment, as the hand ought not to be extended or the bow given unless expected and instantaneously reciprocated.

A young lady should not offer to shake hands with one not expectant of the honour.

Shaking hands on taking leave is, with some few people, a graceful and pleasant fashion of saying good-bye; intimate friends hold the hand while the last words are being said. Women hold each other's hands thus on parting, and some few men take each other's hands; but with them it is rather a foreign fashion, and is principally followed by those who have lived much on the Continent; for, as a rule, an Englishman prefers the hearty English shake of the hand.

A lady having once shaken hands with another, should continue to do so at subsequent meetings, unless a coolness of manner warns her that a bow would be more acceptable.

With regard to shaking hands at a dinner-party with acquaintances: if the dinner-party is a small one, and there is time to shake hands, it is correct to do so; but when there is little time before dinner, and no good opportunity for shaking hands, bows to acquaintances at distant parts of the room, or when seated at the dinner-table, are sufficient recognition for the time being.

At an evening-party it depends upon opportunity whether acquaintances shake hands or not.

The fashion of raising the arm when shaking hands is followed by very few in the exaggerated style in which it was first introduced, but a modification of it has distinctly become the fashion in general society.

The hand, instead of being extended straight out, is now offered on a line or parallel with the chest, a trifle higher than the old-fashioned style, and the fingers of the hand are held and gently shaken, but the palm is not grasped or even touched.

Walking, Driving, and Riding
Married ladies can, if they please, walk out unaccompanied or unattended in places of public resort in town or on the parades of fashionable watering-places. Married ladies, especially if they are young, usually prefer the society of another lady, not so much, perhaps, for propriety as for companionship, as to walk alone, either in town or at fashionable watering-places, renders a lady more or less conspicuous, especially if she is attractive and well dressed.

A young lady can now also walk by herself in the Park for the purpose of joining her friends and acquaintances, both in the morning and in the afternoon, but she should not sit alone. Again, young ladies may walk alone in the fashionable streets, but they should not loiter when alone at shop windows as they pass, but walk at a quick pace from shop to shop, or from street to street.

In the quiet neighbourhoods of towns, suburban towns, and watering-places, young ladies walk unaccompanied and unattended to visit their friends residing in the near vicinity of their homes, or to attend classes, or for the purpose of shopping, etc. Indeed, great independence is generally accorded in this respect, the line being drawn at evening hours—that is to say, at walking alone after dusk.

At watering-places, and at all public promenades, it is usual for gentlemen to join ladies with whom they are acquainted, and to walk with them for a short time when it is apparent that their company is desired, but not otherwise.

Ladies and gentlemen, whether related or not, should never walk arm-in-arm, unless the lady is an elderly one, or an invalid, and requires this support.

When driving in an open or close carriage or motor-car it is quite immaterial whether the owner occupies the righthand or the left-hand seat. The seat she occupies depends upon which side she enters, as the lady driving with her should enter before her and should seat herself on the furthest seat.

A visitor should always enter the motor-car or carriage before the hostess.

When three ladies enter a motor-car or carriage the young unmarried lady should take the back seat and the two married ladies should occupy the front seat; this is a matter of courtesy on the part of a young lady due to married ladies and not strictly demanded by etiquette.

A husband should sit with his back to the horses, or by the side of the chauffeur in the case of a motor-car, when a lady is driving with his wife.

A gentleman should be the first to get out of a motorcar or carriage, with a view to assisting the ladies to do so.

As a rule the hostess should leave the carriage or car after her guest and not before her, unless it is more convenient to do otherwise.

When a lady is merely calling for an acquaintance to take her for a drive, she should not descend from her car or carriage for the purpose of allowing her to enter it before her.

In the afternoon young ladies may drive alone in the public thoroughfares, unaccompanied by married ladies. It is permissible for a young lady to drive alone in the Park or in the streets. A married lady can, as a matter of course, drive unaccompanied.

It would be unconventional were a lady to drive alone with a gentleman in his motor-car, unless he were nearly related to her, or unless she were engaged to be married to him.

It is usual for the owner of a carriage to sit with her face to the horses; when a married lady is driving with her she should sit beside her. When young ladies are driving with her in addition to the married lady they should sit with their backs to the horses.

When a lady is driving with her husband, and a young lady accompanies her, she should not offer the front seat to the young lady, but should retain it herself, and even should the offer be made, a young lady should not avail herself of it.

It is thoroughly understood that a lady may ride in the Park alone—that is, unaccompanied or unattended—for the purpose of joining her friends. It is argued, in these days of woman's emancipation, that no possible harm or annoyance can arise from the fact of a lady riding unattended, beyond the always possible chance of an accident.

Although great latitude is now allowed to young ladies with regard to riding alone, many parents still prefer that their daughters should be attended by their grooms.

Two ladies frequently ride together, unaccompanied by a gentleman and unattended by a groom.

The Court Presentation

During Victoria's reign, the Court Drawing Rooms were held in Buckingham Palace at four stated periods every year–two before Easter and two after. Levées, hosted by the Prince of Wales for the presentation of gentlemen, were held at intervals during the like season in St. James's Palace. Though of lessening distinction as the Victorian period wore on, the delicious prospect of being presented to the Queen or Prince of Wales continued to be a beacon to ambitious social climbers.

When the date of a drawing room was announced, letters poured into the Lord Chamberlain, suggesting names of ladies for presentation. Everyone who had kissed the Queen's hand was able to nominate another for presentation. But it wasn't guaranteed that any name submitted was accepted. The list underwent careful scrutiny by both the Lord Chamberlain and the Queen, Her Majesty only receiving those who "wore the white flower of a blameless life."

There were only three qualifications for admittance to the throne room:

1. The lady wishing to be presented should be of good moral and social character.
2. Presentation had to be made by someone who had already been presented.
3. The status of the actual presentee. The most obvious candidates, the wives and daughters of the aristocracy, had the privilege of being kissed by Queen Victoria (though no kisses were received if the Princess of Wales were acting as stand-in, and the practice was dropped entirely in the Edwardian era), then came the ranks of those candidates whose presentation would be sealed by the action of kissing the Queen's hand. These included the daughters and wives of the country gentry and Town gentry, of the clergy, of naval and military officers, of professional men such as physicians and barristers, of merchants, bankers and members of the Stock Exchange, and "persons engaged in commerce on a large scale."

Summonses were sent out three weeks in advance, allowing ample time for the excited debutante or newly married lady, to practice the complicated court curtsy and order the regulated costume demanded for presentation, as laid out, *via* the Lord Chamberlain's Office, in Lady Colin Campbell's *Manners and Rules of Good Society*, 1911 edition:

Full Court Dress: low bodice, short sleeves, and train to dress not less than three yards in length from the shoulders. Whether the train is cut round or square is a matter of inclination or fashion. The width at the end should be 54 inches. It is also imperative that a presentation dress should be white if the person presented be an unmarried lady and it is also the fashion for married ladies to wear white on their presentation unless their age rendered their doing so unsuitable The white dresses worn by either debutante or married ladies may be trimmed with either colored or white flowers according to individual taste.

High Court Dress: dress of silk satin or velvet may be worn at Their Majesties Courts and on other State occasions by ladies to whom from illness infirmity or advancing age the present low Court dress is inappropriate. Bodices in front cut square or heart shaped which may be filled in with white only either transparent or lined at the back high or cut down three quarters height. Sleeves to elbow either thick or transparent. Trains, gloves, and feathers as usual. It is necessary for ladies who wish to appear in High Court Dress to obtain Royal permission through the Lord Chamberlain. This regulation does not apply to ladies who have already received permission to wear high dress.

White gloves only should be worn excepting in case of mourning when black or grey gloves are admissible. As a lady on presentation does not now kiss the Queen's hand as formerly she did she is not required to remove the right hand glove before entering the Presence Chamber. This order therefore is no longer in force and a lady wearing elbow gloves and bracelets will find it a great convenience not to be to take off her glove.

It was compulsory for both Married and Unmarried Ladies to Wear Plumes. The married lady's Court plume consisted of three white feathers. An unmarried lady's of two white feathers. The three white feathers should be mounted as a Prince of Wales plume and worn towards the left hand side of the head. Colored feathers may not be worn. In deep mourning, white feathers must be worn, black feathers are inadmissible.

White veils or lace lappets must be worn with the feathers. The veils should not be longer than 45 inches.

Bouquets are not included in the dress regulations issued by the Lord Chamberlain although they are invariably carried by both married and unmarried ladies. It is thus optional to carry a bouquet or not, and some elderly ladies carry much smaller bouquets than do younger ladies. A fan and a lace pocket handkerchief are also carried by a lady on presentation or on attending a Court but these two items are also altogether optional.

Armed with the proper arsenal, the young lady or new wife was ready to take London by storm. Queen Victoria held her presentations in the afternoon at 3 o'clock, which caused a traffic snarl of monumental proportions. It was common for the débutante to queue up in her carriage for hours down The Mall towards Buckingham Palace, boxed in on both sides by other equipages and the throng of curious onlookers. Then, once she alighted from her carriage, there was another long wait in the close, sweltering palace antechambers, where neither refreshments nor relief were available.

The young lady who persevered to the end, however, got her rewards. Carrying her train over her left arm, she made her way through the groups of attendants to the anteroom or corridor where one of the lords-in-waiting, with his wand, spread out her train she'd let down, and walked forward to the Throne Room.

Her name was announced as she curtsied before the Queen, so low as to almost kneel, and while doing such, she kissed the royal hand extended to her, underneath which she placed her own ungloved right hand. The peeress or daughter of a peer received a kiss from Queen Victoria.

When the Princess of Wales stood in for Her Majesty, the lady being presented curtsied only and did not kiss the Princess's hand. After passing Her Majesty, the débutante curtsied to any of the Princesses near her and retired backwards in what may be called a succession of curtsies until she reached the threshold of the doorway. The official in attendance replaced her train upon her arm and the presentation was complete.

The reception of a kiss on the cheek from the Queen or the gift of one upon her hand was eradicated when Edward VII came to the throne. Other, more important changes were also made to the presentation ceremony. The ceremony of presentation was sped up, the drawing rooms and levees switched to the evening and held in June, the telephone used to summon a débutante's transport, thus easing the traffic, buffet supper, served from tables laid with gold plate helped to revive waiting ladies, and the court photographers were allotted a room for speedy snapshots of the women.

Levées were conducted somewhat on the same plan as that of the Drawing room but were confined exclusively to men who wore uniform or Court dress. Hosted by the Prince of Wales, later the King, those entitled to be presented to H.R.H./H.M. were members of the aristocracy and gentry, the members of the diplomatic courts, the Cabinet and all leading Government officials. Also, Members of Parliament, leading members of the legal profession, the naval and military professions, the leading members of the clerical profession, the leading members of the medical and artistic professions, the leading bankers merchants and members of the Stock Exchange, and persons engaged in commerce on a large scale. An exception to the rule as regards retail trade was made in favor of any person receiving Knighthood ,or when holding the office of Mayor, or being made a Justice of the Peace, or on receiving a Commission in the Territorial forces.

The workings of the levee were similar to those of the drawing rooms: dates announced and names submitted, and specific court dress required:

The Dress to be worn at Courts State Functions and Levees: Full dress uniform is invariably worn by all gentlemen entitled to wear it. All officers Scottish kilted corps should wear the kilt irrespective their being mounted officers or not. Gentlemen who do not wear uniform may wear either velvet Court dress new style; velvet Court dress old style; cloth Court dress.

The new style velvet Court dress is of black silk velvet. The body of the coat lined with white silk and the skirt with black silk. Steel buttons. Waistcoat of white satin or black silk velvet. Breeches of black silk velvet, black silk hose, patent leather shoes, steel buckled, white bow necktie, white gloves, sword, black beaver or silk cocked hat.

The velvet Court dress old style is very similar to the foregoing with the addition of a black silk wig bag at the back of the neck and lace frills and ruffles.

The cloth Court dress consists of a coat of dark mulberry claret or green cloth with black silk linings, gold embroidery on collar, cuffs, and pocket flaps, gilt buttons with Imperial Crown, waistcoat of white corded silk or white Marcella, breeches of cloth color of coat, black silk hose, patent leather shoes, sword, white bow necktie, white gloves, black beaver or silk cocked hat.

On certain days of the year, the so-called Collar days, high diplomatic and distinguished personages wear the collars and badges of the Garter, Thistle, St Patrick, Bath, and other Orders of Knighthood.

The rules and regulations for being presented at a drawing room or levee were strictly adhered to, but the practically "open sesame" granted towards those who wished to enter society (with a little "s"), the air of exclusiveness granted court circles in the early decades of the Victorian era had nearly dissipated.

Under the aegis of the convivial and *bon vivant* Prince of Wales, later Edward VII, anyone who could entertain and be entertained was welcome in his circles. It was a trend that, if not the numbers of middle-class men entering Parliament, the self-made millionaires being ennobled or knighted, or the hordes of Americans and Continental aristocrats flooding British shores for the season, hunting, shooting, racing, and other amusements—and vice versa—sorely tried the aristocratic and royal prerogatives that kept social climbers firmly out.

By the 1880s, American writers cynically shared that "*in time it became possible to achieve a Court introduction without the intercession of the American Envoy, simply by arousing, through means it would not be discreet to name, the interest of some English noblewoman whose exchequer was at a low ebb.*" Nevertheless, this brief brush with royalty continued to be considered a stamp of social approval by nouveaux riches and foreign nobodies until its demise in 1958.

How to Curtsey at the Court Presentation

From the *Everywoman's Encyclopaedia*, volume 4:

In the first place, a Court curtsey is much lower than an ordinary curtsey, and quite different to the curtsey in a minuet or gavotte, where the front foot is extended.

A Court curtsey is always made on the right foot. The learner should practise standing with her feet slightly apart, then move the left foot sideways and a little forward.

Next draw it gradually round with a circular movement till it is behind the right foot, but not touching it, and resting on the toe only.

Then bend both knees, sinking gradually towards the ground, and bending the head slightly forward. The greater part of the weight is on the right foot when bending down, and is transferred to the left foot on rising. This is done slowly when the learner has bent down as far as possible.

The body draws back a little towards the left foot, which bears all the weight, so that the right foot is perfectly free to start a second curtsey or to walk on.

This curtsey should be practised carefully and slowly till it can be made without jerks either when sinking or rising. And the learner must be careful not to stoop forward from the waist when doing it, but only to incline her head gracefully as her knees bend.

How the debutante should enter the Throne Room and present her card to the Lord Chamberlain, represented at the rehearsal by the figure on the right. Her train is shown as it would appear after being spread at the entrance by the pages.

Rehearsing the first curtsey to the King. In the class the seated figures represent their Majesties. The debutante should hold her bouquet in her right hand just beyond the right knee as she sinks gracefully down in her obeisance.

After her second curtsey, which is made to the Queen, the debutante should rise into the position illustrated, and move train sweeping behind her, and the regulation bouquet held in her right hand.

When the debutante reaches the exit door of the Throne Room, she should turn and extend her left arm for a page (the figure on the right) to place her train over it.

Marriage

The typical Edwardian woman wished to see her name printed in the newspapers but thrice in her lifetime: at birth, at marriage, and at death. Fortunately for the press-hungry, a woman's wedding was cause for pages and pages of articles devoted to announcements, details of the ceremony, and advice for the blushing bride.

No more so was this seen than with the highly anticipated weddings of society women, whose trousseaux, bridesmaids, groom, and wedding gifts were newspaper fodder even for those invited! To regulate the demand for lavish weddings and press access to the impending nuptials, the already dozens of etiquette books on the market were supplemented by books devoted explicitly to pulling off a beautiful and unforgettable wedding ceremony.

By the late 1900s, afternoon weddings had become very popular, with 2:30 pm as the most fashionable time, despite the legally recognized time for marriage ceremonies being between 8 am and noon. To counteract this legality, a special license was obtained (during most of the 19th century, only a few were in position to obtain them) from the Archbishop of Canterbury, after application at the Faculty Office—though a very special reason had to be given to meet with his approval. This license cost on average about £30. Two other options for marriage in England were marriage by "banns" and marriage by license. The "banns," from an Old English word meaning "to summon", were the public announcement in church that a marriage was going to take place between two specified persons. They were required to be published in three consecutive weeks prior to the marriage in the parish in which the groom resided and also that in which the bride resided, and both bride and groom were advised to reside at least fifteen days in their respective parishes before the banns were announced.

A marriage by license was a bit quicker, as either the bride or the groom were required to reside in their chosen parish for at least fifteen days prior to the application for the license, either in town or in the country. This £2 license was obtained at either the Faculty Office, the Vicar-General's Office, the Doctor's Commons, or at the chosen church where the bride and groom were to be married.

On top of these fees, the officiating clergyman needed to be paid (usually according to the position and means of the groom), and the clerk who legalized the marriage required a tip. All fees relating to marriage were paid by the groom, and most of the marriage details were left on his shoulders, including the purchase of the bride's wedding ring and her bouquet, as well as the bouquets and trinkets for the bridesmaids.

Wedding presents were sent to the bride's new residence immediately after the wedding and were supposed to be put in their rightful places and definitely not arranged for the purpose of display.

The most important parts of the wedding were the bride's gown and trousseau. The traditional attire for a bride was a gown of soft, rich cream-white satin, trimmed simply or elaborately with lace, a wreath of orange-blossoms, and a veil of lace or tulle. The skirt had a train, and except at an evening wedding, waists cut open, or low at the neck, or with short or elbow sleeves (unless the arms were covered with long gloves) were not approved for brides. A wedding gown was supposed to be sumptuous and of the most costly materials, for the bride was privileged to wear her wedding down for six months after her marriage at functions requiring full dress. The train averaged eighty inches in length, though very tall brides wore ninety-five inch trains.

For men wedding attire was much simpler: morning dress— top hat, striped trousers, waistcoat, and tails.

Before the wedding, there was a wedding-breakfasts, where the bride, groom, and their families, sat down to a delicious champagne brunch to toast the impending wedding.

The actual service was an equally lavish affair: the bride was driven to the church with her father, where relatives and guests awaited. Once the bride alighted from the carriage, the bridesmaids and ushers preceded her, two by two, as her father escorted her down the aisle. As the bridesmaids and ushers reached the lowest altar step, they moved alternately left and right, leaving space for the bridal pair.

When the bride reached the lowest step, the groom took her by her right hand and conducted her to the altar where they both kneeled on an elaborate kneeling cushion. Formerly, brides removed the whole glove for the groom to place the ring on her finger, but by the turn of the century, gloves were made with a removable left ring-finger, to facilitate easy access. After the ceremony, the bride and groom marched down the aisle to a choir and strewn rose petals and were immediately driven home.

When it was time for the bride and groom took leave of their families and guests, they were conducted in a four-in-hand to their destination.

Widows marrying for a second (or third) time held noticeably simpler weddings. They were advised not to wear bridal veils, a wreath or orange blossoms, nor orange-blossoms on their gown, nor should they be attended by bridesmaids–though she could have pages should the wedding be a smart one. A widow could be given away by her father, uncle or brother, but it was optional after the first wedding, and many a quiet wedding did not feature the widow being "given away."

Formerly, widows married in gray or mauve, though it was later thought permissible for her to wear a cream or white dress, though some wore pale colors, with a matching hat or toque, and a bouquet comprised of mauve, pink, or violet flowers. Interestingly enough, the subject of a widow continuing to wear her first wedding ring was of importance, and etiquette advised the young widow to remove her first band, though she should not cease to wear it until she has arrived at the church. However, it was more usual for a formerly widowed bride to wear both rings for the remainder of her life.

The German custom of celebrating Silver weddings became a vogue in Britain of the late 1910s. The entertainments given to celebrate such an occasion were either an afternoon reception and a dinner party; a dinner party and an evening party; a dinner party and a dance; or a dinner party only, of some twenty or thirty covers. The invitations were issued on "At Home" cards three weeks beforehand, the cards being printed in silver with the name of the husband and wife, and the date and the time on them.

Each person invited was expected to send a present in silver, and these were exhibited in the drawing room on the day of the Silver Wedding with a card attached to each bearing the name of the giver. At the afternoon reception, matters were much as at an afternoon wedding, with refreshments and a large wedding cake in which the wife made the first cut much as a bride would do. At the dinner party, the husband and wife went in first, followed by the guests according to precedence, and a wedding cake occupied a prominent place on the table. At the dance, the husband and wife danced the first dance together, and subsequently led the way into the supper room arm-in-arm, where their health was toasted.

In the country, some Silver Weddings were celebrated in festivals ranging over three days, and balls, dinners, and treats were given to the neighbors, tenants, villagers and servants. At this celebration, the wife wore white and silver, or gray and silver.

Prohibitions to Marriage

From *The Book of Church Law: being an exposition of the legal rights and duties of the parochial clergy and the laity of the Church of England* (1890 edition)

Minors
Where both or either of the parties between whom the banns are published are under the age of twenty-one years, and the parents or guardians of such parties openly and publicly declare, or cause to be declared, in the church or chapel where the banns are published at the time of such publication, his, her, or their dissent to such marriage, such publication of banns shall be void.

Consanguinity
A Man may not marry his:
Mother or stepmother
Widow of his father, father-in-law, uncle, brother, son or stepson, or nephew
Aunt, Sister, Daughter, or Niece of himself or his wife
Daughter or Stepdaughter of his own or his wife's children

A woman may not marry her:
Father or Stepfather
Widower of her mother, mother-in-law, aunt, sister, daughter or stepdaughter, or nice
Uncle, Brother, Son, or Nephew of herself or her husband
Son or Stepson of her own or of her husband's children

The Deceased Wife's Sister Act, which allowed a widower to marry his dead wife's sister, was passed in 1907 after decades of bills being presented to Parliament. The law allowing a widow to marry her dead husband's brother (Deceased Brother's Widow's Marriage Act) was not passed until 1921.

Married Women's Property Act
From the *Englishwoman's Year Book* (1900 edition)
By the Married Women's Property Act, 1882 (45 and 46 Vict. c. 76), a married woman is capable of acquiring, holding, and disposing by will or otherwise of any real or personal property as if she were a *feme sole* without the intervention of a trustee, and may

enter into any contract and carry on a trade. A woman married after 1st January 1883 is entitled to keep the whole of her property, present and future, as her separate property.

She has the same remedies, civil and criminal, for the protection of her property as a *feme sole*, but she cannot take criminal proceedings against her husband whilst they are living together, nor for any act done by him when they were living together, except with regard to property taken by him when deserting her. Her liabilities in respect of his property are the same. If her husband become chargeable to the parish, she is liable to support him out of her separate property, and has the same liability to her children and grand-children as her husband. The Act does not extend to Scotland.

In Scotland, the Married Women's Property Act, 1881, provides that in marriages contracted after the passing of the Act, all the movable or personal estate of the wife, acquired before or after marriage, shall be vested in the wife as her separate estate, and shall not become the property of the husband, nor liable for his dents, provided it is invested in the name of the wife herself or in such terms as to distinguish it from the money of the husband. The income shall belong to the wife alone; but she cannot spend or dispose of the principal without his consent.

Divorce

The law of England regarded marriage as a contract, a status and institution. Up until 1857, divorce was administered by ecclesiastical courts, who created such a long, frustrating and expensive route to end a marriage, most unhappy couples had no choice but to remain together.

Upon the passing of the controversial Divorce Act of 1857, the jurisdiction was passed from the ecclesiastical courts to a new civil tribunal, and absolute divorce was sanctioned with permission of remarriage on proof of adultery on the part of the wife, or adultery and cruelty on the part of the husband.

For the miserable couple willing to weather the scandal and the exclusion from the choicest circles, if not the still considerable expense, the application for divorce would be made by a petition to the Probate Divorce and Division of the Court of Justice. The party seeking relief was called the "*petitioner*" and the party against whom the petition is brought was called the "*respondent*".

If the wife was accused of adultery, the party with whom she committed this "criminal act" was the "*co-respondent*." However, the person with whom the wife alleged her husband had committed adultery was *not* a party to the suit–but a woman implicated in a divorce suit could, upon proper application, be allowed to secure an order permitting her to attend the proceedings as an "*intervener*."

While a husband was entitled to a divorce if his wife committed adultery, a wife had to jump through hoops. Besides adultery, a husband had to commit incestuous adultery, bigamy, rape, sodomy, bestiality, adultery coupled with cruelty, or adultery coupled with desertion without reasonable excuse for two years or more. Incestuous adultery was adultery with a woman within the prohibited degrees (sister, grandmother, mother-in-law, etc).

Furthermore, a wife would not be granted a degree of divorce on the grounds of cruelty and adultery, unless the cruelty consisted of bodily hurt or injury to health, and at least two acts of cruelty on the party of the husband were required. Thankfully (in this instance at least), the communication of venereal disease when the husband knew of his condition was considered an act of cruelty.

Barring *condonation* (where a matrimonial offense, which was a sufficient cause for divorce, was condoned or forgiven by the spouse aggrieved), *connivance* (where the adultery complained of was committed by the connivance or active consent of the petitioner) or *collusion* (the illegal agreement and co-operation between the petitioner and the respondent in a divorce action to obtain a judicial dissolution of the marriage), the couple was on its way to receiving a *decree nisi*. If, after six months, it was unaffected by any intervention by the King's Proctor or any other person it could be made *decree absolute* upon proper application.

For the gentleman or lady who desired lose an undesirable spouse, there was no greater a solicitor than Sir George Lewis of Ely Place, Holburn. Described by contemporary portraits as a "pleasant-voiced, white-haired, dapper little man" who was the "depository of so many scandalous secrets," it was he who helped society's brightest extricate themselves from sticky situations–such as the time when Lady Charles Beresford attempted to blackmail the Countess of Warwick into breaking off her relations with Lord Charles, and Lady Warwick brought in the Prince of Wales to back her up.

The divorce court itself was a source of entertainment. On almost any day, particularly if a scandalous case was being tried, a line some fifty or sixty people deep, made mostly of women, queued up at Royal Courts of Justice the for a seat in the public gallery. This was a considerable annoyance to junior barristers, who, especially when an aristocratic trial brought a crush, were perpetually unable to find a sufficient number of seats.

Despite collusion nullifying a petition for divorce, it was a standard procedure for couples who just couldn't stand one another. To spare the wife even greater scandal, she would hire a private detective to follow her husband on an appointed night, the husband himself having hired a lady to impersonate his lover, and there would be proof of adultery. On the other hand, a wife could publicly refuse to share her husband's bed, and he could sue for divorce based on her repudiation of his conjugal rights. If divorce was unobtainable, a couple could petition for a legal separation, which was easier to receive, but the prospect of a future divorce was made a bit more difficult.

The most difficult part of an English divorce were the children. Unlike in France or America, where children of divorced parents lost nothing and were at liberty to watch over their bringing-up, according to English law, a guilty mother was entirely deprived of their custody and even access (however, it *was* allowed for a faithless father). Under no circumstances, if the mother was found guilty, would she have custody of the children regardless of their ages. In divorce, the guilty woman lost everything: income, custody and access to children, reputation, and even in some cases her husband's name.

Bibliography

Campbell, Lady Colin. *Etiquette of Good Society*. London: Cassell, 1893.

Fenn, Henry Edwin. *Thirty-five Years in the Divorce Court*. Boston: Little, Brown & Co., 1911.

Flanders, Judith. *Inside the Victorian Home: A Portrait of Domestic Life in Victorian England*. New York: W. W. Norton &, 2003.

Gibbs, Philip. *The Eighth Year: A Vital Problem of Married Life*. New York: Devin-Adair, 1913.

Gosling, Lucinda. *Debutantes and the London Season*. Oxford: Shire, 2013.

Harland, Marion, and Virginia Van De Water. *Everyday Etiquette*. Indianapolis: Bobbs-Merrill Co., 1905.

Harris, Janice Hubbard. *Edwardian Stories of Divorce*. New Brunswick, NJ: Rutgers UP, 1996.

Kingsland, Florence. *The Book of Weddings; a Complete Manual of Good Form in All Matters Connected with the Marriage Ceremony*. New York: Doubleday, Page & Co., 1902.

Randall, Rona. *The Model Wife: Nineteenth-century Style*. London: Herbert, 1989.

Ringrose, Hyacinthe. *Marriage and Divorce Laws of the World*. London: Musson-Draper, 1911.

Sherwood, Mrs. John. *Manners and Social Usages*. New York: Harper & Bros., 1912.

Sproule, Anna. *The Social Calendar*. Poole, Dorset: Blandford, 1978.

Wood, Edward J., and Carrie Chapman Catt. *The Wedding Day in All Ages and Countries*. New York: Harper & Bros., 1869.

Amusement

Country Society

The country house and its society was taken very seriously by the British. Unlike their Continental counterparts, whose society adhered closely to the movements of the court or remained in major cities, the British long acknowledged the countryside as the backbone of the country. The Englishman actually preferred to live in the country, finding on his land a range of sporting activities and like-minded tenants and neighbors; his home was his country seat no matter how much time he spent in London or abroad.

According to T.H.S. Escott, the country house as a social entity first appeared during the time of Chaucer, and cemented its purpose as a center of social and political life by the time of the Tudors. By the Edwardian era, the country and the country house had begun to lose a bit of its importance, but anyone and everyone within Society knew the quickest way to establish roots and display one's wealth was to buy a country estate and a few acres, and regularly host house parties.

The years between 1861 and 1914 were considered the "golden age" of country house entertaining. Country house parties existed prior to this time, as seen in Lord Byron's poem "A Country House Party," where he described "[t]he politicians, in a nook apart, Discuss'd the world, and settled all the spheres;" but never before was it undertaken in such militaristic order. During this golden age, the house party was it considered a vital part of the year-long social season, and was an extremely expensive undertaking. It was this great expense—much of it spent entertaining the easily bored Prince of Wales—that opened the door for the entry of wealthy Anglo-Jewish families into British society.

This lavish expenditure had its casualties. Many of Bertie's closest friends bankrupted themselves in their quest to entertain him and keep up with the ultra-wealthy Anglo-Jews and Americans who hosted vied for social prominence. These casualties included Bertie's "court jester" Sir Christopher Sykes (his sister-in-law had to buttonhole Bertie to get him to pay Sir Christopher's debts), the rakish horse racing enthusiast Harry Chaplin (who had to sell his estates and his possessions), and former mistress Daisy, Countess of Warwick (who threatened

George V with the publication of Bertie's love letters to her in order to keep bankruptcy at bay). But while the fun lasted, boy did they have it! House parties sometimes lasted a week, but they were typically held from Saturday to Monday (hence the name "Saturday-to-Monday," since the phrase "week-end" was considered a vulgar Americanism), and each day was packed with activities.

Many house parties were held during the Season at the recesses in Parliament, but August and September were the months earmarked for country house parties, as this was the height of the shooting season. August was the time for family parties, and many houses focused around cricket or tennis matches. The first week of September, harvest permitting, was when the crack guns appeared. Etiquette required different form for small shooting parties, large shooting parties, parties to which royalty was invited, and shooting parties held for intimates or relations, but all types lasted three days.

Many etiquette books of the time stressed that the success of the house party mainly depended upon people knowing one another—this was important for the men out in the field with the guns, and of particular importance to the ladies, who were expected to amuse themselves while the men went out shooting. Most people visited the same houses year after year, and if there was an awkward gap between the ending of one house party and the beginning of another, a relative or intimate of the hostess was permitted to remain until departure–the unknown, however, was advised to leave and remain in town until it was time to depart.

Shooting was considered very important to Edwardian men. Landowners vied with one another to produce the biggest "bags" each year, and the numbers increased by leaps and bounds. At the home of the Earl of Pembroke, three days produced 1,236 head, 1,142 head, and 2,276 head, respectively, and this was thought normal. This competitive streak led to the most infamous shoot in 1913 at Hall Barn, a Buckinghamshire estate owned by Lord Burnham, of 3,937 pheasants—which led to even King George V remarking "perhaps we overdid it today." Against the boom of guns, ladies usually scribbled letters, a practice of much amusement to foreigners who could not imagine how busy an

Englishwoman's life was, creating the need for correspondence on political, social and household topics.

Besides sport, food was one another preoccupation of a country house party. Guests were free to arrive at breakfast when they so chose, but the proper hour was usually between nine and half past ten. Far from the simple repast enjoyed at the beginning of the nineteenth century, Edwardian guests would feast on fruits, eggs, potted meats, fish, toast, rolls, tea cakes, muffins, hams, tongues, pies, kidney, fried bacon and were given tea, coffee, hot cocoa, and juices to drink. The sportsman's breakfast was even more substantial, including game pie, cold beef, deviled turkey, broiled ham, kippered haddock, collared eels, spiced beef, shrimp, cold fowl, curried eggs, toasted mushrooms and broiled mackerel among other things, and though tea and coffee were taken, a tankard of beer or a cherry brandy were the drink of choice.

Luncheon was included at some houses, though many remained old-fashioned and stuck to the meal times of breakfast, dinner and supper. Luncheons were both formal—with everyone seated by rank—and informal—the gentlemen served the ladies and sometimes children were invited down. The dishes served were a little fancier though similar to breakfast, and beverages included claret, sherry and a light beer. Dinners were more formal, and suppers were the typical sumptuous, formal affairs. Afternoon tea was a given, of course.

Indoor amusements such as word games, charades and practical jokes were the norm, but a passion for gambling overtook the fast set during the 1880s. Baccarat was the initial game of choice and no hostess threw a country house party without a baccarat game. The Prince of Wales was a particular fan of this illegal card game, and until the scandal at Tranby Croft, he carried his own set of counters on his person at all times in case of an impromptu hand. Because of the publicity, society abandoned baccarat, and just as quickly as that went out, bridge came in.

The craze for bridge swept women in particular, and during the early 1900s, the conversation of the most obsessed centered around bridge, bridge, bridge! Ladies were known to play hands in between eating, before going to bed, and would neglect dancing in favor of sitting down for a game in a drawing room. The founding of ladies' clubs in the mold of gentlemen's clubs fostered this obsession, for now women would give the same excuse as their husbands as to why they were late to supper and had to hurry into their evening dress.

However, the most engrossing activity of the country house party was sex. Love affairs were the tune of the day, and once a gentleman and a lady had made it known to their hostess that they wished to consummate their attraction to one another, the hostess knew she'd better arrange room assignments to facilitate this. An Edwardian love affair was not an instantaneous matter. The couple in question might spend a few months, or even a few years expressing their affection to one another through letters, and with the amount of clothing involved and the presence of observant servants, getting into bed with one another was not an easy deal—even at a neatly arranged country house party.

Anita Leslie tells the story of Lord Charles Beresford who, groping in the dark for his lady love's bedroom, pushed open the door and leaped into the bed with a "cock-a-doodle-doo!" only to discover he'd slipped between an Archbishop and his wife. Another embarrassing story is that of a hungry guest who wandered through the halls in search of a bite to eat and found a plate of sandwiches on the floor in front of a bedroom door. He satisfied his hunger, ignorant of the intentions meant by the plate and the gentleman hoping for a "yes" from the lady was left disappointed by the tray's barren surface.

More innocently (or perhaps not), the house party was the last hurrah of that season's marriage mart. Mama's who hadn't caught a suitable gentleman for their daughter that season could count on a house party and its sympathetic hostess to bring the girl in contact with the man of her or her parent's choice. Activities such as picnics, walks, riding, croquet, billiards and lawn tennis could show off the young lady at her best angle and prove to the gentleman her intelligence and worthiness of being his bride. Another important use for the country party was its original purpose: politics. The Souls, a social and political clique centered around Taplow Court, the home of Lord and Lady Desboroughs, and Stanway House (the Earls of Wemyss). Nancy Astor's home at Cliveden formed the setting for a band of Boer War veterans and Pro-Rhodesian Imperialists known as Milner's Kindergarten. Arthur Balfour, Prime Minister from 1902 to 1905, and a member of

The Souls, was a prodigious golfer, and his intense interest in this Scottish sport led to its adoption by hostesses as part of the country house program.

So important was the country house that even royalty took part. After extensive renovation in the 1850s and 60s, the Prince of Wales and his family hosted many an important party at Sandringham House in Norfolk. Here, the clocks were set forward half an hour—not to accommodate the Princess of Wales's habitual tardiness as many memoirs claim, but to allow more time for shooting. Because of this, that half-hour ahead was known as "Sandringham Time." The motor car made it easier to get to country house parties, and newspaper reports of the 1910s bemoaned the emptiness of London due to the dash of society to the country every Friday evening in their motors. Though the Great War further decimated the political importance of the country house, it remained and has remained a symbol of social and political influence in British society.

Country House Etiquette
According to the etiquette column in the *Every Woman's Encyclopaedia*, a typical invitation to a house party is as follows:

> "My dear Mrs. Whyte, – Can you and Mr. Whyte spare us a few days next month? We should be so pleased if you could come to us on Monday, the 17th, and remain till the 24th. The Hunt Ball comes off on the 19th, and I know you are fond of dancing. Hoping you can come, and with kind regards to you both, believe me, very truly yours, – Constance Greene."

The reply should not be delayed too long. The mistress of a country house has to plan out her relays of guests and fit in her friends so that all those she is anxious to have shall be included. Therefore, a delay in answering is not common politeness. In sending an acceptance it is usual, and convenient, to mention not only the day of arrival, but also the date of departure, that suggested in the invitation. This prevents any misconception on the point, such as arises occasionally from indistinct writing, the similarity between the figures 3 and 5, 7 and 9, etc.

If a refusal is sent, the regret expressed should be all for oneself, and a good reason should be given. A prior engagement is the usual one. It covers everything, and is therefore adequate. An inadequate excuse is a rudeness. It shows so clearly that the writer is declining for the simple reason that she Would rather stay away, and has trumped up some futile excuse for want of a real one.

In writing to accept any invitation the present tense, not the future, should be used.
It gives me great pleasure to accept," not "It Will give me." Acceptance is done in the present, though the visit itself is in the future.

On receiving an acceptance the hostess Writes again, expressing her pleasure at the news that her friends are coming, and giving them information about the trains, saying that the visitors will be met at whatever hour they may decide to arrive at the station. In wealthy circles, where many travel in their own motor, the capacity of the garage is referred to as adequate, or otherwise, to the accommodation of another.

For instance:
"There will be room for your car between the dates mentioned, as the Greys leave us on the 16th, taking theirs with them."

A supply of notepaper bearing the address of the house, of blotting-paper, ink, pens, pencils, stamps, and telegram forms should be provided on a table in the bedroom.
Plans for the day were usually discussed at breakfast, and unlike during the Victorian era, the guests made their own plans for amusement.

Tips

The butler will expect a sovereign for a few days' visit. If there have been many motor-car rides, the chauffeur will expect from half a sovereign upwards. If he only meets the guest at the station and drives him back to it, five shillings or three half-crowns will do. This, too, will meet the case of a woman visitor.

For a week-end visit she will give five shillings to the maid who looks after her room, half a crown to the footman or parlourmaid who carries down her luggage when she is leaving, and a similar amount to the coachman who drives her to the station. A chauffeur will expect more. If her luggage is sent on some other vehicle, she will find the driver of it waiting to be remembered.

For longer visits the tips would be in proportion to the length. A girl is not expected to give such liberal tips as her married friends. Married couples pay their tips separately, the man giving something to the butler, his wife to the parlourmaid and housemaid, sometimes to the housekeeper if she has to avail herself of her services in any way. Should a man-servant have valeted the husband, the latter should give him a tip.

At the conclusion of a ten-days' visit to a house where there is no shooting, the money spent on tips sometimes amounts to five pounds.

Dinners and Dining

Nothing preoccupied the mind of an Edwardian hostess so much as the planning of a dinner party. From matters of food and drink, table service, the guest list, and matters of precedence, every detail was of the utmost importance. A dinner of tepid or cold food, of dull guests, and of seating arrangements that did not take the rank and form of each guest into account could doom a lady's social aspirations in one evening.

Since dinner giving was the most important of all social observances, gentlemen and their wives held them much more frequently than balls or other social occasions; a dinner was considered more intimate, and invitations were sent to those one was intimate with or with those the host and hostess hoped to become *intimé*. In the greater scheme of the inner workings of society, a dinner party was both a test of the hostess's position and the direct road to obtaining a recognized place in society.

When issuing invitations to a large dinner party, it was customary for the hostess to give three weeks' notice, though, by the 1910s, the notice was extended to four to six weeks in advance. This permitted sufficient time for the guests to bow out in case of an emergency–though the acceptance of the invitation was socially binding. Invitations could be purchased at stationary shops, and were blank save for lines where the hostess or her social secretary would fill in the names of the guests, the date, and the time of the dinner. These were sent in the name of both the host and hostess as following:

The dinner hour was approximately eight to nine, and guests were expected to appear at least fifteen minutes prior to the time listed on the invitation. The long, slow, and heavy meals of the mid-nineteenth century had disappeared by the Edwardian era: now hostesses preferred their dinner parties swift and filling (though this was taken to the extreme by Gilded Age hostess Mrs. Stuyvesant Fish, who would hurry her guests through eight or nine courses in forty minutes), most likely to make time for evening entertainments.

On arrival, ladies and gentlemen would take off their cloaks in the cloakroom or leave them in the hall with the servant before entering the drawing-room, where the host and hostess awaited them. The vogue for pre-dinner cocktails was strictly an American custom until about 1910, and once the host and hostess greeted each guest, the ladies sat and the men stood, chatting lightly until the last guest had arrived. If any parties were unacquainted, the hostess would introduce the guests of the highest rank to one another. At very large dinner parties, however, the butler was stationed on the staircase and announced the guests as they arrived, and no introductions were required.

According to Arnold Palmer's *Moveable Feasts: Changes in English Eating Habits*, the custom of pairing off to go in for dinner did not begin until early in the reign of William IV, and this was refined throughout the nineteenth century until it morphed into its usual form: The host would take the lady of the highest rank present in to the dinner, and the gentleman of the highest rank took in the hostess. This rule was absolute, unless the highest ranking male and female were related to the host or hostess, in which case his or her rank would be in abeyance, out of courtesy to the other guests.

Another don't was for a husband and wife, father and daughter, or mother and son, to be sent in to dinner together. The hostess was advised to invite an equal number of men and women, though it was usual to invite two or more gentlemen than there were ladies, so that married ladies would not be obligated to go in to dinner with each others' husbands only. Should the numbers be skewed, if there were more women than men, the ladies of highest rank would be taken into dinner by the gentlemen present, and the remaining ladies followed by themselves. In there were more men than women, the hostess would go in to dinner by herself, following the last couple. Prior to entering the dining room, the hostess would inform each gentleman whom he would take in to dinner.

The host remained standing until the guests had taken their seats, and he motioned to each couple where he wished them to sit. When the host did not indicate where the guests were to sit, precedence took over, and each lady and gentleman sat near the host or hostess according to their rank. The host and the lady he took in to dinner sat at the bottom of the table, she sitting at his right hand. The hostess sat at the top of the table, and the gentleman who brought her in to dinner sat at her left. According to precedence, the lady second in rank sat at the host's left hand, and the other female guests sat at the right of the gentleman who took her in to dinner. Place cards with the names of each guest were used at large dinner parties, and in some instances, the name of each guest was printed on a menu and placed in front of each cover. The menus themselves were placed along the table, each viewable by one or two persons. These menus could be simple or elaborate, depending on the hostess's tastes, and the dishes available in each course were written in French.

For table decoration, there were a number of variations available, though they were largely a matter of taste than of etiquette. The basic table setting was of a mixture of high and low center pieces, low specimen glasses placed the length of the table, and trails of creepers and flowers laid on the tablecloth. The fruit to be eaten for dessert was usually arranged down the center of the table, amidst the flowers and plate. Some dinner tables were decorated with a variety of French conceits (centerpieces), whilst others were sparse, save for the flowers and the plate. Lighting was an important feature, and though electric lights were in vogue when possible, it was not uncommon to dine by old-fashioned lamps and wax candles. Accompanying the decorations and lighting was the "cover," which was the place lain at the table for each person, and consisted of a spoon for soup, a fish knife and fork, two knives, two large forks, and glasses for the wines being served.

Dinner-table etiquette was strict—an uneducated or uncouth person who appeared innocuous enough, would reveal his or her inexperience in a finer milieu by displaying such shocking customs as eating off a knife, or tucking a napkin into the collar of their shirt. When a lady took her seat at the dinner table, she removed her gloves at once, though were long gloves, they were usually made to allow the glove to be unbuttoned around the thumb and peeled back from the wrists. Both ladies and gentlemen would unfold their serviettes and place them in their laps.

Soups were, of course, eaten with a soup spoon, though one spooned away from themselves and never ever slurped. Fish was eaten with the fish knife and fork, and all made dishes (quenelles, rissoles, patties, etc) were eaten with a fork only. Poultry, game, etc were eaten with a knife and fork, as was asparagus and salads. Peas, the test of true breeding, were eaten with a fork. In eating game or poultry, the bone of either wing or leg was not touched with the fingers; the meat was cut from the bone with the knife. Jellies, blancmanges, ice puddings, and practically any substantial sweet, were eaten with a fork. Cheese was eaten daintily, with small morsels placed with the knife on small morsels of bread, and the two conveyed to the mouth with the thumb and finger. When eating grapes, cherries, or other pitted fruits, they were brought to the mouth, whereupon the pits and skins were spit discreetly into the hand to be placed on the side of the plate.

Dessert was served to the guests in the order in which dinner was served. When the guests had helped themselves to the wine and the servants had vacated the dining room, the host would hand the decanters around the table, starting with the gentleman nearest him, as ladies were not supposed to require a second glass of wine during dessert. If she required a second glass, the gentleman seated beside her would fill the glass–she would definitely not help herself to the wine. Ten minutes or so after the wine had been passed once around the table, the hostess gave a signal for the ladies to leave the dining room by bowing to the lady of the highest rank present.

The gentlemen rose when the ladies did, and the women quit the dining room in the order of their rank, the hostess following last. The gentlemen were left to their port and claret, while the ladies retired to the drawing room for coffee. While the ladies drank their coffee, a servant took the coffee to the gentlemen, and after a few more rounds of wine and the cigarettes and cigars were smoked, they joined the ladies. This custom, however, shortened by 1910 or so, and at times, the practice of ladies and gentlemen separating after dinner was abandoned by smarter hostesses.

Dinner ended in town about half an hour after the gentlemen joined the ladies in the drawing room. In the country, it was common to begin games or play cards into the wee hours of the night. There was no etiquette for leave-taking, and after the host and hostess saw each guest into his or her or their carriages, their duties were done for the night.

Sample menu from *Mrs. Beeton's Book of Household* Management (1907 edition)

MENU FOR BALL SUPPERS. Winter.
(Fr. *Souper de Bal.*)
FRENCH. ENGLISH.

Plats Chauds. Hot Dishes.
Consommé Clair. Clear Soup.
Homard à la Diable. Devilled Lobster.
Pigeon sauté en Casserole. Pigeons stewed in Casserole.

Plats Froids. Cold Dishes.
Petits Pates aux Huîtres. Oyster Patties.
Filets de Sole en Aspic. Fillets of Sole in Aspic.
Mayonnaise de Homard. Lobster Mayonnaise.

Chaudfroid de Perdreaux. Partridges masked with Sauce.
Pate de Gibier à l'Anglaise. Game Pie.

Galantine de Dinde. Galantine of Turkey.
Faisan rôti. Roast Pheasants.
Boeuf pressé. Pressed Beef.
Supreme de Volaille. Chicken Creams.

Sandwiches assorties. Sandwiches.
Salade de Saison. Salad.

Chartreuse d'Oranges. Oranges in Jelly.
Crème aux Amandes. Almond Cream.
Charlotte Russe. Russian Charlotte.
Compote de Poires à la Chantilly. Stewed Pears and Cream.
Meringues à la Creme Vanillée. Meringues with Vanilla Cream.
Patisserie. French Pastry.
Glace Napolitaine. Neapolitan Ice.
Glace Crème d'Ananas. Pineapple Ice.

Dinner Service

Service à la française, whereby separate courses were created rather than two or three courses, where everything alike was lumped together, took hold of the gustatory habits of the wealthy at the turn of the 19th century. This imposed new rules on the order in which food was to be served.

The theories of Antonin Carême and Brillat-Savarin expressed the idea that the foods' relationships to one another were an important element of the dining experience, and both believed food should be served in this order: soup, fish, meat, game, sweets and fruits, and the side dishes were to complement these main items.

This method was better than the previous methods of serving dinners, but it was difficult to keep the dishes hot by the time they reached the table from the far-away kitchen. Because of this, *service à la française* was rendered impractical, making room for *service à la russe*, or service in the Russian style, which was brought to France in 1811 by the Russian ambassador.

However, this style of service did not catch on in England until the 1860s and 1870s, where the English style of service (where all the food belonging to one course was placed in suitable dishes before the host/ess and was served from the table) was more prevalent. With the Russian style of service, there was greater emphasis on the presentation of both meals and place settings. With this new emphasis on table setting, as with the influx of the newly rich knocking at the doors of the upper classes giving rise to etiquette books, *service à la russe* created a set of rigid, correct rules for cutlery, china and table adornments.

The table now cleared of food, table setting blended four elements of design: central decorations, flowers, color, and mirrors. Central decoration usually consisted of epergnes or plateaus, the latter of which was a raised mirror, often with silver or gilt decorations on the raised sides, while the former was a tall stand with hanging arms that held either baskets of sweets, or platforms that held glasses containing sweets. The custom of placing flowers on the dining table began in the early 19th century, but by the turn of the 20th century, the use of a heavy candelabra and elevated dishes alternating with low dishes took hold. Large masses of flowers covered the table, nearly crowding out the place settings, and the individual places were often delineated by strands of ivy or other flowers strung between each cover. Color was important to the early- and mid-Victorians, and colored table runners, color glasses such as green hock glasses or ruby-colored wine glasses, added a deep splash of color against the already crowded table.

Added to this were mirrors, which generally reflected peaceful scenes if a mirrored plateau with figures was not being used. The Edwardian era saw a streamlined table setting, where the table was cleared of the masses of flowers and other accouterments in favor of a simple arrangement of candelabra, bowls of fruit and flower arrangements set one after the other along the length of the table. Now, instead of candles, small lamps, shaded by delicate lampshades, cast an intimate glow across the dining table and its diners.

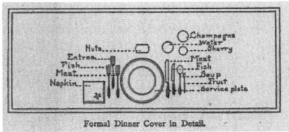

Formal Dinner Cover in Detail.

Beneath the table decorations lay the more important articles of gastronomy: the tablecloth, the dishes, and the silverware. Maids setting the table for dinner were instructed to first lay the silence cloth (of double-faced cotton flannel, knitted table padding, or an asbestos pad) upon the table, then to lay the covers, allowing 24-30 inches from plate to plate.

If the table was bare, the covers were marked by plate doilies. A service plate was then laid for each person, one inch from the edge of the table, and this plate remained upon the table until it was necessary to replace it with a hot plate. The silver placed in the order which it was to be used, beginning at the outside and using toward the plate. Silver for the dessert course was never put on with the silver required for other courses, except for the dinner that was served without a maid. Neither was the table set with more than three forks. If more were required, they were placed with their respective courses. The salad or dessert silver was brought either in on the plate, or placed beside a napkin or tray at the right, from the right, after the plate is placed. The knife or knives were placed at the right of the plate, half an inch from the edge of the table, with the cutting edge toward the plate.

Spoons, with bowls facing up, were placed at the right of the knife, and forks, with the tines turned upward, at the left of the plate. The spoon for fruit or the small fork for oysters or hors d'œuvre was placed at the extreme right or on the plate containing the course and the napkin was at the left of the forks, and the hem and selvage was required to parallel with the forks and the edge of the table. The water glass was placed at the point of the knife, the bread-and-butter plate above the service plate, and the butter spreader across the upper, right-hand side of the bread-and-butter plate. Salt and pepper sets were placed between each two covers.

During the heyday of *service à la française*, the sideboard was used to hold all extras required during the service of the meal. The serving table took its place when the French service was replaced by the Russian, and the sideboard was used for decorative purposes only, usually holding choice pieces of silver.

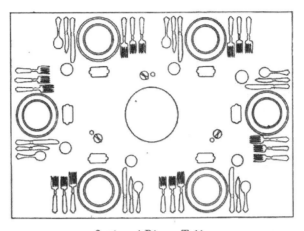

Setting of Dinner Table

Besides this new emphasis on table setting, the most important and enduring development derived from *service à la russe* was the matching of dishes to wines. Before, diners would eat and drink wines to their own tastes, but the Russian service, with its sparser table, made it logical to serve a particular wine with each course. Due to this new protocol of complimentary food and wine, the types of and numbers of wine glasses the diner had to negotiate grew. Now the opening oyster course was to be eaten accompanied by Chablis, the soup and also the hot hors d'œuvre with sherry, fish with hock, removes and entrees with champagne, the meat with burgundy, game with claret, and dessert with port, Tokay, or other fine wines.

Garden Parties

Garden parties were the easiest and most informal manner of entertaining. As part of the duty owed the county, it was expected that at least once a year, preferable in August or September, the beautiful grounds of the lord of the manor were opened for guests to roam about the park, row on the lake, play lawn tennis on the lawn, to wander through the winding paths, to admire the gardens, and saunter through the conservatories. If the sun were too strong, the reception rooms were opened for these guests, allowing them respite from the heat in the cool and elegant interiors of a castle or palace or house mostly closed off to strangers.

Invitations to a garden party were issued in the name of the hostess, and sent three weeks to a week in advance of the date. Rather than formal invitation cards, "At Home" cards were used, with the words "Tennis" or "Croquet" printed in the corner, with the date of the party written beneath the hostess's name, and the time above it. The arrangements for a garden party included a good supply of garden-chairs and seats placed on the lawn and about the grounds, rugs spread on the grass for sitting, and several sets of croquet provided for players. At large garden-parties, a band was necessary, and the band of the regiment quartered in the vicinity was frequently borrowed for the occasion.

A typical garden party began at four, and unless dancing was specified, the party ended around seven or eight o'clock in the evening. When the guests arrived, they were conducted to the garden, where the hostess stood near the entrance or a tent, to receive her guests. The host or son of the house had a duty to starting tennis or croquet on the lawn, arranging the sets, scrounging up players, and directing the game. Cricket matches and golf were also popular amusements, but usually undertaken only if large fields or links were nearby. Since garden parties were open to guests from eight to eighty, the content of amusements varied from the aforementioned sports, to Punch-and-Judy for the children, impromptu musical performances in the drawing room or music room, to archery matches, and beyond.

Sometimes garden parties were combined with bazaars, flower shows, or public afternoon parties, but this was not common. Since the gathering was both informal and athletic in nature, afternoon dress was advised, and for ladies, the more delicate-looking gown, the better! At sunset guests adjourned to the house for a substantial supper, after which they drive home. If a dance ended the party, it was done under moonlight on the lawn, or in one of the tents, and the garden and grounds were sometimes illuminated by Chinese lanterns and small coloured lamps hung in festoons from the trees, which made the evening scene as "picturesque as that of the morning."

Balls
From Lady Colin Campbell in her *Etiquette of Good Society* (1893 edition)

The first thing to be considered before deciding to give a private ball is whether you have rooms enough, and whether they are fitted for the purpose. In order to have your arrangements complete, six or seven rooms at least should be set apart for this festivity—two cloak-rooms, tea and refreshment room, drawing-room for the reception, ball-room, card and supper rooms. Card tables can be placed in the drawing-room when a separate room for their use is not available.

For the dance to be perfect, everything ought to be of the best— good room, good floor, good dancers, good music, and good supper; but it is impossible to compass the whole of this list in every case; therefore, the indispensables must be pointed out. We cannot alter the size and shape of our rooms, but one must be chosen as large as possible, and nearly square if possible, for a long narrow room is fatal to dancing; nor can we lay our floors afresh, but we need not fatigue our guests by obliging them to dance upon carpet. There can be no doubt that a polished floor, such as one meets with on the Continent, is the pleasantest and easiest to dance upon, but if our boards are rough ones, a brown holland covering stretched tightly over them will be a good substitute for more substantial smoothness, if properly done, and is far preferable to another device which is sometimes most unwisely resorted to—*viz.*, waxing the floor.

Good music is a sine qua non. If this be not secured—no matter whether the entertainment be what is called a "dance" or a "ball "—it will certainly be a failure. The want of it destroys all chance of enjoyment. It is impossible to dance well to bad music. "Bad music" means uneven, uncertain playing, and this is sure to be the result when amateurs attempt to play for dancers.

Then, too, it is unfair to impose such a laborious and monotonous task on your guests. If the party is to be a small one, have a proficient man or woman to play the piano; if it be a large one, then one or two instruments as well as the piano are necessary, such as violin, cornet, or harp, varied by the addition of bells and triangles.

The list of dances now in fashion is of greater length than it was some years ago. At that time the valse, the lancers, and the galop seemed to occupy the programme. The two first dances still continue to be the favourites, but others have been re-introduced:

the polka takes turn with the valse, and the quadrille sometimes takes the place of that ever-bewildering, never-to-be-remembered maze, the lancers. The coquettish cotillion, the friendly country dance, and the merry reel are frequently danced: of the two latter, the Swedish dance and the Highland schottische are chiefly chosen. Even the stately minuet, the galliards, the bransle, and the torreano, danced by courtly knights and dignified dames centuries ago, are likely to be brought forward again.

All the rooms in the house should be brilliantly lighted, for light induces gaiety and mirth. Darkness engenders silence and gloom. The illumination of the ball-room is another difficulty which besets the giver of dances, especially if the house be a country one. Gas makes a room very hot and oppressive, no doubt, but it is the easiest and most effectual mode of lighting a room, if it is available, and good ventilation can do much to remedy the evils it carries with it. Wax candles are objectionable on these occasions, because, fanned and irritated by the continual motion of the dancers, they drop their waxy tears on coat and dress, the traces of which remain for ever and a day. French lamps, placed on brackets at short distances, and high enough to be out of the way, shed the softest and most pleasing light. If the dance is of long duration, the lamps may require to be re-trimmed one by one during the course of the evening, or darkness will perchance descend upon the scene.

A broad piece of carpet should be unrolled from the hall door to the carriage steps; and where the distance between the two is great, an awning should be stretched over the passage. As the guests arrive, they are ushered into the cloakrooms. A maid should be at her post in that reserved for ladies, to give her aid in straightening dresses, arranging hair, and removing all trace of the slight disorder caused by the carriage drive. She should be armed with needle and thread to sew up the inevitable tears and rents which occur during the evening's campaign. It is also well to number hats, shawls, and cloaks, that they may be restored as quickly as possible to their owners on their departure.

The lady having put a finishing touch to her hair, and the gentleman to his tie, the two are next conducted to the tea-room. Here a table is laid out with tea and coffee, cakes and biscuits, the beverages being dispensed by a servant. After having partaken of a cup of one or other, the new arrivals emerge from this room and are then shown into the drawing-room, where the lady of the house receives her guests Dancing should begin directly there is a sufficient number of people present to make a respectable show. In quadrilles and other square dances, those couples who are at the top of the room always begin the figure.

The fashion of programmes has become almost obsolete at the best London balls, which is a pity, as they were not only pretty souvenirs of the balls of a season, but also most convenient aids to memory at the time being; for if a girl has many partners it is no easy matter for her to remember to whom she is engaged for each dance. However, the capricious goddess for the time wills it otherwise, and only at country balls are programmes still found to survive.

It is considered "bad manners" if a man fails to come and claim his partner when the dance is about to commence, or for the lady to break her promise by accepting any other partner who may have asked for the pleasure of the same dance in the interim.

If a lady declines to dance with any one who may request her, but with whom she does not wish to become acquainted, and has no plea of a former engagement to offer for her refusal, the best course to take is, not to dance that particular dance at all, and then any chance of hurting the feelings of the rejected one is avoided.

The number of times that a lady should dance with the same partner, except under special circumstances, should be limited. Never so often as either to attract observation, or to call forth remarks on the subject.

After a dance the gentleman asks his partner whether she will take any refreshment, and if she replies in the affirmative he escorts her to the room and procures her an ice, offers to hold a cup for her, and when the music for the next dance begins he conducts her to her chaperon, when she disengages herself from his arm, they bow to one another, and he leaves her. It is not customary to promenade much after a dance.

Private balls usually begin at ten p.m., and end about three a.m.; supper at one a.m.

The gentleman with whom the lady has been last dancing generally takes her in to supper.

It is necessary to bid good-night to your hostess, but you go away quietly, that your departure may not be noticed, lest it should tend to break up the party.

Dancing

Until the emergence of the waltz in the early 19th century, the minuet reigned supreme as the courtliest, most aristocratic of dances. It was stately, it was elegant, it was—most importantly— proper; only the hands of the dance partners touched, their fingers clasped ever so gently. When the Viennese waltz set a dainty foot on English ballrooms, it shocked the church and society with the prolonged bodily contact not just of the hands, but of the body. Anglican archbishops quickly denounced the waltz as a lust-inducing, decidedly degenerate action to be left to those hot-blooded, silly foreigners. Needless to say, the more forbidden the dance became the more anxious society was to engage in it—while at the same time considering it scandalous.

However, by 1816, the dance had finally reached respectability, and the waltz firmly fastened itself onto the dance schedules of balls and routs of English society for the majority of the 19th century. Society thought itself safe from unruly and scandalous dances, having only added the polka in the 1840s, and the Virginia reel, germans, and other vigorous dances which did no more harm than red faces and shortness of breath.

Then came ragtime.

By the turn of the century, the syncopated rhythms of African-Americans had slowly but surely invaded the sedate ballrooms of American society. Composers like Scott Joplin, whose Maple Leaf Ragtime made him the first mainstream black artist in American history, created a furor for ragtime and the phonograph. By the time Irving Berlin became an overnight sensation with Alexander's Ragtime Band and Everybody's Doin' It Now, ragtime music had inspired dances with amusing names like the Turkey Trot, the Grizzly Bear, and the Bunny-Hug.

Moralists, parents, and statesmen from America to Russia decried the corrupting influence of these dances on youths, but they only served to make them even more popular. However, nothing prepared the terrified older generation for the tango.

This slinky, sensual dance emerged from the fusion of Afro-Latin-American rhythms and movements. It was said the tango originated from the brothels of Argentina, where the lower classes and prostitutes of both sexes indulged in this uninhibited dance. Upon the migration of Argentineans to Europe, the dance hit mainstream first in Paris, around 1910, making its way to England and the United States by 1913. In reaction to the fluid movements of the tango, skirts suddenly slit to the knee, people began to talk of gigolos, "Tango teas" became the craze, and Latin American music began to supersede the graceful Viennese melodies of the nineteenth century.

History repeated itself once again with the vitriolic protest Pope Pius X launched against the tango. In Milan, priests thundered from the pulpits, warning congregations "not to indulge in the immoral dance; better still not even to watch it for fear of temptation." But as with the waltz, Society turned a deaf ear to the remonstrations and in fact, took to the tango (and those wild ragtime dances) with even more alacrity than with the waltz.

For many, despite the insistence that in order to be fashionable, one must do the dances, the tangos and Boston two-steps and such were too much for their sensibilities. Into the fray leaped an American couple by the names of Irene and Vernon Castle. After a stint in Paris, the Castles introduced sedate versions of the raucous dances into the parlors of America's aristocracy. They placed a firm emphasis on the health benefits and gracefulness of dancing, and as a result of their performances on Broadway, garnered the patronage of thankful matrons such as Mrs. Stuyvesant Fish and Mrs. Rhinelander. The highly-successful couple made the first dance instruction video, wrote a number of popular books on dancing, and opened a series of successful dance and nightclubs in New York before the war.

The average ball or dance stuck with waltzes, the Boston, two steps, and the Cotillion. Quadrilles were danced at State Balls and those balls at which the King and Queen were present. Lancers were occasionally danced at hunt balls.

Types of Balls
- Private Ball—held in private homes and were invitation only.

- Hunt Ball—held during the hunting season for members of the hunt and their family and friends. Usually in a shire hall and decorated with "flowers, shrubs, foxes' heads and brushes, with other trophies of sport."
- Fancy Dress Ball—costume ball. Usually themed, as with the famous ball hosted by the Duchess of Devonshire at Devonshire House, Piccadilly, in 1897. Guests were divided into four "courts" representing royal courts of the 16th, 17th, and 18th centuries. Fancy Dress Balls were also held at Covent Garden—these were considered quite racy, and ladies only attended with the accompaniment of gentlemen and wore masks to watch the goings on from the opera boxes.
- Public Ball—tickets of admission were purchased, though for the most exclusive, it was "necessary to obtain vouchers from the committees or patronesses, when held in town or at watering places." Public balls included county balls, charity balls, and subscription balls.
- Military and Naval Balls; Yeomanry and Territorial Balls—exclusive to whichever branch of the military was hosting this ball, and were by invitation only.
- County Ball—the season for these were between November and February. The composition of these balls was made up of the aristocracy residing in the country, the gentry, and members the professional classes.
- State Ball—two State Balls were given each year at Buckingham Palace, during the London Season. Invitations were issued by the Lord Chamberlain, but the King revised the list at will.
-

Other Fashionable Amusements

George Sims, editor of *Living London*, a three-volume look at Edwardian London, discusses the most fashionable amusements of the day.

"The average foreigner who visits London must indeed be of opinion that we take our pleasures sadly. The loneliness which a chance traveller must almost inevitably experience in a great city is proverbial; but if a foreigner be duly armed with letters of introduction to members of fashionable Society he will speedily discover that the pursuit of the business of pleasure is waged more industriously in London than in any other European capital.

He will find every kind of sport ready to his hand. If he is fond of polo, there are clubs where the game is played at Hurlingharn, Ranelagh, and Roehampton. The most beautiful grounds arc those of the Club House —an early Georgian building—at Ranelagh. At Ranelagh, too, there are driving competitions for ladies, horse and dog shows, balloon ascents, meets of stage coaches, and motor-car races. Automobile gymkhanas are arranged, and a band of one of the Guards regiments makes music merry or sentimental the while. Then, if you have no engagement for dinner, or are not obliged to put in an appearance at Covent Garden Opera House, you may dine in the club's new dining-room, and smoke your cigarette on the lawn afterwards what time the daylight gives place to the mysterious shadows and fragrances of an English twilight.

At Hurlingham the game of croquet flourishes exceedingly. But croquet has become an exact science—almost a duty, instead of a diversion. Yet it is a boon to the occupants of many London houses which have attached to them small gardens. A gardener who will construct a good lawn is never far to seek.

Another form of amusement, this time ostensibly for the benefit of children, is the sailing of model yachts upon the water of the Round Pond in Kensington Gardens. Embryo challengers for the America Cup direct their mimic yachts with considerable skill, although the fathers—many of them sea-dogs who have retired from the Service—stand by to assist in cases of emergency.

On a fine Sunday morning, when the clouds fly high and there is a brisk breeze blowing, there will be found a crowd of spectators admiring the expert manner in which the smartly dressed children adjust the rudders and sails of their toys so that when the craft is once adrift it shall eventually find a harbour in some part of the pond.

Private theatricals have not at present the vogue which they enjoyed at the end of the nineteenth century. This is because the tendency of the age is all for specialisation, and unless an amateur actor can really act people do not want to be bothered by sitting through a performance which is not efficient. Nevertheless, from time to time entertainments are arranged in private houses by leaders of Society which are often of astonishing excellence. Sometimes a theatrical manager is present, and finds talent of such calibre that he is emboldened to make an offer of a professional engagement. This in many cases has been accepted with successful results. The old-fashioned prejudice against acting or singing as a profession no longer exists. For sweet Charity's sake tableaux vivants are also arranged, and various funds in connection with the wants of the widows and orphans who have to suffer for the benefit of the Empire have been materially helped by those who have made a fashionable amusement a means of well-doing for others.

During the winter months Prince's Skating Rink is a favourite rendezvous at tea-time or thereabouts. The artificially manufactured ice on the rink is invariably crowded by skaters; those members who prefer to watch and wait are accommodated with chairs and tables on raised platforms which flank either side of the interior of the building. The cult of the motor-car has had a belated growth in London. The writers who foresaw that, apart from utilitarian reasons, steam or electric traction on the King's highway was a potential amusement were for a time as voices crying vainly in the wilderness. But London has become converted, and even in Hyde Park the drivers of the automobiles speed merrily on the macadam road which skirts the Row that is sacred to equestrians. Many ladies drive their own machines, whether these latter be of English, French, or American make.

As an amusement "motoring" is incomparable; the mechanism nowadays is so exact that complete control is almost absolutely assured to the driver. But the horse is still with us, despite the prophecies of the quidnuncs, and, although the equipages and horses in Hyde Park cannot compare favourably with those to be seen in the Bois de Boulogne in Paris on a fashionable afternoon, there is a certain quality of solid magnificence which is always impressive.

In the early morning, in Rotten Row on a June day, you may see a Prince of the Royal blood cantering side by side in earnest converse with a Cabinet Minister. Passing them comes a popular actor or a King's Counsel; a young stockbroker gallops along at full speed, hoping that he shall ride off the effects of a late supper at one of the Society or sporting clubs which he has left but a few hours previously.

In Regent's Park the game of hockey is very popular. There are several ladies' clubs, and pupils from fashionable boarding schools and colleges for girls can be seen playing the game with a zest only comparable with that with which a Rugby boy plays football. The sport of archery, which was almost the sole outdoor amusement indulged in by ladies towards the middle of the nineteenth century, is not so popular as it used to be. Nevertheless, the Royal Toxopholite Society holds meetings from time to time in the Royal Botanic Gardens in Regent's Park, and it is a very picturesque sight on a ladies' day to watch the fair, up-to-date Amazons drawing the bow, not at a venture, but with nice and exact precision. Some of the shooting is of exceptional merit; the colours of the targets themselves have an Imperial note, which is only fitting when one remembers what a great part the English bow has taken in the formation of our "rough island story."

Tennis—real tennis, the Royal game, as opposed to lawn tennis and its variants—still has its vogue among those who are able to afford the luxury of membership in the pleasant club, the Queen's, which is situated in Kensington. Here, watching from the gallery of the building, spectators, guarded from the fearsome effect of blows from the hard ball used by the players by an iron net, may see this glorious game played by enthusiasts in the great spacious court below.

At Queen's, too, members may play rackets—cousin-german of real tennis—if they be so inclined. Both these games, from the expensive environment which the rules demand, are solely available for the well-to-do strata of Society. Still, they form two facets in the elaborately cut diamond which may be symbolised as London's fashionable amusements.

Lawn tennis is played in the gardens of houses of the more outlying districts, and wherever space permits. Of indoor games billiards still must be accorded a certain standard of authority.

Most large houses contain a billiard room, and nearly all clubs. Fashionable Londoners are whimsical in their adherence to any particular game, and for the moment billiards is somewhat neglected. Nevertheless, every evening you shall see hotly contested games in club or mansion.

In a few houses the billiard table has been sacrificed to a game which bears the sufficiently inane title of "ping-pong." This is practically lawn tennis played upon a table with a wooden or parchment racket and celluloid balls. It was invented by an Army officer who thought it would be an amusing toy; but the toy soon became a tyrant.

"Ping-pong" took the suburbs by storm, and finally even laid successful siege to Belgravia. But the wild enthusiasm with which the game was first greeted cooled after a time, for—as you will notice if you are interested in games—over-proficiency of the few destroys the zeal of the average or amateur many.

Lastly, we come to the all-pervading tyranny of "bridge." This game, which is a form of whist, has (to use a dear old journalistic phrase) shaken Society to its very foundations. Man, who plays it, cannot resist its fascinations; but Heaven knows the havoc it has wrought among us! This is the average day in the life of a Society woman. At noon a few friends arrive for luncheon—ostensibly. Select parties play bridge until two o'clock, when luncheon is actually served. Bridge again from four to six. Then a drive in the Park, followed by dinner, and—bridge until the small hours of the morning. As a natural corollary—since games of cards are rarely played unless the element of gambling in actual specie enters into the matter—the results of this mania will be apparent to everybody. At clubs the card rooms are filled with quartettes of gamblers; nominal points are exacted by the committees, but this is a matter which is easily evaded by very obvious subterfuge.

For the rest, fashionable London has concerts, theatres, cricket matches, balls and cotillons, and many other of the rare shows of civilisation. The restless, soul-harassing pursuit of pleasure goes merrily apace— or tragically, which you will. The matter is interesting when one realises how limited fashionable amusements were a hundred years ago. Who shall say what they will be a hundred years hence?"

Bibliography

A Member of the Aristocracy. *Manners and Rules of Good Society; Or, Solecisms to Be Avoided.* London: F. Warne, 1911.

Allen, Lucy Grace. *Table Service.* Boston: Little, Brown, 1940.

Barstow, Phyllida. *The English Country House Party.* Wellingborough: Equation, 1989.

Campbell, Lady Colin. *Etiquette of Good Society.* London: Cassell and Limited London Paris & Melbourne, 1893.

Escott, T. H. S. *Society in the Country House.* London: T.F. Unwin, 1907.

Ferrer, Horacio Arturo. *The Golden Age of Tango: An Illustrated Compendium of Its History.* Buenos Aires: Manrique Zago, 1996.

Golden, Eve. *Vernon and Irene Castle's Ragtime Revolution.* Lexington, KY: University of Kentucky, 2007.

Hall, Florence Howe. *The Correct Thing in Good Society.* Boston: D. Estes & Co., 1902.

Hill, Janet McKenzie. *The Up-to-date Waitress,.* Boston: Little, Brown, 1922.

Leslie, Anita. *The Marlborough House Set.* New York, NY: Doubleday, 1973.

Murphy, Claudia Quigley. *The History of the Art of Tablesetting, Ancient and Modern, from Anglo-Saxon Days to the Present Time.* New York: De Vinne, 1921.

Schollander, Wendell, and Wes Schollander. *Forgotten Elegance: The Art, Artifacts, and Peculiar History of Victorian and Edwardian Entertaining in America.* Westport, CT: Greenwood, 2002.

Waldo, Terry. *This Is Ragtime.* New York: Hawthorn, 1976.

Wallace, Carol McD. *Dance: A Very Social History.* New York: Metropolitan Museum of Art, 1986.

Church and Religion

Though church attendance and religious observation remained firmly affixed in the everyday lives of most Edwardians, the Church of England itself grappled with the growing disbelief and its seeming irrelevance in the face of modern life. The Church of England also had to deal with the rising numbers of non-Anglicans, as well as the fight for Welsh Disestablishment, which sought the creation of the Church of Wales.

Three Schools
In the late 17th century, the Church of England found its members separated into three "schools" of thought in regards to worship practices, hierarchical structure, and theology.
- High Church: considered "Anglo-Catholicism," where the structure and ritual of Anglicanism was prized. The most conservative of Anglicans.
- Low Church: "Evangelicals," where the personal spiritual journey was prized.
- Broad Church: where the truths of religion were sought to be coordinated with the certain results of science. The most secular of Anglicans.

The Church Handy Dictionary provides a glossary for the Church of England:

Church of England
The Established Church in England is governed by 2 Archbishops and 31 Bishops. Besides these, there are 4 Suffragan (which see) Bishops (Dover, Bedford, Nottingham, and Colchester). There are also 22 retired Colonial Bishops in England. Four new Bishoprics have recently been created, and two more are in course of formation. As assistants to the Bishops there are 82 Archdeacons, and 613 Rural Deans. There about 13,500 benefices in England, and about 23,000 clergymen of every class. The Church sittings number about 6,200,000.

Primate

A "Primate" is the highest in rank in a National Church. The Archbishop of Canterbury is Primate of all England, but is without power in the province of York. The Archbishop of York is Primate of England.

Three Orders of the Church of England

- Bishops: from Greek word *episcopos*, meaning "Overseer." A bishop must be not less than 30 years old, a Priest 24, and a deacon 23, unless dispensed by a faculty from the Archbishop of Canterbury.
- Priests: from a corruption of *Presbyter* (which see). Priests, like bishops, have the power to absolve, to consecrate, and to bless, but not to ordain.
- Deacons: derived from the Greek, and means a minister. Only the assistant of the Priest and may only perform certain spiritual duties--the rubrics of the Prayer Book direct certain parties of the Service to be taken by the "Priest" while the rest is left to the "Minister."

Qualifications for Orders

The papers generally necessary for Deacon's orders are the following—

1. Certificate of Baptism, or a declaration by some competent witness that the candidate has completed his 23rd year and has been baptized.
2. Graduates of Cambridge must have passed either the Special Theological, or the Preliminary Examination for Holy Orders; Graduates of Oxford must produce Certificates that they have attended two courses of Lectures by Divinity Professors. Durham men must be either B.A. or L.Th. Dublin men must be B.A., and hold also the Divinity Testimonial.
3. College Testimonials.
4. The "Si quis," a notice read in the Church of the place where the candidate resides, to give opportunity for raising objections, something like the asking of Banns.
5. Letters Testimonial for three years, or for the time elapsed since the Candidate left College. This Testimonial must be subscribed by three beneficed clergymen.
6. A Title, or nomination to a Curacy.

For Priest's Orders, the Candidate requires 4, 5, and 6, as above. When a Candidate is accepted by the Bishop, he has then to pass an Examination, which slightly differs in the various dioceses, but generally comprehends the following subjects, viz.—The Bible; the New Testament in Greek, and a minute acquaintance with some specified portion of it; The Prayer-Book; The 39 Articles; Church History; Latin; some theological authors, such as Pearson, Hooker, Butler, Paley, &c.; a Hebrew Paper is set for those who care to take up Hebrew.

Parish

"That circuit of ground which is committed to the charge of one parson or vicar, or other minister." Some think England was divided into parishes by Archbishop Honorius, about the year 630. There are instances of Parish Churches in England as early as the year 700. The cause of the great difference in the extent of different parishes is explained by the fact that churches were most of them built by lords of the manor for their tenants, and so the parish was the size of the lord's manor. In 1520 the number of Parish Churches was between 9,500 and 10,000. There are now about 13,500 Benefices; and many more District and Mission Churches, and Chapels of Ease.

Rector

A clergyman who has charge of a parish, and who possesses all the tithes

Vicar

A clergyman who has charge of a parish, and is entitled only to a certain portion of the tithes.

Parson

The Rector or Incumbent of a Parish, when the income of the living is derived from land. It represents two Latin words, 'Persona Ecclesiae,' the ecclesiastical person of a place.

Curate

Properly the person who has the *cure*, or care, of souls in a parish. In this way the word, is used in the Prayer Book. But the word, in common parlance, is used to denote the *assistant* clergyman in a parish. He is licensed by the Bishop of the diocese, and can be removed only by consent of the Bishop after six months' notice. He can, however, resign, after giving the Incumbent three months' notice.

Dissenters

A *civil*, not a *religious* term, and denotes those who have diverged from the civilly established religion of a country. Episcopalians are Dissenters in Scotland, Christians are Dissenters in Turkey. In England all are Dissenters who do not belong to the Church of England, whether they are Protestants or Papists. Also known as Nonconformists—Quakers, Baptists, Unitarians, and The Salvation Army, among other non-Anglican Christians. They were restricted from many spheres in English life and denied educational opportunities until the 1820s and 1830s.

Anglican Religious Orders

Though religious orders were dissolved by Henry VIII, the Oxford Movement of the 1830s saw a revival of interest in them. Brotherhoods and Sisterhoods were established in the mid-nineteenth century.

- The Community of the Resurrection
- Society of St. John the Evangelist
- Society of the Sacred Mission
- The Convent of Bath and Wells
- The Sisters of Charity
- Sisterhood of St. Margaret
- Sisters of the Holy Cross
- St. Mary's Home

Bibliography

Heffer, Simon. *High Minds: The Victorians and the Birth of Modern Britain*. London: Random House, 2013.

May, Trevor. *The Victorian Clergyman*. Princes Risborough: Shire, 2006.

Moorman, John R. H. *A History of the Church in England*. London: A. and C. Black, 1953.

Nowell-Smith, Simon, ed. *Edwardian England, 1901-1914*. London: Oxford UP, 1964.

Scruton, Roger. *Our Church: A Personal History of the Church of England*. London: Atlantic, 2012.

Thompson, Francis Michael Longstreth. *The Cambridge Social History of Britain: 1750-1950*. Cambridge, Angleterre: Cambridge UP, 1990.

Mourning

Mourning customs in Edwardian England toned down the excesses of the high Victorian period, and the toll of World War One hastened the decline of the elaborate parade of mourning. Nevertheless, most held fast to traditional periods of mourning and their accompanying accoutrements into the post-war era, even as the scarcity of material, and the costs of mourning garb and stationery rose considerably.

According to Mrs. C.E. Humphry (otherwise known as society columnist "Madge" of *Truth*):

"When a death occurs in a family, the accepted mode of making the fact known to the outside world is by drawing down all the blinds and tying up the knocker with a piece of crape. An announcement of the death is sent to the papers for insertion in the obituary column, and letters are written to relatives and very intimate friends giving them the sad news." Because women were thought to be in insufficient control of their emotions, the custom arose of forbidding their attendance at funerals. Though this "strict social law" gradually relaxed by the close of the 19th century, women mostly remained at home until after the funeral service and burial had taken place.

Accordingly, mourning customs for women were much more stringent than they were for men. Widows mourned their husbands for eighteen months to two years, whereupon they wore black dresses made of crepe, with "deep trimming of crape on the skirt" for the first twelve months. By 1913, widows wore crepe trimming only, and discontinued its wear after 6-8 months. The elaborate and stiff widow's cap of the Victorian era had given way to the "graceful little Marie Stuart coif, with long ends at the back," and ladies also had the option of wearing a crepe-trimmed bonnet with heavy veiling (this veil was exchanged for something lighter after two months). Jet was the only jewelry allowed, with "a watch chain, brooch, and ear-rings being the usual limit." Diamonds and pearls were not permitted until crepe was taken off. Gloves were of black suede or wool.

Half-mourning was donned after a year and nine months, and was worn for three months. During this half-mourning, touches of white gradually appeared to a widow's dress, and she exchanged her bonnet or cap and veil, for black chiffon toque. Gold jewelry was now permitted. By the end of the full mourning period, purples, greys, and deep mauves joined the black and white, thus signifying the gradual return to colors. During this time, the widow remained secluded from society for the first three months– she neither accepted nor issued invitations–and confined visits to family and intimate friends. After these three months, she gradually entered society, but balls and dances were strictly verboten for the first year.

Mrs. Humphry also mentions a brand new etiquette snafu of the Edwardian era: divorce and separation.

> A woman who has divorced her husband would be guided by circumstances as to wearing mourning for him. Should he have married again and left a widow, it would be too absurd for two women to be wearing weeds for him; but if it should be thought advisable, in the interests of children, or for any other reason, for the woman who divorced him to wear mourning, she should do so, though without any exaggerated advertisement of regret. The children would wear mourning for their father, and it would be in singularly bad taste if their mother were not to don black and avoid colours until their period of mourning had expired. But a woman who has been divorced has no right to wear mourning for her former husband.
>
> Women who are separated from their husbands have, in the same way, to be guided by a number of considerations as to whether they shall wear weeds or merely what is called "complimentary mourning " on the death of the man. An incident that occurred to a lady may be related as showing how difficulties may arise when a couple are separated. She had been living abroad with one of her sons for some years, and meanwhile her husband had formed a temporary union in England with someone else. This latter lady died, and a notice of her death, as wife of Mr. So-and-so, appeared in a great daily paper.

The period of mourning for immediate relatives was less severe: six months in black, the first three with crepe; and three months half-mourning. Seclusion from society ranged from two to six weeks, depending upon the degree of the relationship. For example, a child mourning a parent or a parent mourning a child withdrew for six weeks and did not attend balls and dances for six months.

When mourning a sibling, a grandparent, or an aunt or uncle, the period of seclusion was 2-3 weeks. For a daughter- or son-in-law, the mourning period was six months: four in black and two in half-mourning, or evenly split between to the two forms of dress. In the 1860s and 1870s, men wore broadcloth suits and a tie of dull-surfaced silk for mourning, but by the 1900s, anything black signified mourning. A black hat-band was worn by men mourning various relations; widowers wore black for a year and usually entered society after three months.

Servants were provided mourning attire by their employers—and the men usually just wore black armbands—and they wore this for the same period as the family.

The First World War obviously changed these many of these customs, though society held on to them as long as possible.

In the August 18, 1915 issue of *The Sketch*, fashion columnist Carmen of Cockayne considered the question of mourning "one of the most prominent dress problems of the day." The suggestion of laying aside mourning to wear a white band around the arm was ignored, but it was recognized that "elaborate mourning is in the worst of bad taste, [and] a morbid exaggeration of dolour is equally so." Widows' mourning was reduced to eighteen months, with half-mourning for a few months more, and a small cap with small veil replaced the bonnet and widow's cap. For dress, the first few months were spent in black cashmere with touches of white crape, and for the afternoon, dull black silks were permitted. Overall crepe was left to the widow's personal taste. Periods of mourning morphed as well, with the mourning for a son lengthened to one year, and six months for a brother and three for a nephew. As with most advice for mourning during the war, the style, depth, and length of mourning was left to an individual's taste and feeling rather than being standardized and regulated. After the war, this streak of individuality intensified.

(Left) An afternoon frock suited to the modern hip line, it hem stealing from cuff to cuff of the correctly long sleeves, and pointed panels falling below the hem. It is of black georgette crepe and black crepe, which makes cuffs and girdle. The beautiful drapery at the corsage and the chiffon veil which falls from one side are no less correct for being extremely smart, from Thurn

(Right) Social life in its simpler forms is now resumed before the end of mourning, and one wears such charmingly draped gowns as this of black crepe marocain. Chiffon appliqué in leaves and braid trims it, while the belt is of rolled crepe. The cape of black chiffon carries out the flower motif with a petal collar of chiffon and crepe above its many flounces; Thurn

In the June 1922 issue of *Vogue*, the fashion writer remarked:
"A generation ago there were absolutely strict rules for mourning, and in this respect no one who believed in the propriety of the conventions would have broken them. Today, every phase of life is being reexamined in the light of individual opinion, so that even mourning has become largely a question of personal feeling and the ultimate decision rests with the individual. However, there are still rules—or at least accepted conventions—for what is correct; and if one is going to break rules successfully, one must first know them thoroughly.

It is generally conceded that whatever the degree of mourning, all black should be worn for the funeral and for the first few weeks. After that time. the black may correctly be relieved with a small distribution of white. such as organdie collar and cuffs or a slight facing for the hat. All white is as strict mourning as the entirely black costume, but a more or less equal division of black and white, or grey and violet, is the accepted convention of second mourning.

One of the most marked changes in the etiquette of mourning is the decided abbreviation of the time that it is worn. The widow of twenty years ago wore the deepest mourning for two years. and half mourning for the rest of her life, if she did not remarry. To-day, the widow rarely wears the long crape veil for more than a year; some young widows, and even a few of the older matrons, now consider six months a sufficient period of deep mourning, but this is a very modern interpretation and is not the accepted convention. it has thus become customary for the widow. after the first year. to substitute a simple face veil, perhaps with a border of crape or chiffon or georgette crape. It is not, however, considered correct for her to assume half mourning until after the end of the second year.

For a member of the immediate family, meaning a parent, a sister or brother, or a child, a year of deep mourning and a year of second mourning is the strictly correct usage. The crape veil worn in this case is somewhat shorter than the widows veil, and usage varies considerably as to the length of time for which it is worn. In strictly conventional mourning it is worn for six months, but the general tendency in mourning is to be less strictly conventional.

A small amount of jewellery is permitted by even the strict conventions of etiquette. The women who have fine pearls wear them although in the deepest mourning. However, even pearls must be discreetly used—for instance. a single string for the daytime or one beautiful rope in the evening. Also, a little black jewellery, such as onyx or jet set with diamonds. is smart and relieves the often dull appearance of the textiles. There are two reasons for wearing mourning. The first is to show respect for the person who has died, and the second is for the protection of the person who is wearing it. Mourning may be smart, but it should not be conspicuous, and it may and should be becoming, for there is never a time when a woman is not right in seeking to look her best. Above all, it is important that the apparel of mourning should be always in good taste."

Periods of Mourning in 1913

For Parent or Child	Twelve months; ten months black, two months half-mourning, or eight months black and four months half-mourning. The black may be relieved with touches of white after three months. Crape is optional; many prefer not to wear it at all, others as a trimming.
For Brother or Sister	The longest period of mourning is six months, the shortest period four months. During the longest period, black worn for five months, with a little white after two months, half-mourning for one month. During the shortest period, black should be worn for two months, half-mourning two months.
Grandparent	Longest—six months; shortest—four months. Longest period: black for three months, relieved with white after six weeks, half-mourning for three months. During the shortest period black should be worn for two months, half-mourning for two months.
Aunt or Uncle	The longest period of mourning is three months, the shortest period six weeks. For the longest period, black (no crape) should be worn for two

	months, half-mourning for one month. During the shortest period, black for three weeks, half-mourning for three weeks.
First Cousin	The longest period is six weeks, the shortest one month. During the longest period black for three weeks, half-mourning for three weeks. During the shortest period black for one month.
Daughter-in-Law or Son-in-Law	Six months. Four months black and two months half-mourning, or three months black and three months half-mourning.

Mourning Notepaper

Those in mourning were expected and socially required to write letters and other correspondence on specially created notepaper. This paper was heavy, and was available in cream, azure, or grey, with borders ranging from a thick one inch, to a very thin quarter of an inch. Widows were expected to use notepaper with the thickest border for the first three months of mourning, after which the black-bordered edges decreased in size as her mourning progressed. Envelopes and correspondence cards specifically for mourning followed the same design.

Burial

Old customs and practices of burial lingered well into the twentieth century, but the custom of cremation took hold in most Edwardians' lives due to the campaigning of Queen Victoria's surgeon, Sir Henry Thompson, in the mid-1870s. Cremation was considered economical and hygienic, thus combining two of the most important worries of the day. Yet, the Edwardians poor and rich, still splurged on burial and funerals.

There was a great trade in mourning ware and funeral services in all major cities, and London in particular. T.W. Wilkerson, in his article "Burying London" in *Living London*, describes the "showcases of the principal firms which ca, on occasion, put ladies in black in twenty-four hours. Wreath-makers, ranging from the manufacturers of the artificial article to the open air and the hot-house florist...the principal stand of outdoor vendors of 'natural' wreaths forms an oasis in Upper Street, Islington." A variety of funeral homes existed to cater to an equal variety of budgets, ranging from "the small men, whose 'leading line' is the thirty-shilling headstone; in the west, north, and south are the imposing shops of firms whose book orders for memorials costing £2000 or £3000 and erect mausoleums representing a small fortune." London was the headquarters of the British Institute of Undertakers, and their symbol—"an undertaker and his men engaged on ominous-shaped boxes—were encountered quite often in this period.

Wilkerson goes on to describe a certain establishment he declares the "heart of the 'black trade'," which could be Jay's London General Mourning Warehouse, or Peter Robinson's Court and General Mourning Warehouse, both of which were found in Regent's Street (and were established in the early Victorian era). Harrods too had "a large mourning department, including coffins, gravestones and every possible item of funerary fashion."

"Within its walls the retail undertaker can find every requisite, from a bit of furniture to a coffin or a tombstone. Nowhere are life and death more strangely intermingled. A vast stock of wood, such as would set up in business two or three timber merchants; shop after shop full of whirring, buzzing machinery; men at work everywhere, some on marble, some on brass, some making harness, some repairing carriages, some in a battery-room for electro-plating; coffin furniture by the ton, including handles worth £1, a pair; an enormous stock of "caskets" of all sizes and all materials, paper and wickerwork at one extreme, lead and brass at the other, from which customers can pick a fit as the needy purchaser in Petticoat Lane picks a suit — these are a few of the main features that impress themselves on the memory. But there are many others, notably a fine stud of glossy, long-tailed funeral horses, those high-strung, sensitive Flemish blacks which draw or follow the chariot of Death."

Cemeteries were also an important and lucrative business in Edwardian London. The principal cemeteries were Kensal Green, Abney Park, Highgate, Nunhead, Canning Town, and Brompton, all of which were established in the 1830s and 1840s after London's population more than doubled in the first half of the nineteenth century. London also boasted several burial grounds for their non-Anglican residents, including Japanese and Chinese residents, who mostly chose to bury their dead in the East London Cemetery. Each of the largest cemeteries employed a "small army," who repaired the tombs, cared for the graves and mausoleums, and tended to the gardens. At Highgate, the most fashionable of London's great cemeteries, the floricultural department employed a staff of twenty-eight gardeners, and "merely for bedding-out some 250,000 to 300,000 plants are raised every year."

Highgate also had a large columbarium, where cremations took place. "Peering through the gate beneath, you see a small chamber lined with pigeon-holes, in which are urns of various shapes, each containing a handful or two of dust—man in his most inglorious stage. The number of such receptacles is, however, no measure of the popularity of cremation, because in many cases the incinerated remains are buried."

The largest cemetery was Brookwood, located in Woking. This was the headquarters of the London Necropolis Company, and the company had its own private station for the carrying of funeral parties and coffins to the cemetery.

"One minute we are in the thick of London's seething, roaring traffic; the next on a platform of a station which anybody who reached it blindfolded might momentarily take for a rural terminus. Nothing is lacking—even the big-faced clock, now indicating 11.45, is there—except hobbledehoy porters and other rustic types. A glance round, however, dispels the illusion. The waiting-rooms—one of which is allotted for the exclusive use of every party of mourners attending a private funeral—are bright and furnished in admirable taste. While there is nothing funereal about them, no gloomy black with its morbid associations, they are free from any jarring note.

The same good taste is shown in other parts of the station, which contains every convenience that can possibly be desired, including a beautifully fitted mortuary chapel. At the platform stands a train — the train of the dead. On the door of the guard's van are two or three small cards bearing names, one of which, you notice, is the same as that on a similar ticket at the entrance to a waiting-room, while some of the compartments are reserved in like manner. Two mourners are already seated in readiness for the journey, silent, thoughtful, a little sad maybe. They are Chelsea pensioners, and they are taking to his rest an old comrade whom Death has claimed at last.

Thus are London's dead conveyed to Woking, normally at the rate of three or four thousand yearly, though as many as fifty bodies have been sent down in a day. Sometimes a 'special' is ordered for the funeral of a great man, but as a general rule all classes alike go down in the regular daily train."

Bibliography

A Member of the Aristocracy. *Manners and Rules of Good Society; Or, Solecisms to Be Avoided.* London: F. Warne, 1911.

"Burying London" by T.W. Wilkerson in George R. Sims' Living London (1902)

Campbell, Lady Colin. *Etiquette of Good Society.* London: Cassell and Limited London Paris & Melbourne, 1893.

Humphry, Mrs. C. E. *Etiquette for Every Day.* London: Grant Richards, 1902.

Lovric, Michelle. *The Mourning Emporium.* London: Orion Children's, 2010.

Bibliography

Books

Allen, Lucy Grace. *Table Service*. Boston: Little, Brown, 1940.

Asquith, Lady Cynthia. *Remember and Be Glad*. New York, NY: Charles Scribner's Sons, 1952.

Asquith, Margot. *The Autobiography of Margot Asquith*. London: Thornton Butterworth, 1922.

Aston, George. *Secret Service*. New York: Cosmopolitan Book, 1930.

Baedeker, Karl. *Great Britain: Handbook for Travellers*. Leipzig: K. Baedeker, 1910.

Baedeker, Karl. *London and Its Environs. Handbook for Travellers,*. Leipzig: K. Baedeker, 1892.

Baedeker, Karl. *London and Its Environs; Handbook for Travellers*. Leipzig: K. Baedeker, 1911.

Balsan, Consuelo Vanderbilt. *The Glitter and the Gold*. London: Heinemann, 1953.

Barstow, Phyllida. *The English Country House Party*. Wellingborough: Equation, 1989.

Battiscombe, Georgina. *Queen Alexandra*. Boston: Houghton Mifflin, 1969.

Beavan, Arthur H. *Tube, Train, Tram, and Car; or Up-to-date Locomotion*. London: G. Routledge & Sons, 1903.

Beeton, Isabella. *Mrs. Beeton's Book of Household Management*. London: Ward, Lock&Co, 1909.

Blunt, Wilfrid Scawen. *My Diaries; Being a Personal Narrative of Events, 1888-1914*. New York: A.A. Knopf, 1921.

Brinnin, John Malcolm. *The Sway of the Grand Saloon: A Social History of the North Atlantic*. London: Macmillan, 1972.

Brooks, David. *The Age of Upheaval: Edwardian Politics, 1899-1914*. Manchester: Manchester UP, 1995.

Brown, Jonathan. *The Edwardian Farm*. N.p.: Shire Library, 2010.

Busbey, Katherine Graves. *Home Life in America*. New York: Macmillan, 1910.

Caffrey, Kate. *The 1900s Lady*. London: Gordon Cremonesi, 1976.

Campbell, Lady Colin. *Etiquette of Good Society*. London: Cassell and Limited London Paris & Melbourne, 1893.

Cannadine, David. *The Decline and Fall of the British Aristocracy*. New York: Anchor, 1996.

Clayton, Joseph. *The Rise of the Democracy,*. London: Cassell, 1911.

Cooper, Lady Diana. *The Rainbow Comes and Goes*. Boston: Houghton Mifflin, 1958.

Cooper, Nicholas, and Henry Bedford Lemere. *The Opulent Eye: Late Victorian and Edwardian Taste in Interior Design*. New York: Watson-Guptill Publications, 1977.

The Countess of Fingall, and Pamela Hinkson. *Seventy Years Young: Memories of Elizabeth, Countess of Fingall*. New York: E.P. Dutton, 1939.

Cowles, Virginia. *Gay Monarch: The Life and Pleasures of Edward VII*. New York: Harper, 1956.

Cowles, Virginia Spencer. *1913: An End and a Beginning*. New York: Harper & Row, 1967.

Crow, Duncan. *The Edwardian Woman*. New York: St. Martin's, 1978.

Currell, Melville. *Political Woman*. Lanham, Maryland: Rowman & Littlefield, 1974.

Dyhouse, Carol. *Girls Growing up in Late Victorian and Edwardian England*. London/Boston: Routledge, 1981.

Edes, Mary Elisabeth, Dudley Frasier, and James Laver, eds. *The Age of Extravagance: An Edwardian Reader*. New York: Rinehart, 1954.

Escoffier, A. *The Complete Guide to the Art of Modern Cookery: The First Translation into English in Its Entirety of Le Guide Culinaire*. London: Heinemann, 1979.

Escott, T. H. S. *Social Transformations of the Victorian Age. A Survey of Court and Country*. London: Seeley and, 1897.

Flanders, Judith. *Inside the Victorian Home: A Portrait of Domestic Life in Victorian England*. New York: W. W. Norton &, 2003.

Frances, Countess of Warwick. *Life's Ebb and Flow*. New York: W. Morrow, 1929.

Gardiner, Juliet. *Manor House: Life in an Edwardian Country House*. San Francisco, CA: Bay, 2003.

Gathorne-Hardy, Jonathan. *The Public School Phenomenon: 597-1977*. London: Hodder and Stoughton, 1977.

Gladstone, W. E., and James Bryce Bryce. *Handbook of Home Rule: Being Articles on the Irish Question*. London: K. Paul, Trench, 1887.

Hale, Oron J. *The Great Illusion: 1900-1914*. New York: Evanston, London, 1971.

Hayes, Carlton J. H. *British Social Politics; Materials Illustrating Contemporary State Action for the Solution of Social Problems*. Boston: Ginn, 1913.

Hill, Janet McKenzie. *The Up-to-date Waitress,*. Boston: Little, Brown, 1922.

Horn, Pamela. *Ladies of the Manor: Wives and Daughters in Country-House Society, 1830-1918*. Gloucestershire: Sutton Pub, 1991.

Horn, Pamela. *High Society: The English Social Elite, 1880-1914*. Gloucestershire: Sutton Pub, 1992.

Horn, Pamela. *The Rise and Fall of the Victorian Servant*. Dublin: Gill and Macmillan, 1975.

Horn, Pamela. *The Victorian and Edwardian Schoolchild*. Gloucester, UK: Alan Sutton, 1989.

Humphry, C. E. *A Word to Women*. London: J. Bowden, 1898.

Jackson, Alvin. *Home Rule: An Irish History*. London: Phoenix, 2004.

Jalland, Pat. *Women, Marriage and Politics, 1860-1914*. Oxford: Oxford UP, 1988.

Jenkins, Roy. *Gladstone: A Biography*. New York: Random House, 1997.

Jullian, Philippe. *Edward and the Edwardians*. New York,: Viking, 1967.

Kee, Robert. *The Laurel and the Ivy: The Story of Charles Stewart Parnell and Irish Nationalism*. London: Hamish Hamilton, 1993.

King, Charles Thomas. *The Asquith Parliament (1906-1909): A Popular History of Its Men and Its Measures*. London: Hutchinson &, 1910.

Laver, James. *Edwardian Promenade*. Boston: Houghton Mifflin, 1958.

Leslie, Anita. *The Marlborough House Set*. New York, NY: Doubleday, 1973.

Lord Montagu of Beaulieu, and F. Wilson McComb. *Behind the Wheel: The Magic and Manners of Early Motoring*. New York: Paddington, 1977.

Lucy, Henr W. *A Diary of Two Parliaments: The Gladstone Parliament 1880-1885*. London: Cassell, 1886.

Lucy, Henry W. *The Balfourian Parliament, 1900-1905,*. London: Hodder and Stoughton, 1906.

Lucy, Henry W. *A Diary of the Home Rule Parliament: 1892-1895*. London: Cassell, 1896.

Lucy, Henry W. *A Diary of the Salisbury Parliament, 1886-92.* London: Cassell, 1892.

Lucy, Henry W. *Peeps at Parliament, Taken from behind the Speaker's Chair*. London: G. Newnes, 1903.

Lucy, Henry W. *A Diary of the Unionist Parliament, 1895-1900*. Bristol: J.W. Arrowsmith, 1901.

Lucy, Henry W. *Later Peeps at Parliament.* London: G. Newnes, 1905.

MacColl, Gail, and Carol McD. Wallace. *To Marry an English Lord.* New York: Workman Pub., 1989.

MacDonagh, Michael. *The Book of Parliament.* London: Isbister and Limited 15 & 16 Tavistock Street, Covent Garden, 1897.

Macqueen-Pope, W. *Carriages at Eleven: The Story of the Edwardian Theatre.* Port Washington, NY: Kennikat, 1970.

Martel, Gordon. *The Origins of the First World War*. London: Longman, 1996.

Marwick, Arthur. *The Deluge: British Society and the First World War.* Basingstoke: Palgrave Macmillan, 2006.

Massie, Robert K. *Castles of Steel: Britain, Germany, and the Winning of the Great War at Sea*. New York: Random House, 2003.

Masters, Anthony. *Rosa Lewis: An Exceptional Edwardian.* New York: St. Martin's, 1978.

McGee, Owen. *The IRB: The Irish Republican Brotherhood, from the Land League to Sinn Féin.* Dublin, Ireland: Four Courts, 2005.

A Member of the Aristocracy. *Manners and Rules of Good Society; Or, Solecisms to Be Avoided.* London: F. Warne, 1911.

Middlemas, Keith. *The Pursuit of Pleasure.* London: Gordon Cremonesi, 1977.

Mitchell, Sally. *The New Girl: Girls' Culture in England, 1880-1915.* New York: Columbia UP, 1995.

Murphy, Claudia Quigley. *The History of the Art of Tablesetting, Ancient and Modern, from Anglo-Saxon Days to the Present Time*. New York: De Vinne, 1921.

Nelson, Carolyn Christensen. *A New Woman Reader: Fiction, Articles, and Drama of the 1890s.* Peterborough, Ontario, Canada: Broadview, 2001.

Nowell-Smith, Simon, ed. *Edwardian England, 1901-1914.* London: Oxford UP, 1964.

Pakenham, Valerie. *Out in Noonday Sun.* New York, NY: Random House, 1985.

Pascoe, Charles Eyre. *London of To-day. An Illustrated Handbook for the Season 1897.* London: Bemrose & Sons, 1897.

Pascoe, Charles Eyre. *London of To-day. An Illustrated Handbook for the Season.* Boston: Roberts Bros., 1902.

Pearsall, Ronald. *Edwardian Life and Leisure.* Newton Abbot: David & Charles, 1973.

Petrie, Charles. *Scenes of Edwardian Life.* London: Eyre & Spottiswoode, 1965.

Picht, Werner, and Lilian A. Cowell. *Toynbee Hall and the English Settlement Movement.* London: G. Bell and Sons, 1914.

Plumptre, George. *The Fast Set: The World of Edwardian Racing.* London: A. Deutsch, 1985.

Priestley, J.B. *The Edwardians.* New York: Harper & Row, 1970.

Purvis, June. *Emmeline Pankhurst: A Biography.* London: Routledge, 2002.

Raymond, E. T. *Mr. Lloyd George.* New York: George H. Doran, 1922.

Reid, Andrew. *The House of Lords Question.* London: Duckworth, 1898.

Rowan, Richard Wilmer. *The Story of Secret Service.* New York: Literary Guild of America, 1937.

Ruffer, Jonathan Garnier. *The Big Shots: Edwardian Shooting Parties.* [Kingston upon Thames]: Debrett's Peerage, 1977.

Schollander, Wendell, and Wes Schollander. *Forgotten Elegance: The Art, Artifacts, and Peculiar History of Victorian and Edwardian Entertaining in America.* Westport, CT: Greenwood, 2002.

Sebba, Anne. *American Jennie: The Remarkable Life of Lady Randolph Churchill.* New York: W.W. Norton &, 2007.

Service, Alastair. *Edwardian Interiors: Inside the Homes of the Poor, the Average, and the Wealthy.* London: Barrie & Jenkins, 1982.

Sims, George R. *Living London: Its Work and Its Play, Its Humour and Its Pathos, Its Sights and Its Scenes.* London: Cassell and, 1902.

Smalley, George Washburn, and T. H. S. Escott. *Society in the New Reign.* London: T.F. Unwin, 1904.

Sproule, Anna. *The Social Calendar.* Poole, Dorset: Blandford, 1978.

Stanley, Louis T. *The London Season.* Boston: Houghton Mifflin, 1956.

Tannahill, Reay. *Food in History.* New York, NY: Stein & Day, 1973.

Thompson, Paul Richard. *The Edwardians: The Remaking of British Society.* Bloomington: Indiana UP, 1975.

Tuchman, Barbara Wertheim. *The Guns of August.* New York: Ballantine, 1994.

Tweedsmuir, Susan. *The Edwardian Lady.* London: Duckworth, 1966.

Vincent, Howard. *How We Are Governed: Guide for the Stranger to the Houses of Parliament.* London: Vacher & Sons, 1906.

Whistler, James McNeill, Joseph Pennell, Dudley Hardy, and W. Beatty-Kingston. *Homes of the Passing Show.* London: Savoy, 1900.

Wilson, C. Anne. *Eating with the Victorians.* [Stroud, Gloucestershire]: Sutton Publications, 2004.

Zimmern, Alice. *The Renaissance of Girls' Education in England: A Record of Fifty Years' Progress.* London: A.D. Innes, 1898.

Periodicals, Newspapers & Magazines
The Bystander
The Illustrated London News
The Graphic
The Lady's Realm
The Ladies' Field
The Sketch
The Strand Magazine
The Harmsworth Monthly Pictorial Magazine

Online
Wikipedia
Manor House - PBS Masterpiece Theater
The History of Hinchingbrooke House
BBC

Fiction

Allen, Grant. *The Type-writer Girl*. Peterborough, Ont.: Broadview, 2004.

Buchan, John. *The 39 Steps*. New York: Popular Library, 1961.

Burnett, Frances Hodgson. *The Shuttle*. Leipzig: Tauchnitz, 1908.

Childers, Erskine. *The Riddle of the Sands: A Record of Secret Service*. New York: Dover Publications, 1976.

Forster, E. M. *Howards End*. New York: Knopf, 1991.

Forster, E. M. *A Room with a View*. New York: A.A. Knopf, 1923.

Glyn, Elinor. *The Visits of Elizabeth*. New York: Duffield, 1909.

James, Henry. *The Ambassadors*. Harmondsworth: Penguin, 1985.

James, Henry. *The Golden Bowl*. New York: Knopf, 1992.

James, Henry. *The Wings of the Dove*. New York: Modern Library, 1937.

Oppenheim, Edward Phillips. *The Double Traitor*. New York: Review of Reviews, 1915.

Sackville-West, Vita. *The Edwardians*. London: Virago, 1983.

Wharton, Edith, and Marion Mainwaring. *The Buccaneers: A Novel*. New York, N.Y.: Viking, 1993.

Woolf, Virginia, and Julia Briggs. *Night and Day*. London: Penguin, 1992.

17195203R00163

Made in the USA
Middletown, DE
11 January 2015